OLYMPIC GOLD RUN

OLYMPIC GOLD RUN

BRITAIN'S GREAT BOBSLEIGH VICTORY!

BRIAN BELTON

Pennant Books

First published in paperback 2010
by Pennant Books

Text copyright © 2009 by Brian Belton
Foreword & Epilogue © Victor Emery

The moral right of the author has been asserted.

British Library Cataloguing-in-Publication Data:
A catalogue record for this book is available on request from
The British Library

ISBN 978-1-906015-36-7

Design & Typeset by Envy Design Ltd

Printed and bound in Turkey by Mega Printing.

Pictures reproduced with kind permission of Tony Nash and Robin Dixon.

Every reasonable effort has been made to acknowledge the ownership of
copyright material included in this book. Any errors that have inadvertently
occurred will be corrected in subsequent editions provided notification is
sent to the publisher.

Pennant Books
PO Box 5675
London W1A 3FB

www.pennantbooks.com

This book is dedicated to the sporting example of three men at the 1964 Winter Olympics: Tony Nash, Robin Dixon and Eugenio Monti, whose collective lifetime achievements were in many ways informed by the humanity and dignity of their time in competition.

CONTENTS

FOREWORD

When Brian Belton invited me to write the foreword to his book about the NASH/DIXON Olympic victory, I was hesitant. Many articles had been written about bobsledding in our time and I've long since learned not to believe reports from third parties. Besides, while I was flattered by the invitation, the two Italian sleds which Nash and Dixon narrowly beat for their Olympic gold were piloted by two wonderful characters who we all wish were still with us and therefore in a position to do the honours bestowed on me. However, they are not . . .

SERGIO ZARDINI was not only the boblet pilot who won the silver medal in the 1964 Olympic competition but also the world champion four-man bob pilot on the same track in 1963. Tragically, he died instantly in a crash on Lake Placid's bob track in the 1966 International Diamond Trophy event. Sergio's crew were Canadians, comprising the flamboyant Paul Levesque, subsequent manager/coach of Canada's 1968

Olympic luge team, Bob Storey, current President of the FIBT (Federation Internationale de Bobsleigh et Tobogganing) and brakeman Michael Young. (As a novice, cousin Michael was my brakeman in our third-place finish behind Nash and Dixon in St Moritz's 1965 World Boblet championships and was on our winning team in the World Four-Man championships a week later.)

Fortunately, both Levesque and Storey were thrown clear in the Zardini tragedy, occasioned by a melted overhang in Lake Placid's then particularly dangerous Zig-Zag curve. It was a time before artificially refrigerated tracks and Mother Nature could be cruel. Zardini's head was crushed and Young suffered severe face and head injuries; he eventually recovered to take his place in a bobsleigh again and also to enjoy an exciting business career over the ensuing decades.

It was an extremely sad bobsleigh contingent which attended the Zardini funeral in Montreal's Eglise de Notre Dame, we Canadians as pallbearers. The Zardini tragedy had followed on the heels of the German pilot Pensberger's death in the World Four-Man Championships just two weeks beforehand, in Cortina, where we too almost lost control on the boards above the same Curvo Bandion. However , we managed to bang our way down through to the finish and live another day.

Such were the dangers of bobsleighing and the degree of camaraderie amongst our fraternity in the 1950's and 60's. Throughout the ages, young men choosing risky adventures have done so believing that tragedy won't happen to them. In contrast with most of our fathers, involved in the ravages of World War I, perhaps bobsleighing for us was the alternative to being called up.

EUGENIO MONTI is universally acknowledged as the greatest bob pilot of our era – if not of all time – and was certainly a sportsman without parallel. He was our friend and to many bob pilots, particularly Tony and me, he was our mentor. Wanting to win only against the best, his constant assistance and advice encouraged us to become as good as possible. Even when his students became his fiercest competition, he didn't back off.

You will read how both Tony and I owe our Olympic golds to Eugenio. When he came third to each of us in the two and four-man '64 Olympic competitions, I suspect that Tony was as relieved as me to have another team sandwiched in between him and us – just as we were similarly ecstatic when he came out of retirement to achieve his long sought-after Olympic golds in both the two and four-man competitions in 1968. You will read much about Eugenio in this book. No account of our era would be complete without full reference to him.

This is a very well-researched book which – far better than anything else I've read – captures the spirit of international amateur sport as it was played out in the 50's and 60's, and the makeup of some of the main characters in the bobsleighing segment. As a fringe sport, bobsleighing appealed to those willing to pay for the privilege – sometimes with our lives and certainly with our pocketbooks – because of what we must have considered deep-down to be a favourable reward/risk ratio. From the exhilaration and the competitive challenge through to the international camaraderie and (yes) the glamour of the international resorts where the sport is practised, the risks seemed worth it. I am grateful therefore to be given this opportunity to provide a little personal insight into our era of bobsleighing.

The year before Nash and Dixon took up bobsleighing, under the tutelage of the Spaniard Portago and his American colleague Nelson, I was thrown into the deep end of the sliding sports. Starting with the macho Cresta Run, bobsleighing followed in the same month after I was picked up by an eccentric Englishman driving a British bob lorry to the 1956 Cortina Olympics. I was attempting to get there from St Moritz on cross-country skis but had run out of snow somewhere near Merano. The lorry driver was the British bobsleigh captain Keith Schellenberg, who not only introduced me to the bob sport then but also (eight years later) to Jenifer Wontner – a British girl who, in 1966, became my wife for 22 years.

What a decade that initial indoctrination kicked off! Following our first World Bobsleigh Championships in '59, we Canadians were invited by the Italian Federation to the '60 World Championships in Cortina, where it became so warm that we repaired at one point to Venice to informally compete in a *Gondola a Quatro* race through the canals. When we were finally able to proceed with the bobsleigh version, holiday time was running out for some of us, and so I conscripted on to my team a very gutsy Brit – Bill Shand Kydd who, years later, completed a unique 'double' by competing in both Grand Nationals – the Cresta and the rather more famous Aintree version.

By a whisker in '60, we missed flying out of the Cortina track on the same curve which killed Pensberger and almost got us again six years later. That near-miss pre-dated Bill's horse-and-rider tumble in a team steeplechase some 37 years later, which has left him to soldier on as a quadriplegic for the past 12 years. Bill is of the breed which embraces risk for the exhilaration, beggar the consequences, and I am certain that no one has come close to matching his stiff upper lip when the tables were turned against them.

From the outset, speaking more or less the same language and enjoying life to the full, the British and Canadians developed a close rapport, exchanging team members on occasion and generally trying to climb the competitive ladder together. The parents of Andrew Hedges, a member of Nash's four-man team, were particularly hospitable all year round, receiving my brother, 'Dr John', whenever he could escape from an internship at Oxford's Churchill Hospital, and myself whenever I visited England. I spent my pre-wedding night in their country home. 'Mum Hedges' was the surrogate mother of Canada's bobsledders and I am still, to this day, 'Brother Vic' to all of the family.

Which brings me to the core of this book – the friendships, the fun, the tragedies and, of course, the Nash/Dixon story, filled with insight and gripping moments. The book will flood all of us who competed during those years with vivid memories of those halcyon days. I would like to think that international sport still rewards the spirit in the way that we were rewarded then. However, ours was an activity of choice when we had the time and money to practise it. I wonder if the singularly-absorbing lifestyle that ambitious sportsmen have to adopt today is nearly so satisfying.

Tony and Robin were true champions of the old style, working hard with good humour over many years to get to the top, then not only defending their title successfully but carrying on to endure the inevitable toppling as younger competitors and equipment refinements came into play. And by staying in the hunt through 1968 they also ensured that Eugenio's Olympic victory, when it finally came, was not an empty one for lack of their presence.

In signing off this foreword, *chapeaux* also to Brian Belton – for digging deep into a period that preceded so many of the extreme sports practised today. In our time we were at the extreme end, but it didn't feel like it, just as I suspect the youth of today feel comfortable about some activities we would not have remotely considered in our day. While I would doubtless be accused of overstatement in suggesting that ours were the best of times, most of us are still alive and kicking today. That has to be worth something in life's all-too-short cycle!

What is not overstated is how those bobsleigh years affected so many of our lives. Apart from whatever an Olympic victory does to set one apart, in my case bobsleighing gave my life an international dimension which ultimately took me and my family to England. And for the past eight years, I have been spending a great deal of time in Norway and elsewhere with Olympian Liv Jagge – an alpine ski racer from those same 1964 Winter Olympics

Victor Emery
Canada Bob '56-'66
Oslo, November 2009

INTRODUCTION

In February 2010, the athletes of snow and ice will be summoned to the 21st great arctic endeavour, in Vancouver. It will by then be close to half a century since Great Britain achieved one of its most remarkable feats at the Winter Olympics. Back in 1964 it had been a dozen years since the country had won a medal, and close to 30 years since a British crew stood on the Olympic podium after winning perhaps the most hazardous and exciting event: the bobsleigh.

Indeed, there had been only two British successes in the entire history of the Winter Games (three, if the Bronze won by David Earl of Northesk on the skeleton sled in 1928 is considered). But when the 1960's were still young, Tony Nash and Robin Dixon.[1] Their chosen sport required coordination, explosive energy and nerve. They became the greatest ever

1 For most of what follows, by mutual agreement I refer to the man who is now Lord Glentoran by his name at birth. This is the name he was known by for most of his sporting life, and it communicates some of the natural informality of the man and his approach.

British exponents of their event, riding steel and iron down cold corridors of speed. Since that time the nation has briefly tasted success in the same hazardous field, but it is difficult to imagine a more extraordinary saga than the British triumph of nearly half a century ago.

Bobsleighing is said to have started in 1890, when one Wilson Smith randomly decided to nail two toboggans together and invited three friends, apparently equally insane, for a hair-raising ride down a mountain at St Moritz. That initial bobsleigh jaunt epitomises British Victorian inventiveness, but then the Italians, the Swiss and the Americans added steel runners, steering wheels, crash helmets and specially constructed bobsleigh runs, and in turn came to dominate the sport.

It took Britain until 1936 to make a mark on the Olympic runs. In that politically troubled year, in Garmisch-Partenkirchen, Germany, Frederick McEvoy, James Cardno, Guy Dugdale and Charles Green took bronze in the four-man competition. By the time the athletes regrouped in Austria for the IX Winter Olympics, it had taken a long time to find another bobsleigh team capable of scaling the most hallowed rostrum in sport, and the Innsbruck Winter Olympics remains the last time that athletes from the United Kingdom generated gold from the chilly fire of the glassy Olympic runs. The story that follows is told with the help of the men who made the winter of 1964 an historic time in the chronicles of world sport; it is a celebration of a time and a place when their exploits truly made a winter's dream come true.

This book is dedicated to celebrating their legendary achievement, but it will also delve into the glorious myths that surrounds one of bobsleighing's greatest golden eras. This in no way undermines what was achieved, but honours the multifaceted discipline of sport, its combination of mind, body and spirit. Perhaps this is why the Olympic ideal has endured over the millennia since the earliest years of civilisation. With all their excitement and colour, the competitions and sports that make up the Winter Games have now perhaps become something of a circus of daring for the millions that watch them across our planet. Regrettably, the spectators hardly ever understand much about the individual participants, even though the stories of how they got to play on that great global stage are often as engrossing as the events they take part in. The personalities of the champions and those they defeat are rarely glimpsed in anything more than a flash as they tear down a slope or thunder toward the hockey goal. We perceive them only in a flashing blur of intensity. Even afterward, on the victory podium, as these fleeting heroes accept the medals and the applause that is their due, we see little of them behind a brief smile, a wave and occasionally tears of relief and pride.

This transitory acquaintance has become an Olympic tradition; the next spectacle awaits and time is short. But these winners and losers are a cross-section of athletes who have come to prominence on the wintry slopes of their native Colorado, the Great Glen, the Tyrol, the Russian Artic circle, the Swiss, German, French or Italian Alpine hamlets, the Rocky Mountains, Finnish Lapland – or even the leafy counties of England; whether likely or unlikely, these are the settings out of which the first glints of great skill or purpose shone.

The story that follows tells of a journey, over years and miles, to the Olympic arena in Innsbruck; more specifically, it describes a couple of days in a small mountain village, a time and place where lives would be defined. And it continues, these few hours and days evolving into the future of the men involved, their subsequent victories and disappointments.

The exploits of Nash and Dixon are far from forgotten. As

Tony Nash said to me, "People of all ages still know and are interested in what happened and we still get requests for autographs; before reunification a lot came from East Germany, bobsleighing seemed to be quite a thing for them at the time. Up to a few years ago it wasn't unusual to get something every week."

However, for most of us, bobsleighing is something we don't tend to think of until the Winter Games come around. Other triumphs of the sport usually go unsung, while even the great moments on the Olympic runs are sometimes soon forgotten. Moments of drama and disaster from St Moritz or Cortina d'Ampezzo live longer in the mass consciousness than any glorious victory. A mistake while travelling at breakneck speed on glittering ice may end with an obituary, which is harder to dislodge from memory. It is the speed, the race, the contest that is remembered, albeit dimly, as the sun sets over the shivering chutes of the bobber's world.

Bobsleighing has traditionally been associated with the international champagne set and has been referred to as the 'sport of kings'. Until his father ordered him to give it up, Prinz Wilhelm of Imperial Germany raced bobs, as did Baron Edward Alexander von Falz-Fein of Liechtenstein (whose wife insisted on his retirement from the runs). The Marquis de Portago of Spain, Lord Suffolk of England, Baron Jonny de Crawhez of Belgium, Prince Michael of Kent and Airman Third Class 'Smoky' Williams of Scotland Neck, North Carolina were also bobbers of note.

Until the second part of the 20th century, bobsleighing was for the most part the sport of persons of title or rank. It was this elite stratum who had brought the sport what minimal fame it had managed to gain. This said, throughout its evolution, bobsledding (as it is known across the Atlantic) has attracted not only the well-to-do but occasionally drawn from the ranks of the working classes. Most participants have been adventurers of one sort or another: airmen, soldiers, polo players, racing drivers, athletes and speedboat racers have mixed with dreamers, carpetbaggers, thrill seekers and the odd lunatic. But there have also been insurance adjusters, students, funeral directors, lumberjacks, accountants, plastic surgeons, teachers, geologists, bankers, butchers, doctors, business people and clerks.

For all the danger and excitement, the annals of bobsleighing tell of comparatively few bad accidents and disasters. However, in the early to mid-1960's, any incident that took place at speed on the rough, unforgiving plane of a bob run was not an attractive prospect. The 'natural' tracks that were prevalent in the 1960's were not the smooth rides offered by the artificial chutes of later eras. Sometimes hitting over 140kph, any mishap spelt danger for the four-man bobs that moved faster than their two-man sisters.

While bobsleighing at the top level has always demanded considerable skill and courage, at the time of the IX Winter Olympics one might still feasibly break into the world-class category with comparatively little experience compared to a top-ranked skier or the best figure skaters. But most top pilots took years to perfect their skills, and a thorough understanding of the run (even before the competition) was necessary not only for success but to avoid disaster. Crucial fractions of a second could be gained if a turn was taken well, but precious time could also be lost if anything but the runners so much as scratched the precipitous ice banks.

'Line'[2] has always been a decisive factor. While the best of teams work together on it, it is the pilot who tends to dictate this aspect of bob racing. Eugenio Monti, perhaps the greatest

---

2 Identifying the swiftest, most efficient route down a run.

ever exponent of the art, tended to go high on a bend and swoop down into the straight. Tony Nash took the middle line, while racing driver Bill McCowen preferred to stay relatively low. But personal tactics are nearly always overridden by conditions and no one really knows if circumstances are right for a fast run. The state of the track and the consideration of who has run previously, their style and their performance, are all of relevance. The combinations of temperature, humidity and air speed are also sometimes crucial factors that can sway for and against a decent time. As such, the variables for consideration are endless.

(In early 1960's St Moritz, the best times were usually made between 3.20pm and 3.40pm. No one was certain why!)

Survival and speed have always been the preeminent considerations in bobsleighing. Both are the product of team-work and, in 1964, the Italians had perfected the balance. Post-World War II, they had become the dominant force in the sport. Their two not-so-secret weapons were the Cortina Run, which provided a unique level of access for practice, and their genius for building sleds. The Italian Podar was the best machine available and, although most of the top performers used these sleds, the Italians had an intimate familiarity with their manufacture and performance.

RIDING THE WIND

The first time you heard it – a rumble like a cavalry galloping in the distance or an express train thudding along the metal tracks – you might not have registered the origin of the noise that was echoing around your ears. Then, as the volume increased, you might feel a vibration starting at the soles of your feet and moving up your legs. In a blurred flash something which looked like a metal coffin screamed paSt There should be a shout but nothing human can be heard. You might briefly glimpse a pilot, helmeted and goggled, glaring grimly ahead, with the brakeman's face buried in the driver's back. Together, they might resemble some strange ice creature – half-human, half-metallic clawed beetle.

In fact, in the early 1960's this strange vessel was around £500 worth of precise engineering, designed and built to hurl its riders down a narrow ice gulley at an average speed of more than 80kph, the only separation between this world and the next being a sheet of metal not much thicker than a couple of coats of paint.

You might wonder at the things humanity will do in the sacred name of sport; perhaps bobsleighing is best thought of as the blood sport of winter, a pursuit that exacts a penalty of pain and injury (at best) for the slightest slip in focus or deviation from an optimum line. In this unfathomable test of soul, physique and courage, the most inexplicable thing is how the pilot keeps the thundering sleigh on its course while hurtling from bank to bank. Tony Nash's superlative achievement was to steer impeccably at great speed, hardly distracted by any bump or crack, without touching the gully walls.

Steve Holcomb, part of the first American team to win the two-man world bobsleigh title in 2007, explained his own involvement in the sport by saying, "I'm a thrill-seeker at heart. When it comes down to it, I'll take a dare." Russian Olympic silver and four-time world championship medallist Alexsandr Zubkov tells how he "switched to bobsled from luge when my wife told me to get a better job. I don't think this was what she had in mind."

It seems that no top-class bobsledder can adequately explain why they embrace the life-threatening risks of the sport. Unlike some forms of car and motorcycle racing, it offers no great financial rewards; those that have become available over the last 30 years were certainly not on offer when Nash and Dixon were competing. "Why do I do it?" reflected Tony Nash in 1965. "Oh, I suppose one just does . . ."

In the course of writing this book, I have researched and spoken to some of the legends of bobsleighing. To them, the 'why' question almost seems redundant. Most of them seem to have simply found the sport – or perhaps it found them. Their descriptions of their time on the most challenging runs in the world seem inextricably linked to the rest of their existence, and they have been similarly curious about why one asks the question 'why'. The motivation for getting into a relatively frail vehicle – with few of the accoutrements of safety associated with car racing, for example – and placing one's survival in the hands of gravity and a pilot's capacity to predict the almost unpredictable, while reacting at a speed on the very edge of human ability, seemed to strike them as self-evident or else irrational. The danger of the sport seems to add an existential edge. In fact, for most of the people I became familiar with whilst writing this book, bobsleigh racing was explicable only in the doing of it; to adopt their own tautology, one 'did' bobsleighing simply because one did it.

But there is something more than this. As Nash reflected, "What do I really like about it? The camaraderie, the atmosphere is wonderful. You're never alone. The people are terrific."

It is such people that will shape the tale that follows; hence I have included the biographies and exploits of some of Nash and Dixon's great rivals and friends, as it would be impossible to accurately reflect their achievement at that time without doing so. I have focused in particular on Eugenio Monti, chiefly because any chronicle of bobsleighing in the 1960's would be inadequate without understanding the impact this man had on the sport during that decade, but also because his tutelage of those he competed against is such an integral part of the story that follows. I have, in addition, looked closely at the development of the Canadian bobsleigh team, the winners of the four-man event at the 1964 Games, as their relationship with Monti, Nash and Dixon is a seminal aspect. This mosaic of skill, danger, friendship, solidarity and rivalry reveals what made Nash and Dixon's great bobsleigh victory, their Olympic gold run.

THE BEST EVER

No British bobsleigh duo has come close to matching the achievements of Nash and Dixon, with their four medals in the two-man event at the FIBT World Championships: golds (1965) and two bronzes (1964 and 1965). Combined with their Olympic feat, it confirms them as Britain's best ever exponents of the sport. This book might be thought of as a journey into the past, but Nash and Dixon may ride again in the minds and hearts of us all.

I was an eight-year-old, living in the East End of London, when these two men made their audacious bid for golden glory. For as long as I could remember, my paternal grandfather had told me tales of ice and snow. During the Second World War he had played a part in the liberation of Norway and it was there that he taught himself to ski. Jim Belton – who had boxed and played soccer to a high standard in his youth – found the freedom of the snowfields a world away from his life as a gasworks stoker deep below ground, amid the intense heat of the furnaces of Beckton. Apart from their steel boots the stokers stripped bare, drinking pint after pint of milk laced with salt water to stay hydrated.

Toward the end of the war Jim was assigned to Italy, having picked up a grasp of the language from his godfather. It was there, just outside Rome, that he won $175 from two clandestine bare-knuckle prize fights. In the first he defeated a wiry, Bronx-born GI with comparative ease; the second bout was a much more demanding confrontation with a gangling Algerian pugiliSt It took Jim close to 30 rounds to overcome this lofty battler who seemed for the most part to be fashioned out of granite; he was only felled at last by an uppercut that landed flush on his angular jaw, delivered almost from ground level.

Jim used his winnings to make his way to the Alps, to take a chance he might never have again to hone his recently found skills and indulge his passion for the cold outdoors. He was to discover a whole world of winter sports, even managing to bribe his way onto the Cresta Run. Although most of the British exponents of bobsleighing were – in a social sense – foreigners to him, Jim was able to identify with many of its continental practitioners. He would encounter some of the great pre- and immediately post-war winter sportsmen, as the first Winter Olympics since World War II got underway in St Moritz, Switzerland.

Alas, the dual pressures of making a living and family life meant this was the last time Jim would experience such personal liberation, after playing his part in liberating Europe from fascism at the most northerly of its evil tentacles. But, from time to time, his grandchildren gave him the chance to retreat back into that white world where he found peace after the war; the memories had frozen like ice in his blood.

Jim occasionally said that those mid-century snowfields and mountains were his university. In the pages that follow, I have called upon a few of the observations he shared with me, along with the insights of some of the outstanding practitioners from the early years of bobsleighing. Back when I was a boy, as I watched Nash and Dixon on the black and white television screen, such insights made that world authentic but also magically unreal; for the Winter Olympics were a big event, taking place geographically and emotionally far away from my home in the dying docklands that huddled close to a changing industrial cityscape, hanging on to the last vestiges of empire.

Memories of those people rushing toward glory evoke a screen that was dazzlingly bright, with a few dark figures darting about it to the exuberant commentary of David Coleman (who never slipped up once – remarkably). It was an experience both mystical and euphoric. Nash and Dixon became my sporting yardstick. I compared every sporting achievement to theirs: West Ham United's FA Cup win of that same year; Bobby Moore lifting the European Cup Winner's Cup and then the Jules Rimet Trophy; Chris Finnegan winning the Olympic middleweight gold medal in 1968, and many more.

Later, I would meet the likes of Moore, Sir Donald Bradman, Pele, Alf Ramsey, Ferenc Puskas, Eusebio, Steve Ovett, Muhammad Ali, Graham Hill and many other great sportspeople. But it was only during the last years of the first decade of the 21st century – when I first shook the hands of Tony Nash and Robin Dixon, now Lord Glentoran – that I felt I had come full circle, back to where it all began. Their victory opened my eyes to the nature and power of sport, and how it can reveal a meaning, purpose and direction for everyday living. What I didn't know at the outset was that, in writing about that special moment, frozen in time, I would discover even more about the nature of human integrity and nobility than I could have imagined from the television or newspaper reports back when the 1960's were young.

Tony Nash was right . . . *The people are terrific.*

I

NASH AND DIXON

Olympic and World Championship bobsleigh medallist Todd Hays, of Del Rio, Texas, once described a run thus: "I thought the driver must have been unconscious and that we certainly were going to die. You have to remember on these bobsleds, there's no suspension and it's a steel frame mounted to a steel axle. When you start approaching speeds of 140kph you can feel every vibration. It's like some someone pushes a piano on you and pushes you to the bottom of the sled. You go up to the top and you see your buddies doing it over and over again, so you want to continue to do it. As you do it, it gets less scary and more exciting and then you start searching for the speed."

At the outset of writing this book, I had to ask myself what brought two apparently quite conventional Englishmen to this sport. How could I begin to understand what they achieved unless I knew where they had come from, and what it was that might have motivated them to take up this scarily exciting search for speed. Who *were* Nash and Dixon?

In Britain in the early 1960's the sport of bobsleighing meant very little, although there had once been something of a tradition of excellence in international competition. At the inaugural Winter Games in Chamonix, France, the British four-man team had brought a silver medal home, while the second World Championship at St Moritz in 1931 saw the British four-man team (Dennis Field, P. Coote, R. Wallace, J. Newcobe) claim a bronze.

However, the golden years of the sport for Britain started in 1936 at Garmisch-Partenkirchen, when the British four-man team took the Olympic bronze. In St Moritz at the 1937 World Championships, Great Britain won both the four-man (Frederick McEvoy, David Looker, Charles Green, Byran Black) and the two-man (McEvoy, Black) events. This feat was almost repeated the following year when, for the second time, Nazi Germany's four-man team was beaten by the British bob (Chris MacKintosh replacing Black) into the silver position, this time in their own backyard at Garmisch. However, the positions were reversed in the two-man event (McEvoy and Charles Green took the silver in the British sled). In 1939 at Cortina d'Ampezzo, Italy, the German fascist sled was once more bettered by four Brits, but this time Switzerland denied the British (McEvoy, Hoard, Critchley, Green) victory as the Germans got the bronze.

For all this, for nearly 30 years British bobsleighing was notable only for its relative lack of success. But as the austere post-war era met the 'swinging 60's', two Englishmen would change that state of affairs.

*　　*　　*

Born on 18 March, 1936, the driver of Britain's number one bobsleigh at the 9th Winter Olympics was just under 28 years old at the time of the games. Anthony James Dillon (Tony)

Nash was the grandson of Francis Henry Dillon Bell, who became the first New Zealand-born Prime Minister in 1925. Bell's father had been that country's Agent General – the post which would later become High Commissioner – from 1880 to 1891, and another New Zealander grandfather had been killed at Passendale. As Tony tells it, "My grandfather died and my father's mother Amy brought up her children."

Tony Nash first saw light in the leafy English village of Amersham, in the county of Buckinghamshire, although in the early 1960's he lived in what was then Buckinghamshire's smallest village, Little Missenden, at his family's beautiful Mill House. An only child who would become involved in his family's Chesham and Brackley (Northamptonshire) breweries, Tony's early years were influenced by the exigencies of wartime.

"From four to eight I went to school in Whitehill, outside Chesham," he recalls. "During the war we lived very close to the brewery, so my father could walk round there more or less. I then went to the local school, near Bovingdon. I went to prep school in Broadstairs, St Peters – they had just moved back there after the war. So, going to Broadstairs, the whole thing was new to us all. It was fantastic rummaging around, because nobody knew what had been left in 1939. We went in the cricket pavilion and there were bats and balls that had been left where they were standing from before the war. The Americans had taken it over."

It was clear that Tony was always going to be more sports and action-oriented than scholarly. "I should have gone to Rugby, which is the family school, but unfortunately I wasn't bright enough," he happily admits. "Malvern were just leaving Harrow – they had five houses apiece during the war at Harrow – so they were trying to fill Harrow quite quickly. The headmaster of the prep school where I was at was an old

3

Harrovian anyway, so that seemed the logical way to go. So, [as] a Harrow boy, I came home slightly in front of the Eton lad." Tony smiles at his notional victory, recalling how he sat in the front seat of the bobsleigh just ahead of his old Etonian brakeman, Robin Dixon.

"I loved school," he continues. "I was in the first XV in rugby, I was the heavyweight boxing champion at Harrow, Robin was the heavyweight champion at Eton but we never met. We used to play Harrow football[3] in the Easter term because the pitches were so awful it was the only thing you could play – with a medicine ball! Never played cricket; bad eye for a small ball. So I used to go sailing on Elstree reservoir – so I could be off the hill,[4] get to the first film and get a pint in the pub on the way back," Tony laughs.

"I still have a boat but I've given up racing it. I don't like long racing, I like going round the buoys and back in for a gin and tonic on dry ground. I was getting pounded and bruised and I'm not as fit as I used to be, so I've given it up. We go fishing instead now.

"I didn't go to university," he elaborates. "I went straight into the Army from Harrow. I was in the Army before I was 19, doing my National Service. I'd gone through the basics and I met a chap who lived in our village – I was going out with his daughter and I was walking along behind my father, shooting one day, and this chap said, 'National Service, Tony, what are you going to go into?' I said, 'I don't know.' My father was never in the Army. This chap said, 'Better join my

---

3 Harrow football is played mostly with the feet, although use can be made of any part of the body, including – in particular circumstances – the hands and arms to propel the ball. The leather ball, shaped like a huge pork pie, has a diameter of about 18 inches and is a foot deep. It has a propensity to soak up water so it can become very heavy. The game, played exclusively at Harrow School, is one of the forerunners to Association Football.

4 An expression used for being out of school at Harrow.

regiment.' So he gave me the introduction to the Royal Dragoons, which is now the Royals and Blues, but in those days a line regiment.[5]

"I passed the officer training and I passed out as a second lieutenant and went out to Germany. I loved it. I had a great time. You learnt quite a lot about yourself and other people in the Army. In hindsight, I'd get my son to do the army training then go to university, rather than going to university and then going to the Army, which is what a lot of people did."

Despite having a good time during his National Service, Tony sees himself as indelibly connected with his family's industry. "I'm a brewer by trade," he acknowledges. "I came out of the Army to go into the brewery."

The roots of Chesham and Brackley go back more than 150 years. The brewery was founded by Alfred Hopcraft in 1842. Registered in July 1895 as Hopcraft and Norris Limited Brewers and Spirit Merchants, the company boasted 119 tied houses. In July 1946 Hopcraft and Norris merged with Chesham Brewery Ltd to form Chesham and Brackley Breweries Ltd.

As Tony says, "The family had the majority of shares when it became a limited company. I started learning about brewing from the age of six. My father would say, 'Sam, look after the boy,' and I used to be plonked on a barrel and I let everyone know, 'this barrel's full' – the barrels had a sight glass so you could see the level of froth; a barrel had to be full of beer so there had to be a check when the froth had settled. That was my job. I loved it. Brewing went back to about 1885 in my family, back to my great grandfather. He was one of two brothers who originally came down from Bowdon just outside

5 A regiment organised for general service, as distinct from those, like the Life Guards, whose duties are usually specific.

Manchester. One was a lay preacher and an accountant all in one; the other had a farm outside Chesham, and that's where it all started off from."

Tony's father James was keen for his son to get a rounded and realistic induction into the family business, and to start him at the bottom. "It wasn't so much an apprenticeship, more a pupillage. You were a gentleman brewer; I had to go to another brewer as my father refused to have me back until I'd learnt. But his head brewer from Brackley had gone up to Charles Wells, the big brewers in Bedford. My father said, 'He's a good man – you go and learn under him.' So I went to Bedford and I leant all about the trade, from the legal side to malting to brewing. I was there night and morning – every day."

The Charles Wells Family Brewery was established in 1876, to provide beer to the local Bedfordians. The company is now the largest independently-owned, family-run brewery in Britain and the country's fifth largest brewer. They also provided the young Nash with a good grounding in the industry. As he recalls, "I went out to Sweden and then to Denmark with Carlsberg/Tuborg. It was the very early days of lager and my father said this was the coming thing."

Although brewing still took place at both Brackley and Chesham, the company endured for just 11 years prior to a takeover by Taylor, Walker & Co. Ltd. In 1959 the Brackley Brewery was closed. Three years later the tied estate was transferred to Benskin's Watford Brewery Ltd. Meanwhile, Taylor, Walker & Co. Ltd. became part of Ind Coope. The situation was probably a crucial turning point in the life of young Tony Nash.

"The firm was sold over my head when I was in the middle of my time with Charles Wells," he recalls. "I was very, very upset when it was sold. But death duties were a problem and I don't think my father had any other alternative. If I'd have known what was going to happen to the brewery I would have signed on after national nervice.

"I returned to the people who bought us out and found myself down the end of the Commercial Road in Poplar, east London. I had a year of that and I thought, 'Sod it.'

"I came back to my bachelor uncle [Thomas Nash] who had already bought me into the engineering factory[6] in Penn, at Tylers Green just outside High Wycombe. He had nobody else to leave it to. So I thought it very politic that I went and joined my uncle."

It looked as if Nash had come full circle – working close to where he was brought up, in light machinery manufacture. But events would have a different outcome.

*   *   *

When, in 1893, Belfast was born as a city and gained a Lord Mayor, Robin Dixon's great grandfather, Daniel Dixon, was the first person to hold that office. He had risen from humble origins as a builder's merchant but, at a time when Belfast was growing at an unprecedented rate, he made his fortune importing timber and acquiring his own shipping line. In 1906 his company was responsible for building Belfast's splendid City Hall.

In 1902 Daniel was made a baronet and served as an MP for North Belfast. After World War I his second son, Herbert, having fought first in the Boer War, returned home to follow in his father's footsteps, serving simultaneously at Westminster and in the fledgling Northern Irish parliament. He became a leading member of the first Unionist government and was given a peerage, becoming Baron Glentoran in 1939.

Herbert's elder son, Daniel Stewart Thomas Bingham, was

6 Tony was a director of the firm – T. and A. Nash (Penn) Ltd.

born on 19 January 1912; after Eton and Sandhurst, in 1935 he was appointed aide-de-camp to the GOC (General Officer Commanding) in Northern Ireland. On 20 July 1933, Daniel married Lady Diana Mary Wellesley – daughter of the Third Earl Cowley and Clare Florence Mary Stapleton. Diana was the great, great granddaughter of Henry, First Baron of Cowley, who was himself the youngest brother of Arthur Wellesley – the First Duke of Wellington, the legendary victor at Waterloo and twice Prime Minister of Great Britain.

On the day of their marriage Diana was 19 and Daniel was 21. They would stay together for 50 years. The Cowley family owned a big estate in Wiltshire, while the Dixons (who had continued their timber business) were big horseracing enthusiasts, renting the Cowley estate in the winter months while the Cowleys lived in the manor house. Although her father died at the age of 52, when she was just five years of age, Diane took part in the local hunt and shoot and it was through these shared family interests that she met her husband-to-be.

Daniel served with the Grenadier Guards in France, North Africa, Sicily, Italy and, after the Second World War, in Palestine. He was mentioned in despatches, and finished his service career at the rank of lieutenant-colonel. On the death of his father, the First Baron, in 1950, Daniel succeeded him as Baron Glentoran and Ulster Unionist member for Belfast Bloomfield in the Stormont House of Commons.[7] He was to hold his seat for 11 years.

Appointed Parliamentary Secretary to the Ministry of Finance in 1952, Lord Glentoran[8] was the following year

7 Northern Irish peers – unlike all other British peers – are not barred from voting in general elections or from being elected to the House of Commons.

8 The bestowment of a life peerage brought with it a place in the House of Lords, therefore Baron Glentoran was a serving lord.

made Minister of Commerce, a post he held until entering the Northern Ireland Senate nine years later. He was to be Leader of the Senate for three years and took charge, with a large degree of success, of the new industries drive.

In 1961 Lord Glentoran resigned from the Stormont House of Commons when he moved to the Senate as Minister of State. He was the Senate's last speaker, from 1964 to 1972, before incipient Parkinson's disease induced his retirement. He was appointed as a Knight of the British Empire in 1973 and three years later became Lord Lieutenant for Belfast.

Known affectionately by his Northern Irish constituents as 'Danny Glentoran', from 1950 until 1985 he served first as Her Majesty's Lieutenant and then as Lord-Lieutenant. His family's passion for horses had endured from childhood, and it seems it was not unusual for the Speaker of the Senate to be absent during Royal Ascot week. At the other family home, Ballyalloly in Co Down, the stables were well populated with bloodstock and hunters. At a 1961 auction at Ballyalloly eight oil paintings were sold; all but one were depictions of racehorses and one portrayed King William of Orange mounted on his customary white charger.

Lord Glentoran had been a past Master of a Belfast Orange Lodge but, when he was away from Stormont, his place was invariably taken by Nationalist Senator Paddy McGill. Glentoran was always a modest and polite politician, never antagonistic or coarse, and had good relationships with even his most ardent political opponents.

The Second Lord Glentoran died on 22 July 1995, to be succeeded by his first child, the Right Honourable Thomas Robin Valerian[9] Dixon. Lady Diana had died in January 1984

---

9 'Valerian' is a Wellesley family name of Latin origin; its meaning is 'strong, healthy' and it was given to one of Imperial Rome's late soldier-emperors.

of emphysema, at age 70. As Robin now says, "My mother was the biggest influence on my life. We were quite alike and we loved each other very much. Now it's my wife. We are not alike but we are very, very close. I listen to her – she says I don't," he smiles gently.

Diane and Daniel had two sons and a daughter: the Hon. Clare Rosalind Dixon was born two years after Robin (15 November 1937) and lives in London, while their brother, Peter Herbert Dixon, an accountant and financial director, came along on 15 May 1948.

Robin was living in Woking, Surrey in the early 1960's, while serving as a soldier. He was educated at Eton and Grenoble University, France, but at the age of 16 he'd stayed with a working-class family in Bristol before doing a series of shop-floor jobs. Robin served in the Grenadier Guards from 1954 to 1966, which has become something of a family tradition (his middle son was also with the Grenadiers). During his service he undertook a varied range of duties all over the world.

Tony Nash is very complimentary of his old brakeman's qualities, but also remembers his idiosyncrasies. "He was seriously powerful. He was in G Squadron, the Guards, so he basically ran everywhere. A very fit guardsman at any rate," Tony laughs. "Robin was sometimes a pain in the arse. Obviously, living together, we had factions, everybody has arguments but by and large everybody in the bobsleighs was fine because we'd all done National Service and we all knew what was what and if things were going wrong we kept out of each other's way. We worked fine together, but Robin on race day was a complete nutter! He more or less refused to turn up. He got nerves. 'I've got a cold,' or, 'I've got flu.' And we had to drag him out – but once he was there he was alright."

Perhaps there is a connection between brakemen and bad nerves? As Olympic silver medallist brakeman Valerie Fleming once related, "My preference would be to start as early as possible. I get extremely nervous. I can't eat all day long. I just want to get up there and get it over with."

Captain the Hon. T. Robin Dixon, the brakeman with his wavy hair cut in pompadour style, was perhaps the more suave of Britain's top bobsleigh duo. At 28, he'd been a parachutist with the Grenadier Guards. Together with Nash, these two Brits carried on something of an Army tradition. At the first ever Winter Games at Chamonix in 1924, the silver-winning GB four-man bob team had consisted of a colonel, two majors and a captain. In St Moritz in 1928, these same Army men were included in the only ever Olympic five-man bob event. As such, Tony and Robin had a lot to live up to from the start.

II

COMING TO
THE RUN

By continental standards, Tony Nash and Robin Dixon came to bobsleighing late in life. Tony was almost 20 when he first took an interest in the sport. No story of how someone starts bobsleighing is truly typical of the sport, and Nash's involvement might be thought of as characteristic of his curiosity and hunger for life. But there was also something of being the right person in the right place at the right time that brought him into the winter speed-sport. However, at first his involvement was little more than the consequence of a young soldier looking for something to relieve the tedium of Cold War occupation and the routine of National Service.

"Around 1952/53 we had some leave due down in Germany and all the colonels of the four cavalry regiments in the Seventh Armoured Division got together and we'd taken over a wing of a hotel," reminisces Tony. "To make this pay, the subalterns were sent down there if they weren't doing anything else. So I leant to ski.

"It was very basic in those days – lace-on boots and tie-on

skis and you did your own thing. Winter came and there was very little happening in the middle of Germany, so three of us decided we'd go down to St Moritz on the Combined Services Winter Sports Association, which meant as officers you could go first-class to Basle for free and gratis and then from Basle to St Moritz we had to pay.

"The Swiss in those days were very pleased to see the British and the Combined Services Association," he continues. "We stayed in one of the cheaper hotels and had a wonderful time for a fortnight. What we'd said we'd do is go out there because we'd probably never be able to afford it again and do everything that we could do there. So we curled and we bobsleighed, we went down the Cresta and we skied and we just had a ball on very little money!

"I can remember it cost £65[10] for the two weeks each, including all the beer and everything else we could cope with, which was fair enough in those days but we could match it with the pay we were getting and that we hadn't used because we were out in the hinterland with the regiment.

"When I came out of the Army I told my father that I really enjoyed the bobsleighing. I'd had several car accidents – going too fast. He said, 'Okay, we'll have a deal. You want to go bobsleighing and you are going to work for your uncle eventually, so I'll give you some money to go out there and he'll give you the time off as long as you promise us that you'll never go on a motor racing track.' So that was the promise, and I never have been on a racing track. Their theory was that I wanted speed. My father used to be a racing driver at Brooklands and was reasonably good. He used to race a thing called an Air Cooled SARA, which was a French car, and a Dixon Riley.

10 However, it has to be remembered that this was a time when a building craftsman, working in the south of England, did well to earn £9/10s (£9.50) for a 50-hour week.

"I then went back down to St Moritz in 1956/57. I went out with a pair of boots, no team, nothing, moved into our Ski Association hotel. I was prepared to get on anything and I ran into a chap called Gunnar Nelson. He was a 'blood brother' of Marquis Alfonso De Portago. Gunnar was the co-driver when he was killed in the Millie Mlgila."

The Millie Mlgila has become something of a legend. The race was staged in Italy between 1927 to 1957 on public roads. Its name was derived from the distance over which it was contested; 1,000 miles. There was next-to-no crowd control, so competitors needed to be constantly vigilant, keeping a sharp lookout for local traffic, animals and pedestrians. During the 1957 race De Portago, a renowned Spanish international playboy, was just 40 miles from the finish when his vehicle blew a tyre. Travelling at around 250kph, he lost control of the Ferrari and it crashed into a group of spectators who had been watching the race from the roadside. Portago, his co-driver Nelson and ten of the crowd were killed. The consequent outcry prevented the race ever being held again.

Edmund 'Eddie' Gunnar Nelson was just 42 years of age when he died. An American who had married a Japanese wife and lived in Paris, while studying at the University of Illinois he worked as a photographer's model and was elected the 'most handsome male student' on campus, being featured in national automobile advertising at the time. Eddie was also a boxer and was with an amateur team at Pearl Harbour on 7 December 1941, the day of the infamous Japanese raid that brought the USA into the Second World War.

Tony speaks of his time with Nelson, who had taught Portago how to bobsleigh, coached the Spanish Olympic team and finished fourth in the two-man event during the 1956 winter Olympics.

"He used to take people down and race bobsleighs at St

Moritz and I went and braked for him. I got any ride I could because I loved it! The next year I went down again and I ran into Robin. We met in a hotel bar. He was bobsleighing with a chap called Henry Taylor who was a motor racing driver. They wanted someone extra in the team and that was that.

"If you needed someone for a four-man bob in those days you got him pretty drunk the night beforehand, then the next day you'd insist that he'd given his word to go on the sled – cannon fodder!" laughs Tony.

Just under six feet tall and weighing in at 12 stone eight pounds, Robin Dixon was a sturdy and powerful athlete. A heavyweight boxer and track sprinter in his final years at Eton (his 100-yard best was 10.3 seconds), Robin was then a captain in the Grenadier Guards. He ran, played tennis and also competed to a high standard on the squash courts.

As he says "I've always loved sport. I loved getting in the first teams at school and giving the best part of myself that I could. I hate doing things badly in sport. I always got coached if I could find coaches. I always did the training that you had to do. I played league squash when I came back to London in the 1950's, but I wanted to be better than that. I wanted to play for the Army. And a lovely man called Nasrullah Khan[11] coached at the Lansdowne,[12] where I played

"I said, 'Look Naz, I want to get in the Army team next

---

11 Pakistani Nasrullah Khan, a fine squash player in his own right, was a cousin of the famous Hashim Khan. Nasrullah coached Ireland's Jonah Barrington in 1966 when Barrington was preparing for the British Open, then regarded as the world championship. (Barrington won the first of his six British Open titles between 1967 and 1973.) He also worked for Azam Khan, Hashim Khan's younger brother, as his matchplay strategist and tactical advisor, and coached Angela Smith, the GB and England world star, who became a legend herself for taking the ladies' game into the professional league.

12 The Lansdowne Club, 9 Fitzmaurice Place, London W1, is a "social, residential and athletic club for members of social standing". From its inception in 1935, it was the only club in London where ladies had equal standing with men – as they still do.

year because the Army championships are here and I'll be here.' He coached me for an hour every day I could make and he gave me a series of exercises – it was hard but I got into the Army team. I can be quite focused."

Dixon's recruitment to bobsleighing came, as he says, "completely by chance". As he recalls, "I hadn't gone out to St Moritz to bobsleigh but to ski. I was quietly having breakfast in a hotel in St Moritz while on a service break when an old school friend/distant cousin called John Bingham[13] came into the room."

Pausing only to acknowledge his infamous relative, Dixon continues. "Also a Guardsman, he was involved with the British Army bob team. (He had also raced powerboats.) He sat down, had a coffee and asked if I'd ever thought of bobsleighing and I said I'd never heard of it. He then told me that his team had got selected to race for Britain in the World Championships, but as one of the boys was injured they needed someone to fill in and, as I was always a fairly competent athlete and pretty unimaginative,[14] he thought it was the sort of thing I'd like and asked if I'd like to come and have a look. I didn't know anything about it so I went to see what it was all about.

"I went up to the run and got on this thing, had a ride and – that was it. I was on the back," he laughs. "I didn't look at the course all the way down but when we stopped I thought that I'd quite enjoyed it. A week later I was competing in the World Championships, coming last in the four-man event . . . There were only two Brit teams competing. The closest team to us was the British number one team – they finished second last.

13 Richard John Bingham, Seventh Earl of Lucan – the same Lord Lucan who disappeared in November 1974 following the violent murder of the family nanny, Sandra Rivett.

14 Robin makes a joke at his own expense – if he were more imaginative, so the logic runs, he might have seen the folly of risking severe injury!

"Hubert Martineau,[15] who was then the President of the St Moritz Bobsleigh club, asked me to stay on after the World Championships to learn something about the sport and compete in the European juniors in January 1957. He paid the hotel bills and other expenses and wrote to the regiment to get leave for me to stay on for another two weeks. I was quite a bit faster than any of the other brakemen, so that was probably one good reason why he was so supportive.

"He was also the President of the British Bobsleigh Association," Nash recalls of Martineau. "He had a load of money – came from sugar, all the brewers used it at one time – and was a generous sponsor of sport. He lived at Holyport, in Berkshire, Maidenhead way. He used to have his furniture at his own suite at Claridge's, he had a grouse moor; he'd go to St Moritz for a month and then he came back to Holyport, where he organised his cricket through the summer, then on 12 August he would be seen on the grouse moors. He was President of the St Moritz Bobsleigh Club from 1922 to 1969. There was a tradition for visiting test cricket teams to play a Martineau XI as their first match.[16]

"He was in the First World War, a Major in the Welsh Guards, and was invalided out. He was very, very English –

15 Hubert Melville Martineau was born in Westminster on 24 October 1891, the son of Philip Martineau from the sugar refining firm David Martineau and Sons. The company had been established in the St George's in the East area of London in the mid-19th century, and at one time was based in Christian Street and engaged in sugar baking, a trade largely dominated by the German/Hanoverian immigrant community. In 1875 the company, then operating out of Liverpool, acquired along with Henry Tate the rights for the Langen sugarcube-making process – which proved to be, as they say, a gold mine.

16 Like Robin Dixon, Martineau was educated at Eton and, although he did not play for the school's cricket team, he did develop a great love of the game, playing to a good standard and making three first-class matches between 1931 and 1932 as a right-handed batsman and left-arm orthodox spin bowler for HDG Leveson-Gower's XI. He played against Oxford University in 1931 and against Cambridge and Oxford University in 1932.

Club cricket of a high standard was played at his private ground near Maidenhead between 1923 couldn't be more English!" chuckles Tony. "He used to fund private evenings on the bob run and have torches all along the course for night-time races that happened alongside barbeques, etc. That was before the Second World War, it was in the days of the Bentley boys.[17] He was a very rich individual. The bob run at St Moritz wouldn't have been built if it hadn't have been for his money. After the war the Kurund Verkehrsverein, the town council of St Moritz (who knew he wanted the bob run built), said that they only had so many francs – so he just put a load of money into it every year. He has a corner named after him on the St. Moritz run."

It was also Martineau who found Dixon his first bob driver, as Robin recalls. "Martineau got hold of Henry Taylor,[18] then an F2 driver and later F1. Henry and I paired up then as a two-man team."

According to Taylor, "To all intents a bobsleigh is a racing

and 1939, and four national sides touring England began their tours playing against his personal XI: Australia in 1926, New Zealand in 1927, the West Indies in 1928 and India in 1932. Martineau himself played in all those matches with the exception of the 1926 match against Australia.

In 1927 he went on a tour of Egypt with the Free Foresters, playing two matches against the national side. He took his own team to the country each year between 1929 and 1939, and Martineau played in all the tour matches.

17 A group of wealthy British young men who raced Bentleys.

18 Henry Taylor was born 16 December 1932 in Shefford, Bedfordshire into a farming family. Appropriately he started his 'speed career' at speedway in East London before switching in 1954 to a 500cc F3 Cooper. He had advanced to F2 by 1958 and piloted Britain's bobsleigh team at St Moritz before trying his hand at F1. Starting in 1959 with Cooper, along with the likes of Jack Brabham he joined the team that included Stirling Moss at Lotus in 1961.

Taylor was one of a number car racers who doubled as a bobsleigh ace, which included Ferrari driver Alfonso de Portago who, although born in London, won a gold medal for Spain in the two-man World Championships in 1957. The successful F2 driver Robin 'Widz' Widdows (who also dabbled with F1 in 1968) was another member of this fraternity. The son of a Battle of Britain fighter pilot and post-war test pilot, he represented Great Britain at the 1964 and 1968 Winter Olympics in the four-man bobsleigh event (making GB1 in Grenoble). Widdows held the British Record on the Cresta Run for 15 years. Keith Schellenberg, a member of the British bobsleigh team for both the 1956 and 1964 games, also raced cars in the 1950's.

car on runners instead of wheels," which was not a bad description if you look at the Formula 1 cars of the day.

Robin spent a fortnight training with Taylor in St Moritz. As he recalls, they "always did pretty well – Henry was a supremely confident person and his knowledge of organising a speed sport team was excellent. He was a very good competitor."

Taylor and Dixon both then returned to England to prepare for the 1958 World Championships – Taylor to his farm and Robin back to the Grenadier Guards. They would take silver at the European Junior championships in St Moritz that year.

In the final years of the 1950's, Tony became involved with the British four-man bob-team. After being co-opted to join the British bobsleigh squad by Taylor, he had been competing for the four-man team (the fourth member of the crew fluctuated during that period) as the quartet made appreciable progress on the world circuit, establishing themselves as a developing team. From this point, Nash started to take every opportunity to drive. Apart from it being quite obvious that he was never going to make the perfect brakeman, there was something enticing to him about the responsibility of driving a bobsleigh in competition.

Four-time World Cup race winner Shauna Rohbock (2006/07 Calgary and Park City, Whistler and Königssee 2008/2009) has expressed the sentiment that tends to push you to the front of the bob: "I do like being in control. I definitely enjoy being a driver. As a brakeman, you're kind of expendable. I hated being a brakeman because you have no control. That's why I wanted to be a driver . . . I wanted more control."

As his own passion for bobsleighing grew, Nash became immersed in the sport's international ethos. For Tony, it seems to have been the 'personality' of the sport that captivated him, as found in the characters of the flamboyant buccaneers that populated the runs. The 1958 World Championships – taking place for the fourth time in Garmisch-Partenkirchen, West Germany – presented a tableau of the sport at that time, bringing together the diverse range of eccentric and idiosyncratic practitioners. This group of charismatic adventurers and hedonistic swashbucklers was a constant source of entertainment and inspiration to the young Englishman, who himself had a daredevil quality about him.

"The Germans were a pretty rough lot," remembers Tony. "They had locked containers for the sleds. The Americans, who were army from the occupying forces, had star-spangled helmets, they looked like a load of grid iron footballers. They had this great big donkey emblazoned right across the front of their sled – it was locked up overnight, but when they got it out in the morning they went berserk because someone had painted on a great big dong on this donkey! Everybody else thought it was amazingly funny," laughs Tony.

"We were told by the Swiss to stay outside Garmisch with a chap who owned a pub there (the Schützenhaus in Partenkirchen). We always stayed with him in the future. He had represented Germany in six or seven Olympic sports, marvellous man called Franz Kemser.[19] He was a great big bloke. In the 1952 Olympics there was no weight limit[20] in the bobsleigh so the Germans had these enormous people in their team. They were slow at the start of course, but by the time

19 Franz Kemser was born 11 November, 1910. He competed in bobsleighing from the late 1930's to the early 1950's and won a gold medal in the four-man competition at the 1952 Winter Olympics in Oslo. Kemser also won three medals at the FIBT World Championships: two silvers (two-man, 1953; four-man, 1938) and one bronze (four-man, 1939).

20 Because of the growing weight issue (the heavier a bob the faster it would drop down a run) at the 1952 Winter Olympics, the first changes occurred when weight limits were introduced thereafter. Until the weight-limit rule was added, bobsleigh crews tended to be very heavy. Afterward, the maximum weight became 630kg (four-man), 390kg (men's two-man) or 340kg (women's two-woman). Metal weights may be added to reach these limits, as greater weight makes for a faster run.

they got to the finish they were going like the clappers – he was in the winning German four-man sled that year. He had skied, played ice hockey and kayaked, etc – he was a lovely man. He had us and the Swiss at his place too. We'd drink in his Bavarian bar and he insisted that we ate like horses and he'd send us off to bed – he'd pick me up by the scruff of the neck and put me on the stairs. We stayed with him again in 1961 – you could shoot at stags and things from a back window, it was a hell of a place."

Henry Taylor was the natural first-choice pilot for the British crews. But, as Tony Nash tells it, his dissociation from the sport came almost as speedily as the bob run itself.

"In 1960, during the summer, Henry Taylor had a crash at Aintree," remembers Nash. "He went off the course and got a wooden stake through the petrol tank of the car and it went into his stomach, so petrol went into his stomach and he was never ever going to bobsleigh again. Robin Dixon had been Henry Taylor's brakeman and they'd been together for some time. Their team obviously broke up, as did the British four-man crew, because Henry wasn't there anymore. I had been in the four-man team with Henry driving and, because I had begun to drive and get into the teams with other people on the back, it was logical that I took over."

Even if Taylor had not had the accident, the pressures of F1 racing would likely have meant his days as a bobsleigh driver were numbered. Nash had been gradually tutoring himself in the fundamentals of driving a bob. But from a young age he'd needed to wear glasses more or less all the time – not a common feature amongst the top bob pilots of the world. As Robin recalls with some amusement, "Tony was almost entirely self-taught but he was the only driver left in the team. I was initially a little nervous because he's blind as a bat!"

"The problem with glasses was when you put your goggles

down at the start, you had to swing the bob backwards and forwards and the glasses got misted up," says Nash, recalling how he overcame his little problem. "You couldn't get the condensation out of the goggles. We tried the great big visors that Mike Hawthorne [the racing driver} used to wear and that didn't work at all.

"I drove on contact lenses because we thought it was going to be safer. I couldn't bear to wear them for more than four hours at a stretch. I went down without them once or twice," he laughingly recalls, "the man behind was steering.

"This was before soft lenses. I used to wear them four to six weeks before I went out trying to get used to them, but I found them awfully difficult. They used to slip out occasionally and if you were dancing you'd find yourself crawling all over the floor looking for this little mass of glass. It was hell trying to get them in your eye in the morning with a hangover! I wore them for very little else other than bobsleighing and as soon as I stopped I was back into glasses again."

Tony and Robin had been involved in the same four-man team, but it was clear to Dixon that there were other possibilities. "Tony was in a group that was rather more serious than us and they beat us. But Tony and I were pretty fed up with carrying Union Jacks and ending up at the bottom of the list, and somewhere along the line we got together."

At this time Tony was beginning to think about the probability of taking part in the Olympic Games, which were just around the corner. But Nash and Dixon would have to wait for their crack at Olympic glory. As Tony says, "In 1960 the Olympics were held in Squaw Valley in America. They said they were going to hold skiing and skating and bobsleighing, but then they had a bit of a referendum out there and said bobsleighing was too expensive. So in 1960 bobsleighing wasn't part of the Games and we had a World Championships down in Italy."

However, Nash was beginning to look at the possibility of improving the bob. "I'd started to drive and I was experimenting. I was with my uncle in the engineering company so I had the tools to do things with. Between 1959 and 1960 Henry Taylor had organised and undertaken a lot of experiments with de Havilland, the aircraft manufacturer up in Hertfordshire, and they'd built a bobsleigh. But it wasn't right. It was too heavy in the wrong places, but it was the forerunner of everything you see today in that you stepped over the side, it had retractable steps and so on. An awful lot of heavy thinking went into it."

But things really started to happen at the start of the 1960's. "We began to compete as a team in 1961 – the first year we did as well as could be expected. It was Guy Renwick and I who put the team together. He lives up in Northumberland now; he has a very nice shoot up there. He was my best man at my first wedding. We put the two- and four-man team together, got hold of a Land Rover and a trailer and were totally independent, so we got to the tracks slightly before everybody else arrived and got in one or two practice runs before them."

Robin's sporting attire at this time included wire pot scourers attached to the tips of the light, studless rugby boots that provided extra traction during the push-off stage. (Spikes were not allowed on bob tracks.) "I bought the scourers by the dozen to get a penny off the cost," he recalls.

These accessories were part of perfecting a fast start, something that Nash and Dixon were amongst the first to concentrate on. As Tony Nash tells it, "Pushing at the start is much more of a speed maker now than it was in our day, but we knew the difference it could make."

The start for Tony and Robin was 20 to 50 yards of flat ice.

Establishing a momentum with both men outside the sled, they slid the bob gently back and forth to avoid the vehicle digging itself into a trench on the countdown to the off. Working up a rhythm, on the signal to get away both men would ram the sled for the initial few yards, trying to throw over a third of a ton of metal over the crest and onto the plunging track. First into his seat was Nash the steersman, reaching for his ropes. This left Dixon on his own to build up the speed, timing his eventual leap onto the back of the sled to the split second.

The brakeman in a bob – who to the spectator, fittingly perhaps, often seems to be praying as a bob flashes by, his head lowered between his knees – has his part to play, but it is the driver who has to make decisions at all the right times and in the right places. For bobsleighing is essentially a team sport and how teams come together says much about why they succeed or fail. While logic tells us that putting the best performers together will create the best team performance, so often the whole is much more than the sum of its parts. As Pierre Lueders, Olympic gold medal-winning pilot, commented, "We have a game plan. But in the four-man, anything can happen."

Bobsleighs, tracks and people are a set of imponderable variables. As these complex entities interact they can produce chaos, but the high-functioning team – the combination of two, four, 11 or more people – will be underpinned by their individual talents and motivations. The foundation of any team is premised on how they come together. What starts as an unconnected group can develop into a self-reinforcing unit via a chemistry unique to every positive combination of people. In bobsleighing this is an evolutionary process that needs to occur within a nexus including crew, constantly developing technology (the bobsleigh) and a persistently changing environment (the run), and it is this situation that makes a *team* different from just a group, or a gang.

At the start of the 1960's, Tony and Robin quickly reached an understanding as a duo/team. Nash recalls, "When we went over to Lake Placid in 1961 for the World Championships all the European teams went over on one plane. We were met at the airport by the Mayor and taken to a civic reception. We went on by buses up to Lake Placid. Our sled had been brought into a military airport and been shipped down. It was a fairly concentrated time we had there."

As Robin recalls, "In the first run of our first World Championship we broke the course record and did it again in our second run – overnight, after the first two heats, we were leading. We eventually finished sixth but it was quite a good start. It surprised us and quite a few other people," he laughs. "But that was the lowest we ever finished. We had messed up a bit, but it was the first time we had actually competed in any meaningful way. I believed that if we got organised we'd have a chance of an Olympic medal."

Tony Nash recollects his first big event racing with Dixon. "Robin was my brakeman because he was the best. The American track was nothing like a European track – you had to drive the course completely differently. It pulled the best out of us, I think, and the team gelled from then on."

Tony was quick to recognise Robin as his ideal brakeman. 2006 Olympic silver medallist brakeman Valerie Fleming described the role concisely when she said, "You run, you push, you get in and you have no control." But the brakeman does have certain gifts. The physiological requirements are largely self-evident; the brakeman is an engine with a remarkable opening boost quality. But the psychological combination of total reliability and placing complete trust in your driver is perhaps less obvious. This is not something that can be honed in the same way as drivers can sharpen their reactions and ability to read a course. It is probably true that it's the driver who is usually the more studious of bobsleighing technique, but a good brakeman should be a both a partner and a critic.

Deadweight brakemen – passengers whose sole capacity was covering 20 to 50 yards swiftly – were relatively easy to find. An explosive athlete who could also be an active collaborator in negotiating a series of testing runs was a much less common individual.

Nash and Dixon both recall the aftermath of their American odyssey. According to Robin, "It did Tony a lot of good because he stayed on afterwards while the rest of us went home – he got a lot of practice in."

But, of course, the social side of things was not neglected – as Tony relates: "The Americans were funny people. They used to have various clubs. We had a party after the Championships and everybody involved was invited. Very democratic. We were handing out the whiskeys, vodkas and gins, the lot, and the Americans were just knocking them back. Of course, they got absolutely out of their minds. It was a freezing cold day, and we lined them all up outside – this line of stiffs!" he laughs.

"The next year we were invited out to the Diamond Trophy. Went out with Andrew Hedges, a member of the number two team, who used to race cars and powerboats, he was a great character. Because there were just a few of us we got to know the Americans much better. There was a town just over the hill and they invited us for a drink. Everyone in the bar was watching *Robin Hood*. One of the Americans had had an accident and he got the ambulance to stop and he was carried into the bar on a stretcher, shouting, 'Has it started yet?' He wouldn't go to hospital until he'd watched *Robin Hood*!"

Robin and Tony would celebrate their half-century of

friendship in January 2007. Fifty years previously, at first sight they might have seemed an odd couple. A short, barrel-chested, bespectacled director of an engineering firm – who, although clearly a vigorous man, would not have seemed the type to leap into a bobsleigh to plummet downhill and hurtle around the great white walls of a frosty run – one would more likely imagine Tony Nash to be a country gentleman. Even for the early 1960's, he looked and acted like a person who wouldn't look out of place striding with a dog across a meadow. To the layman, he probably didn't evoke the romantically mad environment of bobsleighing at all.

But Nash – who is close to being an almost entirely unflappable man – was passionate about winning or losing in perhaps the most exciting sport in the whole of the Olympic Games (winter or summer). Those who knew him as a competitor and team-mate realised that his composure and steady nerve were the two prerequisites for piloting a bobsleigh.

Dixon was a man adept at keeping his emotions to himself, likely useful in his later life as a politician and diplomat. But he also had the right stamp for his role on the piste or the bob chute. A background of Eton and parachuting might well be the ideal beginning for the evolution of a bobsleigh racer. The tall, athletic, elegant Grenadier Guardsman was rather more aloof than his partner, but he exuded determination and self-confidence – probably born out of flinging himself from an aircraft with nothing but thousands of feet of sky beneath (until the ground came rushing into his face). Carrying a hint of Peter Cook's raffishness, Robin was both the complete contrast and the perfect complement to Nash, a man with the look of a gentleman farmer going to war. They were a very English twosome – but together they were destined to conquer the world.

III

PRELUDE TO DESTINY

Better to die as a wolf than live like a scared dog.
– old Swiss adage

Even the well-trained wolf won't become a lamb.
– Armenian variation on the same theme

One wolf doesn't desert the other.
– Estonian variation

According to the great Swiss six-time world champion bobsledder Fritz Feierabend, "Somewhere in the human psyche there is a meeting point between attitude and application. It is from there that the successful bobsleigh rider finds his course."

For Max Houben, the Belgian athlete and Olympic silver medallist bobsleigher, one of the deciding skills is holding the sled straight in the glare of the ice road that any given run presents. In the narrow straights, each time the edge of the sled brushes against the wall fractions of seconds are lost. At the same time it might cause the bob to be on the wrong line on entering the next turn; smoothness counts. Every time a bob driver is obliged to correct their line, time is lost.

But the quest for the perfect route down a chute is not historically a lonely pursuit. Bobsleighing is marked out as one of the most affable of sports, even at the level of excellence. Most of those taking part would help one another all they could, providing advice, counsel and information to their peers, comrades or rivals. Perhaps, over the years, this ethos might have been eroded somewhat. Traditionally, however, crews did not want to win on the basis of who made the least mistakes. The desired victory was one by which the winner would know they were the best. This was partly about being a 'good sport', but there was also something primal that seeped through the logic, the urge to be the pack-leader; the cold, unforgiving milieu brought out something of the wolf.

While there was much informality in the sporting lives of Nash and Dixon, a fair amount of effort went into preparation and planning. Although much of it was carried out as part of the socialising that seemed to go with the lifestyle of winter sport in those days, as Tony Nash explains: "I loved shooting. The form in those days was that you couldn't get on a bobsleigh track until the weather was right, so we used to sort out what we were going to do from October to November while we were out shooting together. We used to take in the regular ball on New Year's Eve, meet in a club in London on New Year's Day and drive to St Moritz, which used to take about three days."

As Robin Dixon confirms, Tony "was always the boss. No doubt about that. I wasn't part of the whole decision-making process. I was usually working for Her Majesty somewhere overseas, but by hook or by crook I used to get myself back somehow to meet the caravan taking off from London, usually at pretty early hours of the morning as we had to drive across Europe, Land Rover and trailer, on ordinary roads. These were the days before motorways. The first leg we'd usually fetch up in Basle."

Despite his physical appearance, Nash had a charismatic quality that meant people were happy to do what he asked. He describes the regular journey that was made by himself and his team-mates: "We had to tow our load over the mountains. Although it was only about 150 more miles from Basle, we used to see St Moritz in the dark. That was the worst bit of the trip, descending into St Moritz with everything pushing you down the mountain. You had to try to take it as slow as possible, all the time knowing that your mates were down in the town having a good time in the bars, which was quite frustrating," he laughs.

Tony also had a penchant for mixing socially with the other teams – which, as Robin explains, was a great asset to British sledding: "Tony was always sociable and friendly. He got to know the Italians from our trips to Cortina . . . I think it was natural to him, part of his personality. He got on extremely well with them, and over the months and years we got closer to them. By 1962/63 we were practically integrated with them."

While this friendship was certainly a two-way street, from his earliest days in bobsleighing Tony had wanted to learn about how the Italians achieved excellence in his chosen sport. For his brakeman, "The smartest thing Tony did was to take every opportunity to chat with the Italians . . . we both learnt a lot from the relationship that he instigated . . . that had a huge influence on both our futures. They were the best around, there was no one close to them at that time, who better to find out about?"

Tony himself recalls how his thirst for knowledge was

sometimes frustrated: "I took it quite seriously. The Austrians used to call me 'the Profy', 'the Professor', because I was there to win and always used to examine their bobs, getting as close as you could when they weren't looking. Having the engineering company behind me was helpful, although there was very little that could be done because of the time. We were up against competition from the point we got out there till the time we came home and, of course, we had nowhere to go out of season. Now, with the artificial tracks you can go up to April – somebody will keep a track open or something. But we had nowhere to train in the UK so we had to go to St Moritz, which wasn't the cheapest place in the world.

"Our problem was we used to go out to a track with really good ideas; we went to massive lengths to try and get a British bobsleigh, but we never had the time to do it. When you got out there at the beginning of January you were always more or less into fighting for your place in the team with what you'd got and with what everybody else had got. You didn't have time to try things out, and of course there was an enormous amount of variables – the weather, the ice, how fast you pushed off in the first place. It was very hard to get a quantum on the ice.

"When the season ended the Italians went up into the mountains with their bobsleighs and they used to have standard lengths – they analysed their performance over short distances, looking at whether something was good or bad. We never had the chance. Time to test was always the problem."

But, as Tony says, the Brits did make some innovations of their own: "It became very evident that heating runners wasn't going to be good for the track and that went out quite quickly. We kept them in rugs and had the sled upside down as long as possible. The idea about keeping the blades warm was a bit like the way people would heat tyres on the motor racing circuit before a race. We used to put them on the radiator in our rooms, wrapped up in rugs to keep the heat in, then we'd put them on at the last moment; but if we had to do a full lap before the race, we'd put a spare pair on and keep a warmed pair for the race. One of the Eastern European luge teams, the Poles or the Czechs I think, got caught heating up a pot of oil round the back of the start. They had hollow runners and they were pouring the hot oil in them – so they were singeing on the start," he laughs, "bloody great clouds of steam! That was stopped, so then people started putting ether on the runners. Now they have sensors and the technical judge will go round to see if the runners are heated.

"We used to have runner guards, to try and keep the runners as pristine as possible. So they'd put them on at the end of a run."

In the early 1960's there were no sponsors fighting to assist the ambitions of would-be Olympians. The expression 'central funding' was not in the sporting lexicon and the biggest lottery for men like Nash and Dixon was the one they played themselves when careering down a hard ice run at any opportunity.

"At the end of the 1950's and the start of the 1960's I don't think it was that expensive," claims Robin of the financial costs, "but it was Tony who worked out the economics in the main."

"Robin had family and couldn't put much money into it," he says. "We'd be out there from the end of January to the middle of February[21] and £400 would see us through the winter. My father put up the money for the bobs that we bought from the Italians. The old Land Rover we used to get from track to track was from Guy Renwick's estate – we bought that from his father. We had a trailer made for the

21 This six weeks or so was the usual time that Nash and Dixon had for 'cold' training.

sleds, with the same size wheels as the Land Rover because we had a spare for that. Everything weighed about two tons – a four-man and a two-man bob, spare runners and other equipment, the four of us. That was towed for about a month, about 8,000 miles around Europe, every year by that little Mark 1 Land Rover with its 1500cc engine! And it never let us down.

"We had to show everything at every border – we'd throw the tarpaulin off and they'd never seen anything like it, of course.

"Robin usually came direct from wherever he was doing his service. Of course in those days you had to include a dinner jacket in your luggage, in case you were invited out to dinner.

"When we went out to Garmisch for the 1958 World Championships all British bobsleighs were put on a lorry and sent over, and that was paid for by the British Bobsleigh Association. At the Olympics in 1964 we had the transportation of the sleds, our official clothing and our board paid for by the British Olympic Association. We also went round to shops and got some stuff by saying we'd promote them, Jaeger, etc. Our big one was Simpsons in Piccadilly. We used to have a cocktail party there every winter. Dr Simpson [a member of the family that owned the famous retail store, now the flagship of the Waterstone's chain] was a great friend of Hubert Martineau."

The friendly association with the Italians also took Nash and Dixon to Cervinia. This trip was to prove crucial in cementing their relationship with the most advanced practitioners of their sport on the planet. As Tony recollects, "In 1963 we were invited out to train with the Italians and open up their new government-funded bob run in Cervinia. It was a hell of a long way; down to Turin and along the autostrada then up. So we jumped in the Land Rover and off we went."

Robin doesn't remember it as quite as smooth a departure as that: "I came down off the mountain from skiing about 4pm to see the Land Rover and trailer all packed up and Guy Renwick jumping up and down, shouting at me, 'Where the hell have you been?' because we were supposed to be on the road."

When they eventually arrived at the new track, Tony recalls, "We were the only foreign team there. When we got there, Robin and I and our little sled were faced with about three dozen Italians – mechanics, officials and bobsleighers."

According to Robin, "When we arrived in Cervinia for the first time we were met by one of their team, who told us to get something to eat and that they would take care of our vehicle. I walked through a garage area that had around a couple of dozen bobs in it and into the dining room. Competitors, coaches and technical men were sitting around three huge tables. I thought, 'These guys are serious.'"

As Nash recalls the first day of practice in Cervinia, "The day after we got there to open this run, before our first time down, they said everyone takes it very slowly and brakes. After about the third go we were allowed to go flat out down the track, which was a problem because there were two tunnels included in those days. That didn't help with my contact lenses. The track was like Innsbruck – they had built it especially like that to give themselves some advantage. We went down faster than the Italians and they said, 'That's very good, Tony. Off you go to the pub.' But they didn't come with us. They stayed down there for another three or four goes, trying to get a faster time – they didn't dare leave until they did!" he laughs.

"That trip was one of our more notable adventures," Robin concurs. "They were very welcoming and spoke and worked with us as if we were one of their best teams. From that point on we effectively became the Italian number three bob. This was all very genuine. However, at one point, after a couple of runs in front of a fair few press people, we were leading them in a time trial. The Italian team manager even gave us our team instructions. Eventually he came over and quietly informed us, 'This is our show now,' and that there was going to be one more run and we wouldn't be involved."

The experience in Italy gave Nash and Dixon their first direct step on the road to Innsbruck. Tony describes the dash back to St Moritz in 1963:

"After Cervinia we had to get back to St Moritz for the British Olympic trials. We were reasonably sure that we were going to qualify, but we were obliged to race against the others. The trip was dramatic to say the least. One of the bobs had bent an axle and we needed to get to Cortina on our way back to get that repaired. We'd been all day in the Land Rover in the bitter cold, looking to make the border before 11pm when it closed. If we failed to make it that might have meant we would get to St Moritz too late to take part in the qualifying. We didn't make it and had to stay on the border in a guest house until 5am the next morning, when the border opened. It was about 20 below and we had everything over the front of the Land Rover trying to keep it going. We could only tolerate around a quarter of an hour driving at a time because the freezing air came up through the pedals and froze our feet. We got to St Moritz at 11am. Tony Brooke, the team manager, was worried about us. He told us, 'If you're not up to it, just don't turn up on the run,' but we said that we'd be okay. We thawed ourselves out with bacon and eggs – Guy Renwick and Robin Widdows got the sled sorted out and we managed the fastest run of the day. We disappeared after that and weren't seen again for a while," laughs Nash. "It was so cold that winter – even St Moritz froze up."

In the early 1960's media coverage of sport was changing, and it appeared that winter sports would be part of this. Tony recalls that moment in time in Austria with the British bob team:

"All of a sudden it came together, we started to get quite good at it and one took it a lot more seriously than one did before. In 1963, that bad winter, that's when the BBC found us. There was absolutely nothing on television – football, horse racing, everything was off! They discovered that we were doing reasonably well and that we were trying out the course in Innsbruck for the Austrians – the World Championships were down there. That's where we first got on television, which gave us a certain amount of notoriety. It was the first time bobsleighing had got any attention at all from what you might call a mass audience. We also came in third in the two-man and fourth in the four-man, behind the Italians of course, and we thought, 'My God, we really can do it.' In the 1960 Olympics at Squaw Valley there was a little television coverage, but not very much. So 1964 was the first time the general public had seen bobsleighing, certainly in Britain. We got all our parents to chip in and we got all our kit sorted out – we came out looking like a team, normally we had green jumpers but we changed into blue and we looked quite smart."

At that 1963 World Championship, which doubled as the pre-Olympic competition on the Igls Run, Nash and Dixon claimed third place, bettered only by the two Italian teams. This was the highest Britain had been placed in the event since 1938.

When the Brits returned to St Moritz, they were confident that the medals in the Winter Games would be contested between the Italians, the Austrians and themselves. As Dixon says, "By then there wasn't a lot between us. We had grown more determined and focused."

The British bobsleigh team based themselves in St Moritz just before the Olympics; as soon as the Games in Innsbruck closed, they planned return there. Tony recalls the British preparations for Innsbruck:

"Tony Brooke was the British captain. A quiet man and a former bobsleigher, we told him what we wanted to do and he organised things after that. We did have a bit of nastiness – the RAF had a wing commander driving who reckoned it would look good on his CV to be in the Olympics, although he didn't beat us. Tony Brooke sorted that out. He had also been a good racing driver at Brooklands – he had a very rare Vauxhall, there were only two in the world, he loved his old cars and he'd puff on a pipe. He had been a rear gunner in a Lancaster during the war and his stories about that were hilarious.

"We reckoned after 1963 we could get on the rostrum," Nash confirms, "we saw a medal as possible. That's what we were trying to do. Nobody expected anyone to beat the two Italians.

"By 1964 the sleds themselves were making a difference. If I do something I like to do it reasonably well. I don't say I was always going to be the best, but I'd like to try and be competent. And of course I knew a bit about engineering, which helped us get the most out of the sleds. We went back to using a 1961 sled – 'Old Faithful' – rather than the new sled that we had. The Italians had complained that they hadn't got the money, etc, but they had to use the new sleds because they would have lost face if they hadn't. But I was convinced that the new ones weren't as good for the job we were looking to do.

"We worked dreadfully hard in the year prior to the Olympics. I used to run the beagles and played a bit of rugger to keep fit. There was also the task of getting our equipment together."

Robin remembers their schedule in the run-up to the Games: "We trained a bit harder before we went to the Olympics during the autumn – running, circuit training, weightlifting. I was in the services anyway, so I was in the tracksuit every day and just worked a bit harder. We started training around September for the season that began around Christmas. We trained all the time. We spent the whole of the season at it and we did little else.

As Tony recalls, "I was still working for my uncle and went off with his blessing to work on a farm near Goring-on-Thames, Oxfordshire, for most of the year, right through the harvest, and they gave me all the sod's jobs to do. I worked really hard from dawn to dusk and then went off rowing in the evenings. I got very fit indeed."

Nash, a lifelong non-smoker, was a member of the Chiltern Rugby Football Club, playing at front row forward. He was doing a lot of sailing in a Merlin class dinghy with the Upper Thames Sailing Club at Bourne End and the Royal Corinthians Yacht Club at Burnham-on-Sea. He rowed for Wallingford and Marlow rowing clubs during the summer, training intensively in the warm evenings of 1963, and was also prepared to have a go with a cricket bat (though he claims he "had no eye for a small ball") and was a keen fisherman.

Dixon made no special arrangements to keep fit, as he was spending a great amount of time training paratroopers. But, in true army fashion, Nash went on reconnaissance prior to his team's full advance;

"I went out to Innsbruck in the summer with the number two team captain, Bill McCowan, and did some prelim work," he remembers, "to see how the course was, where we were going to stay, and get everything organised for the teams. One of the things we found was that all of the bob teams were going to be in garages allotted to them to keep their sleds in and service them. We took one look at these and thought them too dark and dingy and found a couple of garages behind a place called the Agida hotel – they were heated. We'd stayed there the year before. It was very much one-upmanship on all the other teams and a tremendous boost to our team morale."

Robin confirms the part his team-mate played in laying the ground: "Tony had done all the organising and we knew where we were going. We'd had a nice winter in St Moritz; getting some good practice in . . . We were pretty confident that, as long as we avoided making too many errors, we could take a medal home."

For all their conviviality, the British two-man bob team were a pairing to be reckoned with. Trained in the best public schools, where sport was second only to religion in its observance, both were intensely patriotic with a deep love of everything that was noble about Britain. Nash, an intelligent and focused individual with a sharp engineer's brain and an eye for detail, was in many ways the perfect partner for Dixon. Between 1964 and 1965, Robin had served with the Guards Independent Parachute Company. His unit were involved in the Indonesian conflict that ran from 1958 to 1965, and was subsequently sent to Hereford to become the founders of G Squad SAS.[22] The athletic warrior and the engineer with the fast reflexes really were the best of British, as the world was about to find out.

During training at St. Moritz, before journeying to Austria, Dixon and Nash had equalled record times set by Italian World Championship aces. Most nights during the bobsledding seasons of the early 1960's, from around 11am, the roaring bobsleigh boys who called themselves the *Equipe Nash* (Team Nash) were almost as much a permanent feature of the Cresta Bar – just off St Moritz's ice-blanketed main street – as the antique toboggan that hung on the wall of that establishment. They were larger than life, raucous, unambiguously and archetypically English.

22 'G' Squadron of 22 SAS was so named because it was primarily drawn from personnel of the disbanding Guards Independent Parachute Company, mostly volunteers from the Household Division.

Their roots as a group went back to 1960, before the Lake Placid World Championships. The syndicate had grown around Nash and Dixon and, although its personnel would change, their focus and attitude remained consistent. They included accountant David Lewis; logistics man Guy Renwick, about the same age as Tony Nash, a farmer and the son of a Northumberland garage chain owner; Tony Lesser, a product of Downside, the estimable Roman Catholic Public School, who worked for a City bank; and Tony Holloway, the amiable son of an industrialist, whose first love was motor cars and who also raced catamarans.

After 70 years or so of contact with the English, St Moritz embraced their often eccentric behaviour and maybe even expected their relatively unconventional ways. However, Tony Nash himself did not quite fit the mould. A mild mannered man, he would become something of an icon in Switzerland and across Alpine Europe. But even prior to the Olympics he was becoming recognised as one of the best in his sport; few could rival his stunning flair for manipulating a bobsleigh from the start of a challenging run to a fast finish.

The Brits had developed a 'bob slang' that became part of their own social language. The lexicon included words and phrases like 'sturz' or 'tipping a bob', which meant 'crash', a challenging situation was 'hairy' and a bad start was 'spastic'. The jargon had commonalities with the Brits who sent themselves plummeting singly on 'headfirst skeletons' (fixed steel-runnered sleds) down the Cresta Run, situated close to the larger bob chute at St Moritz.

This group of English bob-enthusiasts raised the first £500 for two bobs, though other bills soon brought the costs up to £1,500; an Austin Mini (Super Deluxe) would have cost you close to that at the time. (At the time of writing a Mini Cooper S will set you back close to £19,000.) But it's impossible to say

41

how much these men spent pursuing what had become both a passion and a dream, though a small fortune probably comes close. But fundraising was possibly the least of their challenges.

For the cheery British *Boy's Own* demeanour belied the total application and dedication of the team. As Nash tells it, "absolute physical fitness isn't essential; it's more of a nerve-wracking sport really, based on preparation and attention to detail."

However, both Nash and Dixon tend to play down the amount of training they did before embarking down the glassy chutes. Although few in Britain had much idea about the demands of bobsleighing, in Switzerland, Austria, parts of Germany, Italy and France the combination of judgement and courage needed to defeat the best on the bob circuits was better appreciated. In Europe, in fine cold conditions, the sled could touch close to 130kph in the straight. On the vertically banked bends, like the infamous 180-degree 'Sunny Corner' and 'Horseshoe' at St Moritz, crew and vehicle slid around at right angles to the unforgivingly hard track like performers on a fairground wall of death. Injuries were not uncommon. On big event days, the fur-coated spectators paid over £1 an hour (a day's pay for some labourers in the UK at that time) for a view of 'Sunny', and if they experienced something of the drama of a near or actual calamity then that would be considered value for money. As such, the spectacle had much in common with the chariot racing of ancient Rome.

A couple of days before the Olympic two-man event of 1964 was due to commence on Friday 31 January, Nash and Dixon finished off a superb week's training on the Igls track. In his second run, Eugenio Monti broke the track record set by Nash and Dixon (1.06.06[23] – the previous record of

23 One minute, 6.6 seconds; for brevity, times are expressed throughout the rest of the book in this fashion.

1.06.42 had been set by Monti in the 1963 World Championships) with 1.05.93.

But on the first run of the next morning the Brits astonished the Olympic bobsleigh spectators with a time of 1.04.91. This did not just surpass the record recently achieved by the first Italian bob, it smashed it to pieces by more than a full second, an enormous margin in a sport where every hundredth of a second has to be worked and schemed for.

However, the initial British joy was tempered by the Italian second pair's second run. Up came Zardini and Bonagura with 1.05.27 followed by 1.04.91, equalling the record set by the Brits.

The British pair were less impressive on their second run of the day. They lost valuable seconds when the back end of their sled struck the wall coming out of a bend; the 1.06.28 it took them to cover the 1,647-yard (1,506 metres) course was something of an anticlimax.

However, the training had demonstrated that Nash and Dixon had it in them to make a significant mark on the two-man event that started 3,500 feet above sea level. A bit more consistency down the 350-foot drop, over the four runs, ideally bettering 65 seconds in each 17-curve heat (which meant averaging 80kph), would almost certainly put them on the podium. But the tiniest mistake could have disastrous consequences.

While it was the Italian second string that made the fastest aggregate for the last two practice runs with 2.10.13, the cagey Monti remained favourite for the real deal on Friday and Saturday. The Britons, finishing second overall with 2.11.19, could congratulate themselves but they only had to take the briefest of glances over their shoulders for a swift dose of reality; Eugenio was only 0.01 of a second behind them; *Il Rosso Volante*[24] cast a long and foreboding shadow on the ice.

24 'Flying red' (Monti was a redhead).

For all this, according to Sandy Duncan,[25] the British 'Chef de Mission' (Olympic team manager), Nash and Dixon were familiar enough with the course to have a real chance.

For his part, legendary Canadian bob pilot Vic Emery[26] recalls how his countrymen performed: "Pete Kirby and I had been working our way through the pack and in the second last day of two-man practice we won both heats, with Monti just behind us. Of course, the press descended on us like wolves and we were not ready to handle that. The combination of a very bumpy run and the added pressure resulted in my grave mistake of holding the ropes too tight on the last day of the practice, moving us way back to 11th place that day. Then everyone thought we were done; however, I was able to work out why things had gone so badly and, while not ready for medal contention in the two-man event, we thought we could be up there with the best. Because we knew what the hiccup was and believed we could address it."

The second British team of Bill McCowen, a London stockbroker, and fellow Londoner Andrew Hedges as brakeman had the fifth fastest last-day practice aggregate with 2.14.19. The Argentine number one bob finished empty. The two riders, Carlos Tomasi and Jurado Rodrigez, came off but escaped injury.

Nash and Dixon's performance was unprecedented. Twice they had smashed records for the jagged peaks of the Igls course, south of the city of Innsbruck. They had put Britain closer to winning an Olympic medal for what many saw as the most daring event in the Games than had been possible for

25 Duncan, a former athlete and talented sports writer, would take the *Chef de Mission* role a dozen times for Britain at various Olympic Games. As a member of the organising committee for the first World Athletics Championship held in Helsinki, in 1983 he was awarded the silver medal of the Olympic Order.

26 Born 28 June 1933.

more than a century,[27] which would be the first British medal since Jeannette Altwegg won the figure skating gold in Oslo a dozen years previously. Indeed, since the first Winter Olympics of 1924, up until 1960, Britain's tally had been just two gold, two silver and six bronze medals. In 1956, at Cortina in Italy, Britain managed only one fourth and one sixth place, and in the last winter Olympiad at Squaw Valley speed skater Terry Monoghan was the best-placed British competitor, finishing fifth in the 10,000 metres.

At the time Dixon, anticipating the start of the competition, said, "It will be a battle of nerves as much as a battle of ice."

"Luck will play a large part," added Nash.

Both men would be proved absolutely right. Six years of training, sacrifice and commitment would come down to just those considerations over a two-day campaign against the best group of sledders ever brought together to contest an Olympiad; these two Englishmen did little by less than a full measure.

A few days before the Games were due to commence, brilliant sunshine shone down on green and russet fields; mountaintops with merely a sugar sprinkling reached up to clear skies. No snow had fallen since mid-December; there had not been so little snow in this region in January since the winter of 1906.

There was a possibility of last-minute falls before the official opening, but at that stage fresh snow could actually do more harm than good. Robin Dixon tells of his team's shock on seeing the snowless Innsbruck on their arrival at the Alps:

"As we drove over the pass and looked into the Inn Valley we saw that the whole place was brown! They'd had absolutely no snow! That was rather depressing. It was bitterly cold, the ground was seriously hard, so they had

27 In 1936 Britain won a bronze in the four-man event in Garmisch-Partenkirchen, Germany.

extremely good ice, but it led to some early tragedies . . . It was a year without snow!"

According to Tony Nash, "The downhill course was being made by hundreds of Austrian soldiers spreading snow that had been loaded on heavy army lorries, shuttling from higher up on one of the peaks. They made the course with earth movers and by lugging wicker baskets[28] of snow which they carried on their backs, or it was pumped up through aluminium pipes. On the Alpine and Nordic runs they were treading the snow in and cementing it with water into hard tracks, so if you made a mistake you were going to go off into something fairly solid."

Ski resorts had learned to cope with the whims of the climate and, as there had been concerns from early on about the possible lack of snow, alternative venues had to be identified at a higher altitude. But at the start of the Games the lack of the necessary basics was something of an embarrassment. Around 3,000 Austrian soldiers, together with local civilian volunteers at weekends, were tasked with transporting a white landscape in piecemeal from the upper Alps. Some 40,000 cubic metres were dumped on the ski courses; another 20,000 metres were set aside for 'emergency withdrawals'. Six huge snowmaking machines, imported from the US and capable of making five tons of snow an hour, were put into action, spraying ice crystals on the bobsled and luge runs; the foundation of the track had to be pieced together using in excess of 20,000 blocks of ice. As such, the bob track was terribly vulnerable to any warming by the weather.

The most difficult job was to prepare the men's downhill course on the Patscherkofel, south of Innsbruck, where the lack of snow was even more acute than elsewhere. The hillside

28 Many of these were laundry baskets loaned from local housewives.

presented an odd picture, with an imported snow track running through partly bare meadow

Work continued unabated night and day in the few weeks prior to the opening ceremony. Finally, days before the Games were due to begin, Austria's Toni Sailer, who won all three alpine skiing events at the 1956 Olympics, took a trial run on the men's downhill. The ski runs might have been considered somewhat narrow and overcast, but he pronounced the imported snowscape to be, "fantastic – like out of a test tube," and all of Innsbruck heaved a mighty sigh of relief.

However, while there was just about enough snow on the runs, they were probably faster than those that might have been provided by nature. This threatened to tempt the less experienced to take risks, while those who were used to succeeding by pushing themselves to the very edge of safety would be obliged to take it even closer than usual to the periphery.

As the Games started, snow only coated the areas where the events were scheduled. The rest of the region gave no hint of an Austrian winter. The skies, on the first day of the greatest festival of winter sport ever staged, continued to be void of snow. The earth was dusty and Innsbruck's narrow roads were clogged with carbon monoxide pumping out of the growing number of cars.

The Winter Games are weather Games no matter where they are staged, but the lack of snow had its advantages for those responsible for communications. Apart from extra flights to Innsbruck's enlarged airport, 296 special trains had been made available. The German railways ran a daily Olympic Express between Munich and Innsbruck, and parking space for close to 30,000 vehicles had been provided near the Olympic sites.

While conditions for the first bobsleigh event of the

Innsbruck Games were far from perfect, the British contingent certainly didn't want the climate to get any warmer – which would threaten the whole event – but neither did they want it to snow. If it did snow then the Italians, who were so much more experienced, would be able to adapt themselves quicker to changed conditions.

Then, a few days before the two-man competition, the forecast was that snow was moving in from the east.

IV

MONTI

From the earliest days of the sport, Britain's bobsleighers have been dauntless. They were usually rich men's sons who learned the sport in St Moritz, where they habitually passed most of each winter. But the Italians of the 1960's were of a different ilk. Sergio Zardini was a hotel-keeper in Alpine Cortina, while Eugenio Monti was, for most of his bobsleighing career, what the Americans call a lumberman in the same town.

The modern incarnation of bobsleighing was born in Italy out of a track in a ski village etched into the side of a mountain. One exponent of the sport arose from this hamlet in the sky to become the best that ever lived. Most of his life was lived as a blur, negotiating dangerous turns made deadly by speed with a skill that crossed the borders of art and science, disregarding gravity and riding on the very cusp of the laws of nature. He existed not for triumph or fame but for a personal mission; chasing time – reaping the temporal wind.

In 1964, it was generally agreed that a small, red-haired man with a smashed-up face was probably the best, most dedicated bobsleigh pilot in the world. The 36-year-old Eugenio Monti, a diminutive native of the Dolomites (standing only five feet six-and-a-half inches, tipping the scales at 11 stone four pounds for his competition weight) from the town of Cortina[29] in the valley of Ampezzo, was known to his compatriots as a *montanaro*, a 'mountain man', meaning an elusive individual of few words. Genio (as those close to him in the bobbing fraternity knew him) was famed for usually speaking only when he had a point to make. However, when he did give an opinion he was likely to deliver it forcefully and passionately.

"The bloke I enjoyed enormously was Monti," says Tony Nash. "You'd watch Monti go down and he used to be as rough as hell, but he used to make up the time . . . He was a magic little man."

Il Rosso Volante was an extraordinary man. In his mother country, because of his quiet charisma and his fascinating ability to control a vehicle at speed, he was considered one of the 20th century's greatest sportsmen – comparable directly with Nino Bibbia, the Italian who claimed 232 first places on the Cresta Run, and often mentioned in the same breath as the great motor racers liker Nuvolari or Ascari.

Bred in the mountains 240 miles east of Torino (the site of the 2006 Olympic games,) Eugenio Monti remains arguably Italy's greatest Olympic hero, a focused athlete with a professional outlook. As Nash says of him, "Monti was

---

29 Monti was born 1,256 metres above sea level in the village of Dobbiaco, close to the Val di Landro valley, on 23 January 1928. Today the village is known as the municipality of the Tre Cime, and is framed by the mountain peaks towering high above the nearby lake of Dobbiaco. Gustav Mahler chose Dobbiaco as his favourite summer resort, writing his famous 'Lied der Erde' there as well as his ninth and tenth symphonies (the latter was never finished).

charming. An authentic mountain man. He was a great skier before he was a bobsleigher, but, anything to do with the Alps, Monti would have been good at it. He married an American wife and she was the mother of his two children. He also built his own ski-lift and had to deal with tourists.

"Monti knew Cortina and the surrounding area like the back of his hand but before his involvement in bobsleighing he'd never really been anywhere else. He had a bad accident where he broke his nose around 1958 at St Moritz; he was dragged down the course under his sled and emerged battered and scraped beyond recognition."

Tending only to drink Seven-Up when not in Italy, in Cortina Monti took a little Chianti now and then but always claimed that he couldn't find good Chianti in the USA. "They mix cheap wines in," he complained. He was typically in bed by 9pm, his gleaming steel sled runners swathed in wool and usually within touching distance. By dawn he could be found polishing and waxing the bright red Podar sled with the white *Italia I* gleaming on its nose.

In the early 1960's, as a small ski area operator in Pocol, near Cortina, Monti cut a sober figure, his piercing blue eyes and red hair, cut in a slightly scruffy style, together with his disfigured nose giving him the look of a fierce competitor. Other drivers said he was the only man who could put the runners of a bobsled within half an inch of the exact spot he wanted them to occupy while moving at terrifying speeds, often at dizzying heights through the turns, weaving through the most difficult curves. He also carried an aura of authority; his daughter, Amanda, described how he only had to look at her to communicate his thoughts as to how things should be done.

For all this, although he embodied an ethos of authority, he was never dictatorial. According to his daughter, her father's friends would relate how he had a way of talking to people that made them feel important, but his most impressive characteristic was his modesty. She said that he never showed her anything pertaining to his sporting prowess, placing all of his trophies in cardboard boxes and never putting them on display.

However, Amanda was to learn from others of her father's Olympic feats and his shining acts of sportsmanship. For Eugenio would come to the aid of competitors he knew to be the biggest threat to his own domination of the icy runs.

Sergio Siorpaes, Monti's lifelong friend and long-serving brakeman, told of how whenever they raced as a team Eugenio would regard all as equal. Canadian Olympian Vic Emery cheerfully recounts how it was rare to meet up with Monti without him wearing a ready smile, and that the Italian maestro was invariably "receptive and never appeared not to have the time to respond to what were sometimes probably rather foolish questions". Robin Dixon remembers how Monti didn't "quite understand why or how he was so good . . . which is often something of a trait of genius . . . but everyone always wanted to know how he did it." Mario Zardini spoke of his friend's intelligence and persistence, his resolve and power, and how he possessed incredible strength in his legs and arms. According to Monti's first ever brakeman, his long-time business partner was no ordinary person but a man who possessed all the personal qualities necessary to succeed in his chosen pursuits.

Monti delighted in the freedom offered by the Italian mountains. He certainly had a passion for the roaring speed and petulance of a bobsleigh on polished ice, and the whispering swiftness of skis on a precipitous, white-cloaked hill. Just before the Innsbruck Olympics, he was asked to give his views about the modest town of Cortina when its winter streets and slopes were clogged with tourists, replying, "They drive too slow. They ski too slow. But they spend money fast."

In 1956, when the winter Games came to Cortina d'Ampezzo, Italy, Monti grabbed two silver medals. He piloted a two-man sled to second place behind his team-mate Lamberto Dalla Costa and a four-man bob behind the Swiss mechanic Franz Kapus.

Although his precise but daring style seemed to have made him practically unbeatable in the two-man event by 1964, in the big four-man sleds Eugenio often got more than his share of bad luck. In the 1957 World Championships he came second again, losing by the slimmest of margins.

Monti hadn't climbed into a bobsleigh prior to 1954, but in the eight years between the Cortina Games and the Winter Games of 1964 he never tasted defeat in a two-man sled. He had won six world titles in that event and two more in four-man bobs. As such he was the most successful bobsleigh driver the sport had known.

Victory in international bobsleighing is usually decided by the cumulative time of four runs down a glassy, curvilinear course which, according to location, differs in length from 1,500 metres to just over a mile. Depending on the span of the course and its condition, the total time for the four runs in the early 1960's was somewhere between four and five-and-a-half minutes. The difference between winner and runner-up was often no more than a tiny fraction of a second. Considering that a single misjudgment could drag a leading team hopelessly back down the field, Monti's domination of the sport for nearly a decade was remarkable. It is all the more extraordinary considering he was a bobsledder not by choice, but by mischance. As Amanda was to say, after she found many photographs of her father participating in other sports, she had no idea about his accomplishments in fields as diverse as car racing, skiing, soccer and water skiing.

One of those photographs is of her father alongside Zeno Colo, the great Italian skier. That image could be seen as a prelude to Monti's career in bobsleighing; according to the great F1 champion Albert Ascari, Monti was *Data di nascita di velocità.*[30]

When asked how he started bobsledding, he often replied simply that he took it up in 1954. But Monti's entry to the sport is an inspirational story of overcoming disaster and turning misfortune to one's advantage. A natural athlete, he was at first a skier and became good enough to hope to compete for Italy at Olympic level. Growing up in a valley protected by the sheer faces of the great Dolomite peaks, he sought out challenge on the ski slopes. The downhill and slalom events offered a captivating multiplicity of demands on body and mind; in 1951, at the age of only 23 in the downhill event, he was pushing the man who would be the Italian Winter Olympic gold medalist in Oslo the following year, Zeno Colo. The Flying Redhead was the best young skier in Italy: he won national titles in slalom and giant slalom and finished third in the downhill event. Skiing was his first love, but events in December of 1951 were to have a decisive effect on the ability to reach his potential in the sport that was so close to his heart. As he recalled, "I was Italy's downhill champion and was favourite to win at the 1952 Olympics."

But, having won two Italian Alpine championships, a 1951 accident while practising for the next year's Olympics in Oslo ended his alpine skiing ambitions. Without fear or caution, Eugenio concluded his career on the piste by launching himself over uncovered ground. According to Amanda, he

30 'Born for speed.'

tore knee ligaments so badly that fairly complicated surgery was his only option.

The young Monti was obliged to say goodbye to all his good friends from a hospital bed as they went off to the Olympics. The ligaments of both knees were injured to such an extent that the damage was irreparable. Monti's public explanation was typically understated: "I was in ski competitions. Then I had an accident and stopped. I didn't stop skiing, just competing."

However, after his retirement from bobsleighing he was persuaded to make a more extensive explanation: "while training I had a terrible accident. Both of my kneecaps were broken and for me competitive skiing was over. Ironically my team-mate, whom I had defeated for the Italian championship, won the Olympic downhill gold medal."

But Monti's craving for speed was nowhere near sated. After a long convalescence (although shorter than his injuries warranted), for a while he turned his hand to sports cars, racing an Osca, but the cost did not justify what was, for him, a relatively modest buzz; nor could his two jobs – one as a timber grader and the other as a ski instructor – pay for the expensive sport and his family's bills. So Monti eventually turned to the raw contests of bobsleighing. In his own words, the transition was, "Just by chance . . . there was a track in Cortina and I thought, 'Why not try?'"

Characteristically this was something of an understatement. Two years after his skiing accident, at just over 27 years of age, Monti was a spectator at the bobsleigh World Championship in Cortina. He recalled later how he went to the championships with friends and found that there were also competitions for people new to the sport. So the companions agreed to have a go with Monti as driver. After a number of practice runs, the group would equal the track record.

Monti went on to win his first Italian championship. Two years after his first run down the Cortina track he would tackle the same course as the driver of one of the two Italian teams competing at the 1956 Olympics, when the Games came to his home town below the ski slopes of Cortina d'Ampezzo. Monti and Renzo Alvera were beaten by Giacomo Conti and Lamberto Dalla Costa; Dalla Costa's aerodynamically superior sled, tested and refined by the Italian air force, was too much for the locals. Nevertheless, it was a remarkable first effort for Eugenio – but for him, ever the idealist, second place was unacceptable. According to Marino Zardini, his friend raced only with the single-minded aim of winning.

For Monti the result seemed to be more of a frustration than a triumph. He felt it should have been easy for him to win: "I knew the course well, every turn. I was very disappointed in the years that followed. I won several World Championships but I wanted an Olympic gold medal."

Monti's American wife, Linda Constantine, saw this drive as central to his achievements, believing that determination, competitiveness and perfectionism were the marks of a good champion. Her husband had a burning desire to win, and the ability to concentrate totally on that ambition.

For Linda, this was Monti's attitude to everything he did in life. Eugenio would rise at 5am to stroll up and down the bob run. If he thought there was too much snow on the track, he would sweep it clear. If there was a chip in the ice he would consign its location and character to memory, so that he could steer clear of it in competition.

His daughter Amanda told of her father's precisionist attitude. He would cut his own wood and stack it outside of the house; sometimes she would help him, but he wanted each individual piece to be perfectly placed in a precise spot. She smiled as she recalled how, if something was not done in the way he wanted, he would quickly point it out.

Monti pushed forward. In 1957 in St Moritz he achieved his first World Championship, confirming that his success in the Winter Olympics a year earlier was no mere consequence of home territory advantage. He won gold in the two-man bob and, alongside Ferdinando Piani, Lino Pierdica and his brakeman in the boblet, Renzo Alvera, also claimed the four-man silver medal.

Subsequently, the diminutive Italian was eager to go to the United States in 1960, believing that at Squaw Valley, California, he would claim the Olympic crown he had waited four long years to make his own. However, it was decided that the Winter Olympics would not include bobsleighing (for the only time in the history of the Games) due to time and economic reasons.[31] Monti found it hard to stifle his disappointment, but resigned himself to look forward to the 1964 Games.

Its removal from the Olympic framework led to fears about bobsleighing's demise. As Tony Nash says, "To keep bobsleighing going the Italians, who were by then all powerful in the sport, decided to hold the World Championships at Cortina. From a driver's point of view that was the finest track in the world at that time. We also liked the Italians and they were really into the sport, so they made the run as good as they could and it was a magnificent course at a fairly low altitude. We would put tape on the various

---

31 The existing track had been deemed unsuitable for international competition. The creator of the Squaw Valley resort that facilitated much of the 1960 Games was owned by Alexander Cushing, who had a big influence on the organisation of events. Veteran Canadian bobsled captain Vic Emery says, "As I understand it Cushing used the excuse that less than the minimum of 12 nations replied in the affirmative to his last-minute request to answer 'yea or nay' for bob participation within this very short time limit."

cuts which you aimed to go round but you had to drive every corner well, taking the run up to the limit. By that I mean that to get the best from the track you had to be just two inches from the top all the time. There were boards above the ice, which were put in place as a safety measure – if you went on the boards they slowed you down and brought you back onto the ice again. So you had to drive every corner through to the maximum, right up to the boards. Unfortunately, in 1966 the Germans went straight over the top of the boards – it killed two of them."

Robin Dixon recalls how, at first, the conditions were less than conducive: "Cortina sometimes had its problems with the weather. In 1960 the snow turned to rain and a crowd of young athletes hanging around an alpine village with not much to do could cause problems." As such, some extracurricular activity was laid on. "Someone had the sensible idea to get us all out of the place and buses were laid on to take us down to Venice."

Vic Emery recollects that, on the way, the idea to organise a race through the canals of Venice was concocted. At a predetermined time, whichever gondola participants found themselves in would be requisitioned. The Canadian smiles as he remembers how the group only just managed to escaped the clutches of the police during this escapade.

According to Nash, each national team made improvised use of pans and oars, or whatever else they could find to propel their respective gondolas. As Dixon recalls, "We were tearing down the Grand Canal in bobsleigh helmets! The prize was purchased by the losers and drunk by all."

Despite the frivolity, this event marked an important moment for both British bobsleighing and the history of sport. According to Robin, it was during the romp in Venice that the friendship between the British and the Italians blossomed.

"We raced hard down the run and we partied about equally as hard . . . we got to know the Italians very well . . ."

After this informal and improvised event at what was seen, at the time, as bobsleighing's substitute Olympics, the weather finally cooperated. Eugenio steered his nation's two-man and four-man teams to victory, streaking over the hard run in their slick fire engine-red sleds. This meant that he had achieved four successive world titles in the smaller sleds. His four-man team won by a 0.2 second margin, pushing the favoured West German crew into second place with an aggregate time of 5:04.75 over the four heats. Before the four-man competition Monti said of his two team-mates (Sergio Siorpaes and Furio Nordio), who rode sandwiched between him and his brakeman Alvera, "All I ask of them is that they sit still. They can even close their eyes if they want."

Up to that point the Italians had won a four-man world bobsledding championship only once before, in 1930. Monti was now one of the finest individual bobsledders alive. But, despite his dominance and his intense ambition, he was also openly generous, providing tutorials to anyone who might show interest. This, according to Marino Zardini, was in the nature of the bobsledding fraternity of the time. For Zardini, when a true talent emerged in the sport then everyone else followed.

Certainly, Monti had become an internationally recognised mentor and something of a guru in the sport. Vic Emery says that Monti's mother "spoke very good English and his was understandable from the start," which was helpful to both his British and Canadian students. But, even though he was now known as the 'theorist of bobsledding', his diffident personality remained.

When he was once asked about what others said about him, he answered with the direct question, "What's true?" He knew that apparent simplicity often camouflages a complex reality. His only concern remained how to accurately direct a bobsled; for him, while piloting wasn't hard, it was still difficult to produce a good time.

Reflecting on Monti's influence, Emery says he believed the Italian to be the master of the sport, and the Canadian spent as much time as he could with him when convenient, walking up the run and asking him, "How did you take that corner?" "What do you do here?" The Italian was always receptive and never shunned an enquiry. For Vic, "it always seemed to be convenient to him."

Among all the bobsledders, Monti was the one of the few to consistently walk up a bob run, sometimes along the edge, sometimes hopping over onto the chute itself to look for cuts that might hinder his progress or the perfect patch that would lead him to victory. At Lake Placid, it was a familiar sound for the public address system to boom out: "Will Monti please get out of the course? There is a sled coming down."

This habit of 'run walking' was passed on by Monti to Tony Nash. "He told me, 'Walk up the track after a run, you'll always learn something.' After that I hardly ever failed to walk up the run and it was true, you invariably picked up one or two things. Sometimes I walked up the course with him. In Lake Placid, when we weren't racing, I walked up the track 29 times a day, about a mile each time. You'd get to know all the people watching on the way up."

Italian sports fans were swift to celebrate Monti's victory as a national triumph equal to an Olympic title. A dozen different nations had taken part in the event and it had effectively saved the sport from possible oblivion.

In trying to explain what makes one driver better than another, bobsleighers often claim that it is the pilot, not those who ride with him or the sled itself, that makes the vital difference. Apart from a good start, a good time is really up to the driver.

Most bobbers by the early 1960's used Podars, and Monti's sled was not really that different from others. He probably spent more time polishing the runners than the majority of his rivals, and he was known, in certain snow conditions, to wax all of the underside of the bob, including the bolts that held it together, to prevent the snow from sticking to the sled and slowing it down.

Coming from a comparatively modest background, Monti was not averse to the sweat of hard work. In the early 1960's he was a ski instructor and the co-owner of a ski lift that he had more or less built himself, quite literally earning his living from snow. But in his bobs he was a man of *ghiaccio, non neve* (ice, not snow) and he hunted for the smoothest line like a prospector might search for gold. Like the majority of the better bob racers of his era, Monti relished slick ice under his runners, gleaming blue sheets all the way down a bob run over which his sled could flash like a beam of light (although Monti was famous for providing a relatively noisy, bumpy ride). He felt nothing but dismay at the sight of snowflakes settling on a course. In 1959, at St Moritz, Monti had won the boblet World Championship but finished in the four-man a long way back, complaining about "too much snow". Even later in life, his mantra was, "Snow slows up the track!" He hated snow on the course like a skilled footballer hates a muddy pitch. Genio was obsessed with speed and snow blunted pace.

Winning and losing bobsleigh competitions could be partially decided by one's place on the rota of starters. For each of the four runs in an event the starting order was shuffled so that no individual sled would need to continually tolerate the handicap of a snowy track; those disadvantaged in one run were assured of a faster track the next time around. While this created safer contests for the more unexceptional drivers, who steered pretty much the same course on any given run, more gifted pilots were sometimes prevented from showing their full range of talent. Monti was a winner, a proven multiple champion, principally because he ploughed different furrows, looking for a superior route, taking the curves high, reaching a precise apogee then diving downward again, stealing a minuscule but precious fraction of a second from less talented or daring rivals while negotiating each camber.

With this said, the Italian was no mere stuntman. In the 1958 accident when his bobsled flipped over twice at St. Moritz, he was dragged down the course under his sled and crashed a quarter of a mile down the run. His nose was crushed and his face scarred. However, the way he drove a bobsled at his peak suggested he might avoid another such incident. By 1964 he had taken his world titles on the five classic courses of the world. He had been victorious on the gorgeous St Moritz track and had pounded the speed out of the Zig Zag bend at Lake Placid, where Frank Beattie was thrown 100 feet to his death in 1955. He had frequently triumphed on the Crystal curve at Cortina where, in 1957, jet pilot Luciano Mozzolo was killed, and had bettered Garmisch, where three bobbers had lost their lives up to 1964. In 1963 Monti had won in Igls, where Swede Gunnar Ahs broke both his legs and sheared off his front teeth, while Claude Brasseur of France left a bloody streak close to eight centimetres wide and over 15 metres in length after losing control. Ice and death were at times grim partners in bobsleighing, but this never caused Monti to lose his concentration or his vision. For him the ice presented the test he desired, a stage on which any victory could be decisively earned.

*   *   *

Organised bobsleigh racing had begun as far back as the early 1890's. Seventy years on, at the start of the 1960's, many of those who tore down the runs at seemingly immoderate speed believed that the best pilot in history was Stanley Benham, a former fire chief from Lake Placid, New York State. But in February 1961, at the World Championships in Lake Placid, the scene was set for a Benham and Monti duel on ice that would long be remembered by those lucky enough to witness it. This was to be Stan's final race and, although there was nearly 15 years between the men in age (Benham was 47), he wanted to show himself to be the best bobsleigh driver in the history of Lake Placid. He had proven himself as a great pilot on his home track, but he had not dominated the sport internationally on the same scale as Monti.

The face-off took place in a four-man event on the Olympic run that had played host to the 1932 Winter Games, on the side of Mt Van Hoevenberg, eight miles outside Lake Placid. It was the only bobsled run on the North American continent, and at that time one of just four on the planet that continued to be used for prestigious international competitions. The mile-long track with its dizzying, plummeting bends, was quicker than Garmisch, St Moritz or Cortina, although the Italian's home run was thought to be more hazardous and technically testing than the old Yankee chute.

In the US national championships of 1956, also held at Mt Hoevenberg, Stan had claimed the four-man track record: 1:08.88. But Monti had recently broken his own two-man record with an astonishing 1:09.22, to win his fifth consecutive world title.

When not being used for competition or serious practice, the New York State Conservation Department offered rides on their bobsleds at $2 a throw. However, down the straights even the aging, sluggish Conservation Department bobs could clock 100kph, while generating enough G-force at some of the more acute turns to bounce an uninitiated passenger's chin off their knees.

As for the Italian-built Podar racing bobs, in the hands of Monti or Benham they would charge down the super-swift Lake Placid course to provide one of the most impressive spectacles in sport.

The rivals had little in common outside of bob racing. Benham, the USA's top pilot for more than a decade, was a two-time world champion and had claimed the runner-up spot on six occasions. He was old-school, a short but powerfully built man with an expansive barrel chest and an impressive stomach. At 210 pounds he had at one time been a comparative lightweight, insisting that the German crew that defeated his team for the gold medal at Oslo in 1952 averaged well over 300 pounds each. (In fact that quartet tipped the scales at just 1,050 pounds, a meagre 262-pound average.[32])

Like many of his ilk Stan worked and played hard, despite his responsibilities as a father of four and his position as the North Elba Township's manager of parks. He was the product of the late nights and determined hedonism that had been part of the tradition of bobsleighing for decades, and had hit the runs with some classic hangovers that might have made death a welcome visitor. That said, men like Stan would often argue they were quicker, superior drivers under such strain.

Benham liked to question those who did not know his sport too well as to why there had been no Olympic run built for

32 The *Federation Internationale de Bobsleigh et de Tobogganing* had ruled that four-man teams should not exceed 882 pounds, so by the mid-1960's the days of the gargantuan bob-bear were over.

the Squaw Valley Games of 1960. He would tell how it wasn't because it cost too much, or because the ice wouldn't freeze hard enough, as some argued, but because, "a bunch of Olympic officials and some of those other people out there said bobsledders drink too much."

Stan might have had a point.

Monti and Benham didn't have the championship to themselves. Germany's Franz Schelle had hit the best practice times; Sergio Zardini, in Italy II, was becoming recognised as an extremely silky pilot, no longer just Tonto to Monti's Lone Ranger; neither could GBI's Bill McCowan be taken for granted. With ten countries in 14 bobs lined up for the first heat on a fresh February Saturday morning, any of them were capable of a leading run – although the Belgians, with only five days' bobsleigh experience under their collective belts (a couple of weeks in early February at St Moritz), were not heavily fancied, especially after they were seen to find the time to wave at spectators on their way down the runs. In fact, they ran the last three heats of the two-man event with their brakes continuously applied.

The emerging Canadians were unlucky, however. Their number one sled, piloted by Vic Emery, had been moving nicely up the ranks in practice when deteriorating conditions caused a front runner to break through the ice, flipping the sled high into the air. The craft came crashing down on Emery, flattening him into the ice with a smashed nose and a massive hematoma on his left leg. Vic was hospitalised for a week and his sled withdrawn from the event. As he recalls, "I sat out the 1962 Worlds in Garmisch." But he made good use of his time, studying for an MBA at Harvard.

The first day of the four-man event was grey and cloudy, with an occasional drizzle. Before long 'Shady', the huge 180-degree turn with soaring 32-foot walls, was deeply scarred.

This monster had seen one of the run's two fatal accidents, in 1949. 'Zig-Zag', the 13th and 14th curves, was also causing everyone problems. Though not as dramatic a sight as Shady, these bends included an almost instant reverse turn entailing a much more violent examination of a pilot's ability.

Zig-Zag had been the site of the third Lake Placid bobsled death in 1955, and it nearly took more casualties on that Saturday. The Spanish bob crashed hard into the protective overhang of ice added in recent times to prevent racers from taking to the skies. The four Spaniards were ejected and suffered a range of bruises, sprains and breaks. Not long after this, Zardini also hit the wall; Romano Bonagura, his brakeman, was flung out of the sled and needed an ambulance to take him to hospital.

Monti's initial run produced an impressive time of 1:09.20, given that the course was rutted and softening. Benham was 0.02 of a second slower. A trio clocking under 1:10 followed: Schelle (Germany) 1:09.38, McCowan (Great Britain) 1:09.74 and Gunnar Ahs (Sweden) 1:09.58.

As was usual, the starting order was switched for the second heat. Benham was first away, making 1:09.48. This made 2:18.70 over the two runs. Schelle, McCowan and Ahs once more all did better than 1:10, as did USAII, piloted by Larry McKillip and matching Benham's second-heat time. However, these crews had not done better than 2:19 for the two heats, and as such it was clear that only Eugenio Monti would pose a meaningful challenge to the old man of Mt Van Hoevenberg.

The Italian got away well and cut down the course like quicksilver. Low down in his red bob he hit Shady fast and high. He fired through Zig-Zag with an air of impudence, shifting like lightning down the long straight into the finishing turn. As he powered under the bridge the 6,000 spectators lining the course roared in approval, sensing a fast run. The loud speaker system broke down and it took close to five minutes before the time went up on the board: 1.09.20 – a total of 2:18.40, a massive 0.3 of a second better than the American vet.

Pouring rain drowned the night and on the Sunday morning the temperature had risen to 45 degrees.[33] The bob run was as good as washed off the side of Mt Van Hoevenberg. Benham, with some regret, commented, "The only way we could race up there would be in row-boats."

The championship would be decided by the two Saturday heats. Benham said that he would have liked to have tried to catch Monti, although "he seems to be a pretty tough guy to catch. Anyway, this is the last one for me. I'm packing it in."

Monti emerged as top-dog on the runs. It was he who was now the man to beat. He had finally broke through to win both the two and four-man championships. After his victory, Genio told how he was "very happy to win, but sorry I not break that record. The run was not fast. Too much snow."

*   *   *

By 1962 at Garmisch, Monti was favourite to repeat his feat of the previous year. Art Devlin, a former Olympic ski jumper who had recently become fascinated by bob-sledding after sneering at it for years, commented, "This guy is an incredible competitor . . . look at his record. He's always coming from behind on the fourth run to win. He just keeps putting on the pressure. If he stays close the first day, you watch him on Sunday. The others may crack, but not him . . ."

For all this, Monti did not compete in the World Championships of 1962. Garmisch had hosted the championships in 1958 and, following his win in the two-man

33 Fahrenheit.

event on a sleek icy track, on the eve of the four-man competition the event officials, ostensibly seeking to make the run safer, ordered snow to be spread on the course. Monti decided there was too much snow on the run and appealed to the officials, but they were not sympathetic.

According to Tony Nash, "Monti knew and the rest of us knew that the Germans would pack snow into the track so the Italians would go down the run comparatively slowly, and of course everybody else would speed up as the snow got scattered. Sure as eggs is eggs, that night the Germans piled in the snow and, about one o'clock in the morning, Monti and his team-mate came along with shovels and shovelled it all out!" laughs Tony.

Motivated by his unwavering sense of fair play in the face of the Germans maximising their home advantage, undercover of darkness Monti and his three team-mates attacked the track, shovelling the newly scattered snow off the run. However, security guards became suspicious about the Italians' car, parked awkwardly close to where the expensive sleds were stored, and the police were called. The Bundespolizei arrived with torches and a dog called Flegel, the hound leading the now sizable party of police and security guards to Monti and his team beavering away at the track, having cleared 50 metres of the detested snow.

As Sergio Siorpaes admitted, "We shovelled until the police came with a dog . . . pulling the peaks of our caps down to hide our faces we remained silent, so as not to be recognised. But Genio said, 'It's me, Eugenio.'"

Unfortunately, by this time the Germans had taken on the stereotypical role of villain in European bobsleighing. According to Tony Nash, "When I started in the late 1950's the Germans were up to some tricks. In 1958 the Germans knew the order of runs the next day and that the Italians would go down first so the Germans left snow in the runs to slow up the Italians while making it faster for their chaps – that's why Monti decided to clear the run. The armed guards caught the Italians at it and they put them in jail for a few hours. They got let out the following morning and we all pissed ourselves laughing."

The next morning, Monti and his team turned up to compete as if nothing had happened, but now all of Garmisch knew of their late-night labours. With some amusement, Siorpaes later looked back on how people were openly identifying them as, "The Italians who came to sabotage the track!"

A penalty (which became to be know locally as *der gerichtsurteil vos Flegel* – 'the judgement of Flegel') of four seconds was imposed against the Italians, thus destroying any hopes they may have had of winning the event. Monti's only defence was a logical one: "All I wanted was a fast run." However, he felt he and his team-mates had been treated unjustly and he told the world, "This is the last time I will race here." As he left Garmisch, kids made shovelling motions in his wake. But when, four years later, the World Bobsleigh Championships returned to Garmisch, Eugenio Monti kept his word. The defending champion in both events did not take part, thus undermining the status and quality of the competition; no one could claim to be world champion until they had beaten Eugenio.

Soon the whole world knew of the events in Garmisch, as *Time* magazine noted Monti's nocturnal excavations. As Germany took the first two places on a carefully engineered run, the whole of the sledding fraternity applauded Eugenio's conviction and audacity, as well as his determination to fight fire with fire (or indeed snow with ice). He even won a prize for his actions, as Tony Nash describes: "After Garmisch, in recognition of his efforts, we gave him a silver shovel because we thought he'd shown 'form'."

Come the Winter Olympics in Innsbruck, Monti was looking to prove a point by winning the two-man title for the seventh time. The 1963 World Championships had been held on the new Igls track, which was a tiger of a course. Swedes, Americans, French, Canadians, Swiss and Germans had been bucked by its contours; ten bobbers were hospitalised, but Monti and Zardini sailed over the course immaculately.[34]

Igls appeared the ideal venue for what Monti planned to be the finale of his bobsleighing career but, following his inspection, he was disappointed with the run, saying it was "too easy". By that point he wished that his final contest had been hosted by his home course in Cortina, which was *tutto ghiaccio e tante curve* (all ice and many curves), or on the exacting Lake Placid course. He would have preferred to have gone out in the slick Italian-built Podar racing sled that had become forever associated with him, with what he saw as an honest test of his skill.

The great Italian athlete understood that the Igls course would tend to leaven the competition, but he would still have one unusual advantage: his brakeman for the World Championships of 1961 and 1963, 29-year-old Sergio Siorpaes,[35] who had also been in Monti's four-man team that won the World Championship in 1960, and defied one of the platitudinous myths that have been laid down for all sports: the claim that, to excel, you must love what you do and have a desire to compete. But world champion Siorpaes was a reluctant competitor who, according to Monti, didn't like bobsleighing but liked him.

Siorpaes agreed, declaring that he had no love for the sport

34 Italy won both the two and four-man competitions in 1963, but Monti did not take part in the four-man event. Sergio Zardini was the driver for the winning crew in the latter contest.

35 Born 20 July 1934.

and on a number of occasions had attempted to give it up. But Monti would not leave him alone; "I do it for Monti," he lamented

"I say to him, 'Come on, you are a good brakeman. You are clever,'" coaxed Monti.

This detachment became a real resource for the Italian pair. Siorpaes was able to look at their performance and their vehicle in a much more objective way than someone who might be passionate about the results and the pecking order in the crew. Recognised as a skilled mechanic in the bobsleigh world, Siorpaes was responsible for a number of innovations in the vehicle.

According to Tony Nash, "Sergio was an Olympic class runner. Later on he helped the Italians produce an articulated chassis[36] – they broke the sled in half and put in a great big bearing in the centre so it would move laterally – they were looking to absorb the shock of going into the corner – it became the standard thing. What they designed was just the best – we didn't know enough about it."

Siorpaes, who had four world titles with Monti under his belt, was trained as a blacksmith. He first rode a sled in 1958 but recalled that, for his initial ten runs, he felt as though he were inside a washing machine. He won his first international medal as Sergio Zardini's brakeman in 1958, a silver in the World Championship, behind Monti and Rebzi Alvera.

Sergio's brother, Gildo Siorpaes,[37] also won a bronze medal in the four-man event at the 1964 Winter Olympics in Innsbruck. Their grandfather, Holy Siorpaes, was a distinguished mountain guide and climber of the most famous alpine peaks.

36 These were not fully developed until after 1966.

37 Born 12 January 1938.

Sergio was a husky, handsome brakeman. According to Monti, brakes were "for stopping at the end", and indeed after a few practice runs no one used brakes – in fact, braking in a race could result in disqualification.

For Vic Emery, "No braking differentiates bobsleighing from almost all other speed sports [motorcycle speedway being a notable exception], and makes bobsleighing much more a sport of precision as opposed to bravado. The risks were high enough without having to challenge ourselves in terms of the amount of braking."

However, Siorpaes provided a great deal in the way of muscular force to get the sled underway at the top of a hill. Monti attached more importance than many of his contemporaries to practising push-off starts, being acutely aware of the valuable fractions of a second to be earned at that crucial stage.

On most bobsleigh teams at that time the brakeman was little more than a passenger. Once they had played their part in getting the bob away as fast as possible, their role was limited to holding on and desisting from applying the brakes until they were needed, usually not until the end of a run. Monti agreed with the general philosophy that, on a four-man sled, the two men between pilot and brakeman needed to do no more than sit still – or perhaps offer up a prayer. But for Genio the brakeman also served as a second set of senses. At the rear of the bob, Siorpaes had a slightly different perception of every curve to his pilot. After each run Monti and Siorpaes compared perspectives, and it was this melding of perceptions on each critical moment that brought them closer to perfection on the next run.

Monti had won the World Championships with another brakeman before Siorpaes, and he could have probably even have won with Dumbo riding on the back. On his four-man team, Monti asked only that the two middlemen push hard at first, then get in and sit very still, declaring, "You can even close your eyes if you want."

Whenever possible, both Monti and Siorpaes made a point of watching how the other bobs performed on the curves, each of them studying the course carefully before a run. The Italian duo were more than competitors, they were students of bobsleighing theory and practice; but it was not about dwelling over every detail, every crack in the ice. It was Monti's habit to devote long minutes to the inspection of a curve, but he was not distracted by minute features. He was intent on absorbing the clean dimension of a bend, the sweep and form of the arc; the feel of it as a thing. For him, the correct position and speed of the bob as it entered a major bend was a manoeuvre that demanded methodical precision, but this could only be achieved by knowing and becoming one with the 'character of a curve'. His greatest strength was an aesthetic appreciation that effectively allowed him to see more than others. Another Italian, Leonardo Da Vinci, was possessed of a similar quality, but Monti's assessment of his skill was typically pragmatic: "I cannot explain it, but I can do it."

Like most other drivers (excepting the Americans), Monti did not steer with a wheel but used two short reins with handles, deploying them like a jockey might when guiding a horse. Some argued that a sled was harder to steer with ropes, as it did not have the gearing advantage of a wheel, but for Genio ropes gave more positive control, providing the pilot with a feel for what the bob was doing.[38]

Monti took curves as high as any of his contemporaries and higher than nearly all of them at times, brushing the tops as

38 By the 1960s, apart from a few Americans, almost no one steered with a wheel.

he entered them then dropping fast, freeing the bob from their force field, using gravity to achieve maximum speed. But he always wanted to go faster. Gary Sheffield, the young Marine corporal from Lake Placid who finished second to Monti in the two-man race in 1961, believed that, "Genio takes more chances than anyone else. But with him, they're not chances."

In Innsbruck, Monti's main rivals included his compatriot, Sergio Zardini,[39] who had consistently been *pericolo numero uno* (number one danger) in terms of Genio's drive for glory. The American driver Bill Hickey also stood a chance, as did Nash and the Austrian Thaler, while most people involved in bobsleighing saw the Canadians as a force to be reckoned with. But, win or lose, Monti's record preceded him. He would never be forgotten in the world of bobsleighing; even if obscurity might have suited him, he was one of the major intellects behind Italian successes in the sport. Attempts by those who pitted themselves against him to explain his gifts may have descended into platitudes, but his amazing resolve and indomitable will to win were undeniable. A natural athlete who could be nervous but also bold and fearless, Monti remains an immortal of winter sport.

But Monti came to the Olympics after a hectic and tiring year. What compensation he received from his sport for attaining a standard of excellence came only in the shape of medals, trophies, respect and high regard; all rare commodities, but they did not translate to financial support. He had to earn a living on the slopes of Cortina's daunting yet fashionable Dolomites, so he built a ski-lift to exploit and enhance the environment he loved. Monti's daughter, Amanda, described how her father was the first person to bring a Sno-Cat from the United States to Italy. It was an old

39 Born 22 November 1931.

Tucker imported from Oregon that had to be dismantled before it was airlifted.

It was during work on this project that Monti was deeply shocked by the death of a carpenter. The craftsman was electrocuted while working during a rainstorm. Eugenio was obliged to deal with this tragedy while close to exhaustion from the rigours of intensive training and the pressure involved in establishing a business, ceaselessly labouring to complete the new lift by Christmas 1963.

As with all tasks he set himself, great or small, Monti's perfectionism was all-embracing; he wanted to be the best and the first in everything he turned in hand to. As Robin Dixon recalls, "He would spend the summer walking the slopes, taking every stone off the hillsides so they were absolutely smooth and perfect when the snows arrived; people would use his lift knowing that they would get a clean run down. He knew what he wanted and how he wanted to do it. He worked at his ambitions until he was living them and they were part of him."

According to Siorpaes, Monti *just* refused to give up, working all hours of the day. According to his faithful brakeman, Eugenio got to the Olympics physically and mentally tired, unable to race at his usual level. His perfectionism had come at a cost

However, according to Vic Emery, "I think the Monti fatigue thing was blown up too much. He was relatively young and had two to three weeks away from Cortina to get on top of things, which we all could do in that timeframe at that age. Apart from the huge pressure he put on himself, I don't think Monti himself would have used the excuse of fatigue."

For all this, in the winter of 1964 Monti was a multiple world champion, unquestionably at the top of his sport for almost a decade. It is also probable that, on the eve of the

Innsbruck Games, Monti was fatigued in a way he had never been before going into a major event. Yet what was to come would define him as a sportsman and, above all, as a man of towering integrity.

V

INNSBRUCK

The first time Tony Nash set off on an adventure it was short-lived: "I ran away from home when I was three or four with a pal of mine and we holed up in some rhododendrons in Ascot. It was the time of the London Blitz and we saw the whole of London burning from there. When we gave ourselves up we got the tanning of our lives – never ran away again," he laughs.

His arrival in Austria in 1964 proved less painful but at least as memorable. The beautiful Tyrolean city of Innsbruck, host to the IX Olympische Winterspiele, led the whole of Austria in welcoming the competitors, officials and spectators in the time-honoured Olympian manner.

Located in the Inn River Valley at the junction with the Wipptal, which provides access to the Brenner Pass some 30 km south of Innsbruck, the city is nestled amidst the soaring Tyrol Mountains. A strategic crossroad located between Germany and Italy, Innsbruck in 1964 was easily reached by train, motorway and air. When the city was chosen as the site of the 1964 Winter Games, Dr Heinrich Drimmel, the Minister of Education and head of the Organisation Committee, said the Games would be "simple and sportsmanlike, as befits a small country like Austria."

Three years later, a somewhat resigned Dr Drimmel was hoping that sport would not be entirely overshadowed by business. The organisers had managed to keep the Olympic sites free from advertising, but elsewhere Innsbruck and its surroundings were covered with advertising posters of all kinds. Souvenirs bearing the Olympic emblem needed, in principle, the approval of the Ministry of Trade, but this rule did not prevent the production of innumerable tacky souvenirs without the five interlocked rings.

The Winter Games was the biggest thing to happen in Innsbruck for decades. Schoolchildren were given a fortnight's 'Olympic holiday' in recognition of this, but this was more from practicality than altruism, their school buildings needed as emergency quarters for the temporary population boom. Some 5,400 university students had a definite grievance as their lectures and examinations continued, which was a problem for many who had taken on jobs as interpreters, waiters or messengers. They were also having problems with their lodgings, as a students' house had been converted into reporters' billets and private rooms had been rented to visitors who were able to pay premium prices, making the students provisionally homeless.

For the first Olympic Games to be held in Austria, the federal and provincial authorities poured £3 million into direct investment (a huge sum at the time), including the finance for opening up and preparation of the Olympic sites as well as other organisational considerations. The expenditure for the events amounted to 217 million schillings (then more than $8m).[40] A great deal more (400,000 million schillings – around $15m) was spent on speeding up public projects such as bridge, road and apartment building. Such developments would have been necessary for the capitol of Tyrol sooner or later, as the town was flooded by tourists and commercial traffic each year, but without the stimulus of the Games it would probably have taken a decade or more.

Although Innsbruck has always been a focal point for both summer and winter tourism (one of the main industries of the city and the province of Tyrol), it obviously became a centre for the sports because of its location in the mountains. About half of the city's 106,000 citizens skied; thousands of fans were able to walk on foot to the Olympic sporting grounds, thereby lessening the potential problem of motor traffic.

Even though out-and-out opulence was avoided, the Olympic Games did not come cheap. Austria, the Tyrol and Innsbruck accepted the financial burden, but their Swiss neighbours would take no such risk in 1968. (The village of Sion gave up the idea of becoming the site for the Games because the citizens voted down a bill asking for three million francs, equivalent to three quarters of a million dollars.) The Austrians were always stubborn in pursuing their goal. They had been turned down in 1955 at a meeting of the International Olympic Committee in Paris by a vote of 32 to 30, when Squaw Valley won the nomination for 1960. But the Austrians repeated their request in 1959 at Munich, and this time they got the proverbial nod. The members of the IOC believed that the Alps should have their turn again, as the skaters and skiers from that region had long shone at the Games.

40 Then around £3million, a huge sum at the time – the cost of building the Forth Bridge, finished that same year, was £11.5 million; the Queen Elizabeth II Bridge in 1991 was £120 million. So the comparative initial investment in Innsbruck for the 1964 Winter Olympics can be taken as in excess of £50million.

The provision of 150 hostesses – stylishly dressed with white fur hats and fur boots – made for an odd combination with the 15 Roman Catholic priests in ski dress, recognisable only by a small silver cross. More ominously, part of the preparation for events was the stationing of three ambulances and ski stretcher patrols at the foot of the runs, and a helicopter to rush casualties to the city hospital. The games of winter were nearly always insistent on a blood payment.

*   *   *

Innsbruck is built on ground which was covered by glaciers in the Ice Age. Findings from the Neolithic and Bronze Ages are evidence that settlement of the area began sometime around then. Between the tenth and 13th centuries, 70 military expeditions from the German kings crossed the Brenner Pass; whole rivers of wine from the South Tyrol flowed to the feudal lords and cloisters in Bavaria. The economic life of Innsbruck was further stimulated in the 13th century when Venice transported its goods from the Orient through the town and across the Alps, en route to the North. The town blossomed into a city in 1239. In 1292 it was destroyed by fire, but in 1336 the province of Tyrol, with Innsbruck as the capital, became a part of western Austria. Although fire once more destroyed the medieval city in 1340, it remained the capital of the federal state of Tyrol.

Innsbruck is rich in historical and artistic monuments. Many old but well preserved buildings and landmarks remain as living witnesses of the past. The peculiar architecture of the old city – the arched passageways, the gables unique to the region – is fascinating, with the sternness of the earlier gables replaced by the baroque and rococo motifs of the 18th century. (Some façades have no building behind them, the town's love of ornamentation stronger than any straightforward functionalism.)

The city has some idyllic sections along the River Inn, and one can still find many invitingly quaint inns along the narrow streets, some allowing a view of the mountains surrounding the town. Majestic churches demonstrate the cultural history of the region's picturesque past, with some remnants of the Middle Ages still visible.

With its awe-inspiring cultural heritage and natural beauty, Innsbruck was an appropriate choice for the 1964 winter Games. However, modern Innsbruck was not beyond criticism, centring on the high hotel and restaurant prices. Although most hotels kept to the published price lists, the hotels association issued strict warnings against supplementary demands, though there was still, of course, plenty of room for private initiative.

It was said locally that the Olympic emblem had only four rings left, as the fifth was being added as an extra nought to Innsbruck's tourist bills.

VI
THE GAMES OF WINTER

Democracy, like the Olympic Games, originated with the ancient Greeks in their hopes for universal freedom and dignity for their citizens. The ideal that the people of our troubled planet could meet in peaceful forms of combat still maintained some semblance of credibility in 1964. Participants and spectators all wanted to be part of the essence of the Olympics.

Homer, author of the ancient Greek epic poems *The Iliad* and *The Odyssey*, as well as *The Homeric Hymns*, tells of Olympus, mountaintop home of the gods: "No wind ever shakes the untroubled peace of Olympus; no rain ever falls there or snow."

This description was unfortunately to be all too true of Innsbruck in 1964.

Television and radio brought the excitement of the competition into homes across the world on a mass scale, for the first time. For those who watched the icy dramas play out, the memory, and spirit of the Games would live on. For many, the torch continues to burn.

Twenty-eight years after the first modern summer Olympics,[41] the winter Games were initiated in 1924. Gold medals for skating events had been added to the Olympics only 16 years previously. In 1920, when the Games were held at Antwerp, Belgium, an ice hockey tournament was staged with seven countries participating, of which Canada came out on top.

Sixteen nations participated in the first Winter Olympics at Chamonix in France, competing in 16 events drawn from seven sports. A total of 293 athletes took part, including just 13 women. It seemed appropriate that the 'sports of ice' were now added to the Olympic itinerary, as Olympus, the fabled home of the Greek gods, was entered by a great gate of clouds presided over by the Seasons.

Innsbruck was a strictly amateur Games – in the sense that amateur athletes participated solely for pleasure and any physical, mental or social benefits that might go hand in hand with the event. For most competitors the sports they took part in were largely recreational, providing them with no material gain to speak of.

(However, the idea that politics could be set aside and a sportsmanlike ethos prevail was, even nearly half a century ago, a little naive. With the Cold War at full throttle, there were big ideological differences at stake.)

Winter sports were a late arrival at the Games. Skiing, although popular in the Scandinavian nations, had only spread throughout Europe just before the end of the 19th century. The first mid-European ski club was founded at

---

41 The ancient Greek Games (777 BC to 393 AD) was revived in its modern incarnation in Athens in 1896.

Munich, Germany in 1890; Switzerland had its first club by 1893 and Chamonix, France was established as a winter resort in the season 1898-99.

Three years after the third Winter Olympic Games at Lake Placid in the US, and a year before the fourth such event in Garmisch, Germany, Robin Dixon had first seen the light of day in Marylebone, London. Alongside Tony Nash, the athletic Guardsman would now make an indelible mark in Innsbruck.

*　　*　　*

On Wednesday 29 January 1964, the opening ceremony for IX Winter Olympic Games took place on Berg Isel, a small hill dwarfed by its massive sisters. At 750 metres above sea level, it had been the site of the liberation battle of the Tyroleans in 1809, when Andreas Hofer, the *Sandwirt*[42] of the Passeier valley, led his compatriots to eventual victory in four battles against a mainly French enemy.

The Olympic ski jump was located at Berg Isel. The facility had been continually improved over decades and was by 1964 one of the best constructions of its type in Europe. The vast natural arena was a fabulous setting, with mountains and pine forests rising all around. Set high above the outskirts of Innsbruck, the silhouette of the city acted as a backdrop to the north. There were 60,000 spectators packed tightly down the side and around the stadium that once had a capacity of just a third of that number; the place was sold out.

The Berg Isel is shaped rather like a huge soup ladle, with

42 Andreas Hofer was born 1767 in St. Leonhard in Passeier, Tyrol. His father was a Tyrolean innkeeper and patriot who led a rebellion against Napoleon's forces. Andreas followed in his footsteps when he inherited the Sandhof inn. Elected into the Tyrolean Landtag, in dialectical German he was known as a *wirt* (proprietor) and thus ever after as *der Sandwirt*.

the snow strip down the centre of the handle acting as the ski jump. For the first time in the history of the winter Games, the opening ceremony was not held in an ice rink. The flags of 36 competing nations were draped around the natural amphitheatre.

But not all the tens of thousands who had bought tickets at 110 schillings each (about £7 at today's exchange rates, quite a hefty price in those days) were able to get to their places. The walkways and passages of the great bowl were hopelessly congested with people. The Austrian President, Adolf Schärf, was received at the entrance to the stadium by Olympic officials, who escorted him to a box where he was welcomed by the national anthem. On conclusion the parade of competitors began, each team dressed in its official uniform, led by their national flag and a shield bearing the name of their country.

The British standard was borne by 35-year-old Clifford Keith Wain Schellenberg, from Stokesley, Yorkshire.[43] He participated, rather ignominiously, in the luge (which most people in Britain at the time would have called 'tobogganing') in Innsbruck, but as the veteran of three Games he had formerly rode the bobsleigh at the Cortina d'Ampezzo in 1956.

The visual impact of the British team's brilliant red anoraks in the vast ski jump stadium, together with their practised marching and proud bearing, won them much applause. Their clothing for the opening ceremony had been mainly supplied to team members by Lilly White Ltd and Simpson of Piccadilly Ltd. The men got white nylon fur hats, brilliant red anoraks, black vorlages and fur-lined boots. The

43 The future husband of the Hon. Margaret de Hauteville Hamilton, daughter of Lt.-Col. Robert Edward Archibald Udney-Hamilton, 11th Lord Belhaven and Stenton, a former Master of the Freemasons of Scotland.

ladies had red hats and cloaks (both trimmed with fur), vorlages and boots. As Tony Nash recalls, "We went to the opening. We all got a mock fur coat that came down to your knees – it was very warm."

Team members were also supplied with special badges and ties, which technical officials also wore of a slightly different design. However, this apparel, plus some subsidiary clothing and travel expenses, seemed to be the limit of material support given to the British participants. According to Tony, "The only thing we got was official clothing from the Olympic Association when we went to the Olympics – no money for the equipment and so on. Our kit was not the greatest and was readily swapped after the ceremony – the biggest problem after being bussed to the ceremony and waiting a long time for it to start was we were all bursting for a pee!"

The procession, in keeping with the custom of the modern Games, was led by Greece, followed by the other teams in alphabetical order with the exception of the hosts, Austria, who in line with custom were the final team to enter the arena. The world's top winter sportsmen and women had not been trained to march as well as they skied or skated or drove bobsleighs. The lines of competitors following their national flags filed past the Austrian President in the main in a happily raggle-taggle manner; no one seemed to mind if the odd person stepped forward to take a quick photograph of friends.

The United States had the largest team, with 109 participants, followed by Germany (West and East combined in one team)[44] with 104 and Austria with 96. The Russians took fourth place with 95. Britain sent a team of 41 athletes

---

44 The Germans competed as a combined Olympic team from 1956 to 1964, but took part as separate entities from 1968 until German reunion.

to contest 17 events, but hopes for a medal before the conclusion of the Games on 9 February were not high – except, that is, regarding the bobsleigh event.

The official brass band turned up in traditional Tyrolean dress with dazzling scarlet frocks, black knee-breeches, white socks and alpine hats decorated with cock's feathers. They supplied the national anthems and the music for the ceremonial songs. The drum beats, horn signals and parading athletes generated the feeling of an international fashion show. But in reality it was a prelude to a series of intense battles that would take place in the quest for Olympic victory.

Many of those sent from all parts of the world to participate or officiate were unable to take part in the opening festivities at Berg Isel, as there was not enough room for everyone. The event had been limited to 1,300, but approximately 3,000 athletes, national officials and support team members would otherwise have been eligible to take part. The procession moved around the stadium before lining up at its centre in a column facing the tribune of honour. When all were assembled, from the middle of the arena a red strip of carpet was unfurled to make a pathway for the speakers. The president of the organising committee gave a speech welcoming the participants; Austria's President Schärf was brief and to the point: "I declare the Ninth Olympic Winter Games at Innsbruck, 1964 open."

Trumpets sounded a fanfare; with the benediction given, the singing of Richard Strauss's 'Olympic Hymn' flowed out over the hills as the Olympic flag was gradually hoisted. The five familiar interlinked rings of blue, yellow, black and red represented the five continents of the earth against a white borderless background, once more signifying the hopes that humankind still can't quite fulfil.

Doves were released as a symbol of peace, ironically succeeded by an artillery salute as the Olympic torch was carried into the arena by Austrian skier Josl Rieder, 1958's world slalom champion. Just after noon, the lone athlete stood silhouetted against the mountains and forests and lit the Olympic Flame with the torch specially brought from Greece by plane. An orange glow awoke like a creature disturbed from a long slumber, gradually gathering and rousing itself to suddenly leap round the bowl and shoot 21 feet into the freezing cold air, as if straining to reach the sky. The ninth Winter Olympic Games were open and their fire – kept alive by a special liquid gas mixture from Britain – would burn for 12 days at Innsbruck.

Paul Aste, the 47-year-old Austrian bob-man and tobogganist, holding a corner of the Olympic flag, delivered the Olympic Oath on behalf of the assembled athletes: "In the name of all participants I promise that we will obey the rules of the Olympic Games as honest sportsmen and that we will compete with fair mindedness to honour our teams and sports!" This was the new version of the traditional pledge. In 1961, the word 'promise' had replaced 'swear' and 'the honour of our teams' had been substituted for 'the honour of our countries' in an effort to eliminate some of the nationalistic content from the Games.

There was also one sad moment, as the crowd stood silent in memory of two athletes who had both been killed in training during the week leading up to the Games. Trying to negotiate a tricky turn on the ice-coated luge run, just a week before the opening ceremony, Britain's Kazimierz Kay Skrzypecki, 50, had lost control of his fragile vehicle and crashed. As Robin Dixon recalls, he "went over the top and was killed – there was no cushion of snow and he landed on the hard concrete."

Skrzypecki was rushed to hospital with a ruptured aorta and a fractured skull, broken arm and pelvis, but despite every effort made by the hospital doctors and the hurried arrival in Innsbruck of his wife and brother, he died 27 hours later – the first fatality in the history of the Winter Olympics.

"Two days before the opening ceremony we were out with the flags at half mast and wondered what the hell was going on," remembers Tony Nash. Several hundred competitors from all over the world observed the mourning of their own volition.

Then there was another shocking death. While practising for the men's downhill race, 19-year-old Australian skier Ross Milne, from Victoria, missed a bend on the frosty slopes and smashed into a tree at over 80kph. He failed to regain consciousness.

Another competitor, Edmund Schaedler, of Liechtenstein, was critically hurt following another accident on the downhill slope, just after Milne's tragic death. "There were no retaining features [such as nets] up on the piste and he went straight into a tree," recalls Dixon. "The fact that snow had to be brought from higher up by regiments of army vehicles meant the piste was laid with no margin for error and there were no safety nets, etc," says Nash.

Not long after this, Norman Barclay, the 34-year-old British luge captain, from Helensburgh, Scotland, would break his arm. Unsurprisingly perhaps, team member Richard Craig then withdrew "for family reasons". But, despite this tragic prologue, none of the courses had become any more or any less hazardous for top international class athletes than they were previously.

The choir sang as competitors left the stadium. After the opening ceremony was over, three gun salutes were fired at the top of the hill announcing the start of the Games. The protocol set by the founder of the modern Olympic movement, Pierre Frédy, Baron de Coubertin, almost seven decades earlier, was embellished by local colouring as the bells of the church at Wilten rang out, instigating all the bells of Innsbruck, the Tyrol and the nation of Austria to sound in unison.

The 1,186 competitors (986 men and 200 women) from 36 countries then returned to the Olympic Village. (It was the biggest number to take part in any winter Games, the previous record being 960 at Oslo in 1952.) Nordic skiers were transported instead to Seefeld, the highest quality quarters made available to any group of athletes attending the Games, away from the noise and bustle of the city. Innsbruck had given an impressively colourful ceremony, the informality of which made it overrun the carefully timed official schedule.

This was a time when all but a very few of the participants wanted to immerse themselves in the temporary community of the Games, including Britain's bobsleigh team. "It was wonderful to be among so many people from other nations," says Dixon. According to Nash, "What stays in my memory is how all the people from all the sports involved stayed in the Olympic Village, pretty much close together and not, as in later Games, spread out all over the mountains. It sounds a bit trite but it really was like one big Olympic family. We got to know the other people from other teams well, playing table tennis with the Italians or table football with the Japanese, American and Canadians. The Canadian bobsleigh team were absolute magic and enormous fun and the Argentineans were marvellous! We hadn't seen them at a bobsleigh track before, but they had decided to come to the Olympics and dropped their wives off in Paris," laughs

Tony. "They were all incredibly rich! They decided to have a barbeque. They had brought over a couple of beasts that had got impounded, but they got some others anyway, and their idea of a barbeque was two kilos of beef per man!"

While there was a strong friendship between the British, Italian, Canadian and Spanish teams (a sorority that the Argentineans later joined), the Innsbruck Games were notably friendly. It seems the village of 1964 would be almost a no-go area for today's less hedonistic athletes. The Brits were housed in what K. S. Duncan (MBE), General Secretary of the British Olympic Association (BOA), described as "excellent conditions" in Block 3 of the Olympic Village, in flats which, after the Games, were to be made available for the use of the inhabitants of Innsbruck. "Every day was a celebration there," according to Canadian four-man bob team member Douglas Anikan.

During the Games, all the competitors in the village were under a regime of pretty strict seclusion, living literally behind barbed wire. The village was made up of eight large apartment houses and set on the outskirts of Innsbruck. It included a 'rest centre', stocked with books, records, indoor games and a cinema, but, as Vic Emery recalls with some amusement, "The bedrooms were pretty Spartan: iron cots with simple spring underpinnings and hay block mattresses – three per cot!"

The task of feeding the several thousand participants, from competitors to technicians, was in the hands of Karl Schmid, a chef who worked for Vienna's International Atomic Energy Agency. Food was distributed from four central kitchens in the Olympic Village, run by 60 cooks and 209 staff, one each to serve German-Austrian, Anglo-American, Latin and Slav-Oriental food.

While friendship and camaraderie were a big part of what

the Olympics were about for most participants in 1964, all the competitors would now start to make their final preparations to contest the 34 gold medals. Their winter's dream was about to begin.

VII

IGLS

The bobsleighing events of the IX Winter Olympics were staged at Igls, a small mountain village high above Innsbruck, about three miles from the city centre. The track had hosted the 1963 FIBT World Championship, but had also, in 1935, staged the two-man event of the world bobsleigh championships when the track ran from Römerstrasses to the Patscherkofel valley railway station. After several fatal accidents at the finishing curve during competition, the course was closed temporarily until safety measures were introduced.

Although not considered too technically difficult, at some junctures the walls of the Igls run were very steep and sleds tended to bang into them. High up on the nearly vertical ice, the course had seen some fearful crashes down its average drop of 9.2 percent over its long history. As Tony Nash confirms, "These were the days before refrigerated tracks. It was down to a small space of time when the ice was right –

middle of January to the middle of February. Now you can go from November through to April if you want to on good ice tracks. But you couldn't then."

It was the 1964 Winter Olympics that motivated the construction of separate bobsleigh and luge tracks at Innsbruck. The two tracks were made from concrete and were built below the Patscherkofel; construction started in September 1961 and was officially completed in July 1963, following test runs of both. But there were 20 injuries during the 1963 World Championships, which led to further changes.

"We had gone out to Austria to test the Olympic track the year before," recollects Tony. "There were various things wrong with it. In practice one day in the four-man we thought there was a bit of a problem with the run. We sat down and we all agreed what to do: GBIII, an RAF team, GBII and GBI all fell in the same place. At the hospital [Crankenhuse] there were so many bobsleighers because the track wasn't running true. There was a young doctor there who was also a bobsleigher and he told me they were running out of bandages, he had to send me down to the town to get as many as I could buy! By the time the Olympics started they had the whole thing jazzed up with helicopters and things. They'd made it an excellent track. They knew what they were doing and they were very bobsleigh-minded."

The 1964 Winter Olympic bobsleigh track was designed by Austrian former bobsleigher and luger Paul Aste.[45] The bob course was made up of 14 turns packed into 1506.36 metres, with a vertical drop of 138 metres and a maximum grade of

45 Aste won seven medals in the European luge championships with five golds (men's singles: 1951, 1953, 1955; men's doubles: 1952, 1955) and two silvers (men's singles: 1952, men's doubles: 1953). He also competed in bobsleigh during the 1950's and 1960's, earning a silver medal in the two-man event at the World Championships in 1955 and a bronze in 1958.

Aste also competed on the bobsled in three Winter Olympics for Austria, his best finish being

14.04%. It was one of the most impressive tracks in the world, and its turns were named as follows:

1. *Startkurve* – Start.
2./3. *Hohes S* – High S.
4. *Stützenkurve* – Support.
5. *Höcker* – Peak.
6. *Fuchsloch* – Foxhole.
7. *Hohle Gasses* – Hollow lane.
8. *Schanze* – Dig.
9. *Hexenkessel* – Witch's cauldron.
10./11. *Nadelöhr* – Needle-eye S.
12. *Burlepautz* – no clear translation.
13. *Weckauf* – Wake on.
14. *Zielkurve* – Finish.

For the 1976 Winter Olympics, the two tracks would be replaced by a combined bob, skeleton and luge track, enabling all the competitions to be undertaken on a single track for the first time. It was the first such permanent combined artificially refrigerated course in the world, serving as a model for other tracks of its kind worldwide.

*　　*　　*

Ever since it was built for the 1932 Olympics, the curves on the bobsled run at Lake Placid, NY, had been considered the most demanding. Plunging through 16 curves, it was so low-banked and broad that the smallest mistake could send a sled

a fifth place in the four-man event at Oslo in 1952. (Luge would not become a Winter Olympic sport until the 1964 Games.) He took three roles at the first Innsbruck Olympics: bobsleigh and luge course designer; taking the Olympic Oath for athletes during the opening ceremony; finishing seventh in the four-man event on the course he'd designed and constructed the previous year.

hurtling madly off line; the track had taken its toll in terms in sledders' lives and dozens of competitors were injured over the years. When the 46-year-old Aste designed the Igls bobsleigh course, he produced a narrower 14-curve run, estimating that it might be slightly slower than the polished Lake Placid chute but much safer. Whether these aims were achieved would prove to be arguable.

Making its debut for the 1963 World Bobsledding Championships, Igls was about three seconds faster for the metric mile than its Lake Placid counterpart. For the more cautious bobber it was close to an idea of hell. On the second day of the boblet competition, a Swedish team piloted by Gunnar Ähs hit over 120 kph[46] as they roared into the ninth curve, *Hexenkessel*. Ähs lost control. The bob tore up to the top of the 12-metre bank, bounced down and rebounded frighteningly from wall to wall. Ähs fractured both his legs in two places each and his upper front teeth were sheared off on the ice. His brakeman broke a leg on landing after being thrown free from the sled.

The next day the American bob, piloted by 30-year-old Joe McKillip, smashed into a soft snow wall as it closed in on the finishing line; McKillip was rushed to hospital with a dislocated shoulder and a badly slashed cheek. The following day saw Canadian driver Monty Gordon's throat gashed practically from ear to ear after he cracked up on a straight; his sled overturned, came badly off the *Hexenkessel* curve and hit a side wall.

The 1963 competition was suspended for 24 hours to allow for the run to be narrowed, in an attempt to make it safer. However, the alterations had little effect on the toll exacted in injury and pain. A French bob ran into trouble in the

46 A similar speed to most other sleds at this point.

Hexenkessel, skidding down out of control, the brakeman suffering severe concussion.

In total, a score of athletes were injured as the teams from 11 countries pitted their skill and tried their luck on the Igls run for the first time. Only the Italians appeared to be resistant to the hex of the 'Witch's Cauldron'. Eugenio Monti was their general, at that point a 35-year-old six-time world champion in the two-man event; then there was Sergio Zardini, the slim, 31-year-old hotel manager from Cortina. The Italian bobs finished the competition in first and second places in both the two-man and four-man bobs. Monti's best time in the boblet was 1.06.4, an average of something more than 85kph (a mile in just over a minute from a standing start).

"The Witch's Cauldron was in the middle of the course," relates Tony. "It was a big corner and went round about 160 degrees – it was spectacular for the television cameras – it used to have a Coca Cola sign at the top and you turned down on the 'C' of the Cola. The Italians and the Germans thought they could take it better by putting out markers, so we went out fairly early and moved their markers about ten yards – there was a lot of gamesmanship. The Italian Zardini was always fairly nervous, so the deal was I stood next to him and someone would rush up and say, 'My God, Tony, have you seen the blood on that turn?' and he went off to the loo," laughs Nash.

Looking back on their careers, it's apparent that Nash and Dixon had a very low accident rate. The reasons why they didn't crash much are manifold: in spite of his short sight, Tony had a gift for taking the bends almost perfectly, choosing the right line virtually every time. This was the same sort of ability which characterised the performances of Stirling Moss, the great British racing driver of the Nash-Dixon era. A mistake of six inches at high speed in the confined space afforded by the bob track would mean not simply the difference between victory and defeat, but between a good run and a spell in hospital.

Tony also had the competitive capacity to produce the fastest run at the most difficult moment. But the Brits had another great asset in the intuitive understanding between Nash and his brakeman, as Robin Dixon could seemingly read his pilot's mind.

VIII

BOLT FROM
THE BLUE

As modern Olympic bobsleigh bronze medallist Shauna Rohbock says, "Nobody comes in here not wanting to win a medal. It's definitely a daydream, coming across the line, seeing that Number One on the clock, feeling that excitement. Everyone thinks of that."

Bobsleigh was not included in the 1960 Winter Olympics programme, but when the sport returned to the Games in 1964, so did Eugenio Monti – alongside his team-mates, he was considered to be among the favourites for both the two-man and four-man competitions.

Monti and brakeman Sergio Siorpaes began their Games with the defence of their two-man world title. It was a cold afternoon. In line with the rules of international competition, the event, which took place two days after the opening ceremony, was run in four heats spread over Friday 31 January to Saturday 1 February.

Nash and Dixon by this point were seen as serious

contenders. Although Britain hadn't won a World Championship since 1937 and a British bob had never won an Olympic title, in 1963 Tony and Robin had finished third in the World Championship boblet event and fourth in the four-man contest, joined by crewmen David Lewis and Guy Renwick.

However, one of the most crucial aspects of the two-man bobsleigh event of 1964 took part before the first push. According to Nash, "Before the first run we had the draw. They mixed up the draw to a formula which was devised to be as fair as possible to everyone. Because of the weather and the state of the track the order you came out for each of the four runs was going to be critical, so we all went down and a very good old girlfriend of mine had been asked to do the draw. The member jury called out the first team to come out of the draw, 'Great Britain I, number seven.' Of course, everybody hooted with laughter because it was my old girlfriend."

("It turned out to be a very good draw," concurs Dixon.)

Although, as in every big competition, the draw was designed to make sure no one had any advantage over anyone else, getting down early in the first heat gave Nash and Dixon every chance to hit relatively smooth ice and establish a good time from the off. It seemed from the start that the fates were on the side of the British. As Tony recalls, "I was walking up the run before the Olympics and I saw Franz Kemser. This great bear of a man insisted I shake his hand and as I shook his hand he had a gold medal in it. He was sure this would be our moment!"

Nash saw how on the ninth corner, *Hexenkessel*, the bobs hit about halfway down the course at the most vital stage of the run. The sled drivers either gained or lost time coming out of this terrifying curve. Nash says he'd deduced that if a bob took the bend at precisely the right point, there would be less resistance to its dive and it would gather extra momentum for the rest of the run. Nash and Dixon, by trial and error, found what they believed to be the most favourable way to take the turn. This technique would provide the Brits with a critical edge.

Although Robin and Tony had arrived in Innsbruck with their morale high, they knew only too well what Monti was capable of. They were part of the fraternity that surrounded the Italian and they had no doubt that he was the competition favourite.

The day of the event began with practice pilot runs by those in the bottom half of the draw, during which the Austrian II bob, manned by Franz and Heinrich Isser, made an alarming mistake in tackling the infamous *Hexenkessel*. Drivers aimed to get up the Cauldron's high wall as early as possible and dive down into the straight as sharply as physics might allow, thereby striking the right balance between gravity and centrifugal force. A crowd of 10,000 had stumbled and trudged up the pine-covered slopes of the mountain, looking in their brightly-coloured ski-pants and anoraks like rivulets of coloured ink spread over the glittering snow. They gathered around the Witch's Cauldron at a cost of £2 10s, as it provided the best chance of witnessing any extreme drama. They gasped in horror as the Austrians went into the curve too low and rose to the top too late. With disturbing inevitability, the sled came off the banking at a painfully acute angle. They had to turn sharply to avoid going over the top as the bob skidded off the banking into the shiny grey wall opposite. There was a violent wobble which almost threw brakeman Heinrich out as the bob went on its mad way.

A gasp from the crowd like a great puncture drowned the rasp of the runners that left a pair of transverse skid marks, telling of the narrowness of their escape. For a few moments speculation was rife that Heinrich might have shattered his arm, but word came from the bottom of the run that he was only bruised – although he'd be replaced for the competition by Reinhold Durnthaler. Happily, that was as near as anyone came to disaster all morning, although there was a collective sharp intake of breath around *Hexenkessel* when one of the Swedish pairs seemed to be hovering on the razor's edge of destruction.

As the sleds flashed down with that menacing premonitory rumble, passing in a haze of blue, red or gold, all the indeterminable variants were writ large. Competitors were locked in the 'now', unable to retreat to the safety of the past and fearful of the immediate future. Controlling this understandable feeling is essential in a sport like bobsleighing.

"On race days Robin was appalling," remembers Nash, "we had to drag him out, he was very nervous before competition but as soon as he was on the track he was fine. Our first Olympic run was a good one."

Indeed, it was good enough to startle the world's bobsleigh aficionados. The Brits held second place behind Canada II, crewed by Victor Emery and Peter Kirby, while Monti was implausibly languishing in fifth position. The Italian found that he was being outraced by his British and Canadian students, now sitting above him on the leader board.

Robin, more than four decades later, still seemed slightly surprised by the situation. "Somehow Monti found himself a fair way behind us after the first run. He knew us extremely well and would have known that the only other people that were going to win were ourselves or his team-mate Zardini."

With that said, although practically everyone had written the Canadians off following their 11th place on the last practice day, they had the fastest first run in the initial heat of the competition and would be close behind in fourth place at the end of the first day. They had to be considered capable of threatening the leaders if they could produce another fast run.

Nash and Dixon had gone off on their first run as the word *schnell* (fast) rippled around the crowd. When the twinkling lights stopped on the scoreboard at 1.05.53, it was confirmed that they had made the fastest time that far. More significantly, they had surpassed one of the Italian pairs. Nash was probably as surprised as anyone. When the Brits' splendid time was announced he bounded out of the sled, rushed up to a pretty girl he didn't even know and kissed her. It was a decidedly un-English thing to do, but he managed to hide his elation for the rest of the day.

Nash had got to the top of *Hexenkessel* at the earliest possible moment and guided the four-year-old dark-blue bob down again as quickly and safely as the line into the straight would allow. A mistake there would have had the witches cackling into their cauldron; as it was, not even they had seen the Britons coming.

Canada II (Emery and Kirby) did better than GBI by over a third of a second. This was a blow, but more importantly perhaps Nash and Dixon's time withstood the challenge of Monti and Siorpaes, who held the top of the wall too long. For all this, things were relatively close; with three runs to go the top six sleds were separated by less than a second.

Standings after the first heat

1. Canada II: V. Emery/Kirby 1:05.15
2. Great Britain I: Nash/Dixon 1:05.53
3. Italy II: Zardini/Bonagura 1:05.63
4. Austria I: Thaler/Nairz 1:05.72
5. Italy I: Monti/Siorpaes 1:05.94

6. United States II: McDonald/Pandolph 1:05.97
7. United States I: McKillip/Lamy 1:06.17
8. Germany II: Maurer/Grasegger 1:06.72
9. Sweden I: Lutteman/Freyberg 1:06.81
10. Germany I: Wormann/Braun 1:06.87
11. Austria II: F. Isser/Durnthaler 1:06.94
12. Switzerland I: Zoller/Zimmermann 1:06.97
13. Romania II: Oancea/Cotacu 1:07.31
14. Switzerland II: Kiesel/Lory 1:07.33
15. Great Britain II: McCowen/Hedges 1:07.47
16. Argentina I: Tomasi/Rodriguez 1:07.59
17. Romania I: Panturu/Pasovschi 1:07.74
18. Canada I: J. Emery/Currie 1:07.85
19. Sweden II: Akerstrom/Eriksson 1:08.01
20. Belgium I: de-Crawhez/Englebert 1:09.63
21. Argentina II: Bordeu/Agote 1:10.15

Before the second run, Monti walked up to the start of the course with an expression of dissatisfaction on his face. The Italian unhappily inspected the curving runway made of ice blocks that appeared slightly blue in colour, considering what he might have done wrong. Where did he lose that 79 hundredths of a second which gave the men from Montreal the lead?

Siorpaes helped his driver seek an explanation. He had accompanied Monti on a string of World Championship triumphs; in the four-man bobs they'd picked up gold in 1960 and 1961, and Siorpaes had also ridden with Zardini to silver in 1958 and 1959. Both men understood that they now had a fight on their hands.

While he made ready for his second run, Monti muttered to himself. Spectators and competitors might have noted his lips moving as he gave himself commandments and reprimands, but no one heard his words. A huddle of Italians prepared their number one sled; the extremely responsive metallic runners were warmed to maximise glide, buffed to a shine that threatened to blind anyone catching their gleam. Preparation of the bob was something of a sacrament for the Italians. Eugenio was not a man to leave anything to chance, his aim was perfection.

Siorpaes and Monti powered their bob into action with a vigorously potent charge, running alongside it for about 25 yards before leaping aboard the blue bullet. From then on, the squatting Siorpaes used his weight to gain speed. Monti looked to steer the missile on what he saw as an ideal trajectory. Ahead were around 1500 metres of solid, shimmering chill, made up of 14 challenging curves. Spectators paid rapt attention as the halfway time was declared. It was the fastest of the competition that far. The redhead from the Dolomites had sped into the testing valley of Olympic bobsleighing like a frosty banshee, living up to one of his soubriquets, 'the Red-Devil'; taking pole position, he'd come back at his rivals.

After he had passed the photo-electric light at the finish his time was announced, clipping 0.01 of a second off of the record Nash and Dixon had achieved in practice.

Tony Nash knew that he and Dixon had done very well, but also understood they would have to at least match their best to be sure of a medal of any hue. But he froze for a second in horror, as he discovered one of the bolts which held the rear axle supporting the British sled's runners, a critical piece of hardware, had been broken.

"We had every spare part but that," Dixon recalls almost in wonder. Over four decades later, Nash can still feel the profound chill of his discovery. "We'd done our first run and the bob had gone back up to the top of the hill. I'd walked up the course as usual to see if anything had gone wrong and watch one or two of the other bobs go down. When I reached the start I saw our guys were scratching their heads. We found a bolt on the back axle was sheared. The back axle was solid and was fitted on the frame with two bolts.

"As soon as we turned it upside down I realised something was wrong with it. Quite quickly we found that one of the essential back axle bolts that attached the runners to the sled had simply broken. We had every spare in the book with us but we just couldn't get a bolt to the top in time and the second run was about to start."

Except for one American bob, specially built by General Motors, all the other sleds in the competition were Podars, made in Italy, but no spare bolt could be found. It was a devastating blow and a British withdrawal seemed unavoidable; the worst-case scenario was that a bolt would be salvaged from GBII, leaving the leading British sled to fight on alone, but even removing a bolt from one bob and attaching it to the other might take too much time. The nearest alternative replacement was in the Olympic Village, miles away. The situation threatened to deny Nash, Dixon and Great Britain a run for glory and the first chance of victory.

Robin Dixon recollects the next few moments: "Monti was actually on the line about to start his second run. Because of our friendship with the Italians over the years the first people I went to for help were the Italian mechanics. Eugenio, who was about to go down, came over with his helmet and gloves on to see what all the fuss was about. He asked what the matter was and I told him very quickly what had happened. He took one look and said in his broken English, 'It's alright, don't worry. I'm going down now; you can have mine when I get down as I will have finished with it for the day. So send an

Englishman down to the finish with a spanner and they can have my bolt.'"[47]

As he uttered these words Monti was 0.41 seconds behind the British pair on the first run. The German Woermann was fastest on the second run but could not overcome his sled's slow start to the competition. The British bob was amongst the most dangerous challenges to the Italians; Nash had previously worked hard to make it difficult for Monti to win the 1963 World Championship on the same run. Frantic questions from the phalanx of bewildered Italian pressmen were showered on Monti when, as soon as he had completed his run, he tilted his sled without hesitation.

As Dixon recollects, "When he had completed his second run we had one of our team waiting with a spanner, he whipped the bolt out and ran it up the hill. It was got up to us in time to get it into our sled. Monti had sorted all this out before he talked to any of the press. But we had actually got another bolt in before the Italian bolt got to the top. It was a tremendous gesture nevertheless."

Nash concurs with this breaking of the spell: "In the end we didn't use the Italian bolt. By the time it got to the top we had another one in."

Mike Freeman, then a young flight lieutenant in the Royal Air Force and brakeman for Great Britain II, was given the task of helping the Italians remove the bolt and getting it back to the top of the run. Looking back, Freeman recalls, "By the time I got to the bottom, Monti was already out of his bob and trying to get the bolt off. Once we got it off he simply said, 'Go quickly, Mike.' My only worry was whether I would get back to the top in time."

47 After this book sees print, in January 2010, a new bobsleigh run will be opened at St Moritz. The start will be named in honour of Eugenio Monti's magnanimity towards Tony Nash and Robin Dixon, almost half a century previously, provisionally christened 'Monti's Bolt'.

It was actually Sergio Siorpaes who removed the bolt. He would later recall, "I took the bolt out and gave it to him ... it was natural. It was a favour done for somebody I knew ... in the same sport. There wasn't the kind of rivalry there is today."

Mike did get back to the start with just moments to spare, but the replacement bolt had already been implanted into the guts of GBI, to enable Nash and Dixon to make their next run.

As Tony says, "We would have got another bolt even if we had to sacrifice our number two team. Most of the sleds were made by the same Italian manufacturer so all the bolts were pretty much standard. But we weren't going to have the time to get to all our spares which were down below. We had spare bolts, we had the lot! We could have done it if we'd had the time. We were going to withdraw the Number Two team. However, by the time Monti's bolt got to us we had resolved the problem. But although Monti, the Italians and ourselves were great friends – we used to go out for a cup of coffee in the evenings and a chat – that gesture of Monti's was quite extraordinary."

Nash and Dixon had the advantage of going down for a second time towards the end of the second heat, after all the other favourites. The Canadians fell back badly, which is what a gap of just under a second can mean in bobbing, and Monti, with his new record for the course of 1.04.90, tugged Zardini in.

Then away went Nash and Dixon. To grab the overall lead, the British pair had to come down the course in 1.05.22. Cries of *sehr gut* (very good) and *sehr schnell* began to echo around the run. As in the initial run, GBI recorded the second best time, but this was enough to give them the overall lead. At the end of day one, the repaired GBI was leading the pack. But it was the Italian pilot who grabbed the imaginations and respect of all his rivals, placing sportsmanship above all else.

Second heat results

1. Italy I: Monti/Siorpaes 1:04.90
2. Great Britain I: Nash/Dixon 1:05.10
3. Italy II: Zardini/Bonagura 1:05.13
4. United States II: McDonald/Pandolph 1:05.85
5. Canada II: V. Emery/Kirby 1:05.93
6. Switzerland I: Zoller/Zimmermann 1:06.20
7. United States I: McKillip/Lamy 1:06.34
8. Germany I: Wormann/Braun 1:06.42
9. Austria II: F. Isser/Durnthaler 1:06.71
10. Romania I: Panturu/Pasovschi 1:06.97
11. Austria I: Thaler/Nairz 1:06.98
12. Sweden I: Lutteman/Freyberg 1:06.99
13. Canada I: J. Emery/Currie 1:07.64
14. Switzerland II: Kiesel/Lory 1:07.70
15. Great Britain II: McCowen/Hedges 1:07.73
16. Germany II: Maurer/Grasegger 1:07.76
17. Argentina II: Bordeu/Agote 1:08.45
18. Romania II: Oancea/Cotacu 1:08.93
19. Argentina I: Tomasi/Rodriguez 1:09.20
20. Belgium I: de-Crawhez/Englebert 1:10.01
21. Sweden II: Akerstrom/Eriksson 1:11.81

The first thing Nash spoke about to the press, as he stepped out of the bob, was Monti's generosity. Sweating from the jolting ride, he told the world: "Well, we've got the lead thanks to Monti. At the end of our first run we discovered we'd broken a back axle bolt. We were looking desperately for another one. Monti came down early in the second run and when he had completed that, and as soon as he heard about our situation, he whipped his bolt out of his bob and sent it straight up to the top so that we could race again. His gesture was one of the finest sporting gestures I have ever come across."

He described his experience of the run a tad more succinctly: "It was like being a piece of ice in a cocktail shaker!"

From the vantage point of decades later, it's hard to decide who was the greatest sportsman. Nash and Dixon stuck to the story that Eugenio's bolt had saved their day and made their victory possible for the next 45 years. They must have made their minds up in the fleeting seconds it took to make that second run, and didn't even let their great Italian friend in on their pact. Admittedly, it would have been awkward to explain that they were given the bolt but didn't actually use it, and perhaps such an explanation might have made Eugenio appear foolish in some quarters. But all that seems of no import at all next to their towering act of solidarity. The fact is that the Brits were prepared to hand over a great slice of the day's glory to their mentor, a man who in turn had demonstratively proved his willingness to lay down his chance of triumph for his own principles of sportsmanship and friendship.

"To this day I think everyone, including me, believed that Monti's bolt was used," says Vic Emery when apprised of the reality. "While I am a bit ambivalent of holding the secret till eternity, it highlights the great model of sportsmanship both ways, which would otherwise have been lost as an example of the power of mutual respect in sport. I'm amazed it didn't leak out over 45 years!"

Until now the legend has remained intact. But the mere fact that another bolt was used makes no difference at all to the spirit of Monti's action or the great fraternal ethos that existed between bobsleighers of that era. Yes, the knowledge of what actually happened changes sporting history, but the awareness adds to rather than depreciates the soul of the Games.

There is no doubt that the Britons had ridden well and deserved to end the day in pole position. Their starts had been swift and smooth; both times down they motored round *Hexenkessel* if not with ease, then certainly with style.

This second heat results left the overall standings as follows:

1. Great Britain I Nash/Dixon 2.10.63
2. Italy II Zardini/Bonagura 2.10.76
3. Italy I Monti/Siorpaes 2.10.84
4. Canada II V. Emery/Kirby 2.11.08
7. United States II McDonald/Pandolph 2.11.82
5. United States I McKillip/Lamy 2.12.41
8. Austria I Thaler/Nairz 2.12.70
10. Switzerland I Zoller/Zimmermann 2.13.17
11. Germany I Wormann/Braun 2.13.29
12. Austria II Isser/Durnthaler 2.13.65
13. Sweden I Lutteman/Freyberg 2.13.80
14. Germany II Maurer/Grasegger 2.14.48
15. Romania I Panturu/Pasovschi 2.14.71
16. Switzerland II Kiesel/Lory 2.15.03
17. Great Britain II McCowen/Hedges 2.15.20
18. Canada I J. Emery/Currie 2.15.49
19. Romania II Oancea/Cotacu 2.16.24
20. Argentina I Tomasi/Rodriguez 2.16.79
21. Argentina II Bordeu/Agote 2.18.60
22. Belgium De-Crawhez/Englebert 2.19.64
21. Sweden II Akerstrom/Eriksson 2.19.82

The crowd had remained engaged and responsive the whole day, cheering at the first run of Erwin Thaler and Josef Nairz in Austria I and applauding the achievement of Nash and Dixon. As Tony recalls, "Having had the drama after the first run, the second run put us 13 hundredths of a second in front of the two Italians at the end of the first day, so we were in the lead. After that second round we were all chatting and I went up to Monti and said, 'Thank you very much, marvellous gesture.' He just shrugged, as if saying that for him it was just one of those things."

It was BBC commentator David Coleman who broke the news to Nash that he had driven into an overnight lead. The smiling British pilot told viewers: "We knew what we had to do, yes, but doing it was another matter."

With a little understandable relish, Robin Dixon looks back on the conclusion of the first day. "It was a day that was hard to sleep on. But we were professional enough to be able to sleep okay. We had a routine. We went back to our rooms, particularly during the Games, as we were in the Olympic Village. We asked the rest of the team to give us peace and quiet. We took an hour or two in the evening to look at the scoresheets and the timings and so on – we went through the same routines and did the same things."

The British team had not made much of a habit of early nights, as Nash explained at the time: "We prefer six good hours to eight or ten twiddling your toes and getting hot and cold."

Robin (who, like Tony Nash, was a non-smoker) told the press: "We both like a drink and are taking a mild wine or two. But we are both too dedicated to success in this risky business to take any chance, particularly on this track."

"Actually we had a couple of whiskeys and we slept quite well," laughs Tony today, "but it was a tense time."

Sergio Zardini, the 1963 world champion in the four-man bob, and Monti were close behind; Eugenio, the sporting saint of the day, had, for the British the capacity to be the next day's sinner.

For much of the evening Innsbruck was buzzing with arguments about what might happen. The field was virtually down to three; the two Italian bobs and GBI. Speculation was intense about Zardini's ability to withstand the strain and the ice-cool Monti was reckoned by many to be the danger man as far as British hopes were concerned. But in a sport where success and failure is finely balanced on the thinnest of lines, the likes of Vic Emery and Charlie McDonald could not have been ruled out of the running either.

Before the final day of competition, the British support team spent as many hours as possible working hard on the bobs, getting them into shape for the final two runs. It was well known that the British bobsleighs were amongst the most diligently looked after in the field, so well polished that they outshone most of the others. Each of the runners[48] had to be ground perfectly until every mark or scratch had been taken out of them then realigned, front with back. These steel blades would be on the track only for another two minutes or so in all, but the ability of drivers and brakemen would count for nothing without the (literal) grind of thorough preparation. Every bolt and axle was checked, rechecked and treble checked – it was boasted that they knew each part on a personal basis.

Not only were the parts of the bob maintained, they were cared for. The blades were carried to the start meticulously wrapped in tea towels and hot blankets; this treatment was estimated to be worth perhaps 0.03 of a second.[49]

There was also intelligence to be gathered. By the time

48 A set of four runners cost anything upwards of £80 – this at a time when a week's full board at a Pontin's holiday camp during the summer cost around £10 per adult. (The same week would now cost around £300.) A bob's runners were approximately the roundness and width of a smooth dinner knife handle.

49 Artificial heating was not allowed but most of the top exponents just knew, without any measuring guide, that cold runners would be slower. The intelligence they gathered was mainly based on how the fastest sleds took the curves.

Nash and Dixon got back to the top after a run, every facet of their opponents' preparation and performances was waiting for them; details of how their rivals organised themselves combined with painstaking statistical data to provide invaluably detailed insights.

All this backup service meant that, at the start of any big race, Nash and Dixon knew their comrades had already given them an advantage over most of their opponents; it was the basis for the necessary confidence needed to win.

Meanwhile, back in Britain the news that Nash and Dixon had an even chance of winning Britain's first Winter Olympic gold for 12 years was lighting up the back of the early editions. For most people this was something that came out of the blue; large sections of the public knew nothing about the Winter Olympics. The 'game of winter' was football; at the start of February, Tottenham Hotspurs were at the top of the old First Division and the London derby against Chelsea at White Hart Lane would have been considered the sports fest of the day for many.

It was possible that Tony and Robin were being set up to fail. The Italians had a reputation of unfailingly being able to pull something out of the hat. Monti's fantastic second run had pulled him right up from fifth to third place and put him back in contention.

Theoretically, the great Italian had the advantage in the last run of the competition, being scheduled to take his sled down the track after Nash and Zardini. He would know the exact time he'd need to win the competition; Nash and Dixon were not so well placed as, in the first run of the day, they would go down between Monti and Zardini. According to Lawrence McKillip, the experienced American 'slider' (as bobbers were called in the States), "The only worse place to start than sandwiched between two Italian sleds is before two Italian sleds."

On the final run Nash and Dixon had to go down before both Italians; they were the third sled to start. Italy II was eighth to take the plunge while Monti would be seventeenth out of the traps. Canada followed as last down.

Just when events seemed unable to conspire against Nash and Dixon, the white stuff fell on the Igls chute overnight; it wasn't just a little either – a covering of nearly six inches was plonked on Innsbruck. The mountains were suddenly a winter paradise with great fir trees and alpine meadows lightly dusted with snow.

Officials said that, having made all arrangements to hold the Games without a fresh fall, they hadn't really wanted one after the start as there was every chance it could destroy the carefully prepared conditions. There was even talk that times on the bob run could become dangerously fast due to the damp snow (much of it had previously been machine-made). And abandonment of the competition would have probably meant the overnight standings would provide the result, but no one – least of all Nash and Dixon – wanted that. But there were also murmurs that the Brits seemed to be at a disadvantage, having an early starting time.

Then, as the first pilot run was undertaken, the snow stopped. Rather than the course becoming faster, the opposite problem reared its unwelcome head; the weather was warming up and the ice was quickly softening. Fortunately, Nash and Dixon were due to make their first run early on, hopeful of avoiding the worst of any deterioration in conditions.

IX

JUDGEMENT DAY

Monti made the first run of the leading teams. The female
German commentator, who lent such drama to the day,
ominously announced over the track's sound system, "*schnell
und ruhig*" (quick and calm), meaning a fast straight run with
no bumping. Her voice would quicken and grow louder as the
competition wore on.

Following their third run Nash and Dixon were contenders
for the silver medal, just behind Zardini. Monti followed and
held third place, closely followed by the Canadians. But the
British recorded their slowest run of the competition, while
Zardini showed himself to be obviously on form.

According to Tony Nash, "One instinctively knows when
one has done a good run or not, the third run wasn't that
good and the Italians came through us."

As Robin Dixon remembers, "I didn't have anything to say
to Tony at that stage. We had no conversation at all. Once we
got into the race Tony knew what he had to do. Tony did what

he always did and walked back up the run to try and see what had happened, get his mind together. Including practice runs and walking back up the track, we'd been up and down it a dozen times. I just had to get on and make sure the sled was in the best possible condition."

For his part, Tony knew there had been a mistake: "Without a doubt I'd made an error halfway down the run and I thought, 'That's done it! We're fairly safely in third place but these two Italians will hold on to one and two.'

"The number two Italian Zardini came down and there was a halfway time – if they didn't get into the 47s they would not be able to pick up on our time, so when we heard it was 48 something we knew we were in second place."

By 1964 Zardini had won ten medals at the FIBT World Championships (one gold, six silver and three bronze) in two and four-man bobs. His triumph in the four-man event a year earlier in Igls had been the pinnacle of his career. He was a seasoned and dangerous competitor, alongside his 33-year-old brakeman, Romano Bonagura, a bobsled veteran with half a dozen World Championship medals to his credit who'd been in Zardini's world-beating four-man crew in 1963.

"As I was walking back up the run there was Franz Kemser again," recalls Tony Nash. "He said, 'You're alright Tony, the weather's breaking!' At the time I didn't quite know what to make of what Franz had said. I just walked on back up the run to get ready for the fourth run.

"But a thermal was coming in over the Alps, which meant the ice would be softening and the run wouldn't be quite so quick.

"On the fourth run we were coming down in front of the Italians, early in the order. As it turned out, the earlier anyone went down the better it would be. Over time the track was bound to slow up, the question was how quickly, which of course no one could answer."

Heat 3 result

1. Germany I: Wormann/Braun 1:05.17
2. Italy II: Zardini/Bonagura 1:05.21
3. Great Britain I: Nash/Dixon 1:05.39
4. Italy I: Monti/Siorpaes 1:05.41
5. United States I: McKillip/Lamy 1:05.84
6. Canada II: V. Emery/Kirby 1:05.96
7. United States II: McDonald/Pandolph 1:06.16
8. Austria I: Thaler/Nairz 1:06.48
9. Great Britain II: McCowen/Hedges 1:06.52
10. Canada I: J. Emery/Currie 1:06.75
10. Romania II: Oancea/Cotacu 1:06.75
12. Germany II: Maurer/Grasegger 1:06.92
12. Romania I: Panturu/Pasovschi 1:06.92
14. Argentina I: Tomasi/Rodriguez 1:07.36
15. Austria II: F. Isser/Durnthaler 1:07.40
16. Switzerland I: Zoller/Zimmermann 1:07.60
17. Switzerland II: Kiesel/Lory 1:07.92
18. Sweden I: Lutteman/Freyberg 1:07.93
19. Argentina II: Bordeu/Agote 1:11.33

Steered by Bill McCowan, with his 27-year-old brakeman Andrew Hedges, GBII's third heat was to be its best run of the competition. The number two bob in dark blue, the new British racing colour, was guided by wheel, whereas Tony Nash used the more customary two ropes. As Vic Emery says, "It was the Americans who usually preferred wheels over ropes because at Lake Placid there was more snow on the long straights. On European tacks there was less snow and more curves, so ropes, being that bit more sensitive, made sense."

But when Bill McCowen, as a highly-skilled motor racing driver, wanted to turn left he instinctively turned the wheel in that direction, swaying his body right. Most people tend to lean with the direction of the turn, and the in-and-out movement of a rope under each hand is more instinctive. The rope altered the angle of the front runners and for some, like Nash, this apparently crude method exerted more control over a bob hurtling down an ice track only six feet wide in places. Of course, ropes are also much softer to come into contact with than a wheel in the event of a crash. But whether rope or wheel, without precision, courage and instant reaction one is quickly bouncing off the wall of the chute; once that starts to happen, momentum and gravity may overcome all human effort.

GBI had lost the hard-earned lead it had won the previous day. The overall placings looked tight as far as the prospect of a British gold medal was concerned; whatever happened, they would need to go faster than Zardini.

1. Italy II Zardini/Bonagura 3:15.97
2. Great Britain I Nash/Dixon 3:16.02
3. Italy I Monti/Siorpaes 3:16.25
4. Canada II V. Emery/Kirby 3.17.04
5. United States II McDonald/Pandolph 3.17.98
6. United States I McKillip/Lamy 3.18.25
7. Germany I Wormann/Braun 3.18.46
8. Austria I Thaler/Nairz 3.19.18
9. Switzerland I Zoller/Zimmermann 3.20.70
10. Austria II Isser/Durnthaler 3.21.05
11. Canada I J. Emery/Currie 3.21.24
12. Germany II Maurer/Grasegger 3.21.40
13. Romania I Panturu/Pasovschi 3.21.63
14. Great Britain II McCowen/Hedges 3.21.72
15. Sweden I Lutteman/Freyberg 3.21.73
16. Switzerland II Kiesel/Lory 3.22.95
17. Romania II Oancea/Cotacu 3.22.99

18. Argentina I Tomasi/Rodriguez 3.24.15
19. Argentina II Bordeu/Agote 3.29.93

As GBI went off on its final run, the now familiar *schnell und ruhig* echoed reassuringly in the background. But soon the word *unruhig* (jerkily) – meaning that precious hundredths of a second had been lost – heralded a feeling of doom in British ears. All had seemed well as Nash guided the sled into the ferocious *Hexenkessel*, by far the highest banked curve on the track. But as they hit the turn that was showing some signs of wear (as were the nerves of British spectators), Tony seemed to gain altitude much more swiftly than before. The British bob took the wicked S turn that was the Witch's Cauldron too high. Roaring out of that dangerous bend, a penalty had to be paid: a couple of resounding hits on the side walls, between the top of the S and the last big curve, signalled that Nash and Dixon had caught the side wall and were bumping badly out of the curve.[50] Nash got the thundering, squirming sled back under control, but the damage had been done and the Brits were unable to take full advantage of the *Hexenkessel* g-drop into the bottom part of the run.

"We had a bad last run and we knew we'd made an error," acknowledges Robin Dixon. Both men knew they had finished 'untidily'. As Tony Nash says, "The track was beautifully made except on the last morning. The weather broke and the track became softer as the morning wore on. We made a mistake coming out of six, which was the first big corner, and slid. I could feel it slide and I thought, 'Hell! Lost some time there.' While we got through the rest of the run alright we had been put off our stride from thereon. We

50 Relatively speaking, there was almost nothing very challenging between the *Hexenkessel* and the S curves before a straight into the big 12 curve. There was just a contra curve before the finishing straight.

were absolutely devastated when we heard the time, how slow it was. But we hadn't a clue that the track was breaking up at that time."

Most of the British supporters had moved to the bottom of the run, out of sight of the gigantic electric timing machine. The inexorable ticking away of the seconds was almost more than they could stand. Both Nash and Dixon looked dejected at the end, the former shaking his head slightly as he got out of the bob. Their total of 4.21.09 seemed well within the capabilities of both Italian teams. As Robin recollects, "We thought we'd blown it. We knew we'd got a medal but we thought it was going to be a bronze one. Tony said, 'Come on, we've had enough of this, we'll go and have a jar.' We'd been pretty Spartan for a while. There was a wee hut just up on the left at the bottom. We didn't say a thing to anybody and left our helmets, so we were fairly anonymous when we went in there. We sat in the corner and had a coffee with a schnapps. We thought, 'Well, we've got a bronze and we've got what we came for,' and just said, 'Bad luck, fellow.'"

Tony Nash remembers the same sort of anticlimactic feeling. "After the fourth run, which was a bit of a disaster (or so we thought), we disappeared down to the café at the bottom to drown our sorrows, knowing that Monti could usually adjust to any track and come down smiling."

The fourth run was the slowest time of the championship for Nash and Dixon. Zardini had only to achieve 1.05.82 seconds to overwhelm them. There was a level of fatalistic gloom and despondency in the British camp. However, an insidious factor was creeping into the equation: the temperature was rising and, as it did, the course started to soften; as it did so, it dragged on the runners and times worsened – heat four was producing the slowest runs of the competition by a long way. Nevertheless, unaware of this situation, Tony and Robin remained more or less resigned to having missed out on a gold run.

The Brits were aware that Monti had many times previously shown himself to be literally capable of anything. For all this, the current leaders Zardini and Bonagura dramatically lost their grip with a very poor time in the fourth heat. GBI was back in the lead!

As Dixon tells it, "About a quarter of an hour, 20 minutes after we'd retreated to the café the race was still going on but we didn't know anything about it. We were both a bit fed up although we were relaxed because we knew that we'd got the bronze, but Tony Brooke found us. Everyone had been looking for us all over the place, but Tony Brooke said, 'I know where they'll be!'" laughs Robin. "He came in and swore at us, saying, 'What the hell are you buggers doing here? You're going to win this race!' We asked, 'What d'you mean?' He replied, 'The course has slowed up! Zardini had an even slower time. You've got to go out and see the others – the Italians are not going to catch you!' They, of course, were the ones who most people thought would beat us. It was only then we realised that Eugenio was highly unlikely to catch us. Tony Brooke roared, 'The world's press is looking for you!'

"So we returned to the finish to welcome Monti, who we still thought would probably win – Eugenio at that time was a nine-times world champion and he could walk on water."

But Tony Nash still had to be convinced, declaring at the time that, "Monti is going to do it once again and catch us on the final run. He is the one man to stand this terrific pressure."

Nash couldn't bear to watch the Italians' final run. He sat on a sledge with his fingers crossed listening to the times. Could the greatest driver in the history of bobsleighing pull off another fantastic win? *Schnell und ruhig* rang out as Monti covered the first part of the course. The noble alpine hero threw his bucking chariot boldly forward in one last attempt to grab at those vital fractions of a second between him and his Olympian ambition. But, as Tony relates, even *il Rosso Volante* was limited by the conditions.

"His halfway time had to be a low 47 – it was a 48. Not even Monti could gain that much back and we were going to win! It was only after the halfway mark that we realised he couldn't catch us."

Robin suddenly knew that it marked the end of Monti's Olympic crusade. "He would have known that too, which wouldn't have helped him."

According to Vic Emery, "While a staggered draw for all four heats was calculated to produce as fair a competition as possible, the early start for the Brits in the last run was truly their 'luck of the draw'! The times got slower and slower as the temperature climbed and track started to break up. As the last sled down, we were confronted by water in the track and were lucky to have enough of a cushion to hold on to fourth place. In fact our last run was possibly better [in terms of performance] than our first [winning] run, beating the sleds just before us by a quite a margin."

Nash and Dixon were the first to acknowledge that a sudden rise in the air temperature after their run had reduced the chances of their nearest rivals. The Italians – who came down later, followed by the Canadians – ran into tougher and tougher conditions. Although, after his final run, Nash had thought the track would hold up, the spring-like weather had given the winners a slight advantage. By nightfall it was raining and the temperature was well above freezing point.

For all this, conditions affect most outdoor sports from cricket to open water swimming; the concept of a 'level playing field' is just that, a notional ideal striven for but hardly ever in place throughout an event. This aside, the 1964

Olympic bobsleigh competition was won and lost over two days and four runs. While it seems typically British to count up the advantages Nash and Dixon had on the day via the weather, the luck of the draw, etc, they had probably as many telling disadvantages – besides the fact that there was no British national bobsleigh track.

For instance, the final run required the Britons to follow the Argentineans, who had scarcely been on a bob run before that winter. Although a courageous and affable cavalier crew, the polo-playing, bullfighting, aircraft-flying, parachuting, car, motorbike and powerboat-racing daredevil gauchos cut a very erratic, messy and shaky track for the next bob down. But such was the luck of the draw.

The British Olympic team were out in force to support Nash and Dixon, the white fur hats they were provided with as official headgear conspicuous all along the track. A mighty roar went up that echoed around the hills from this small but vociferous contingent when the Italians' time was announced. British reserve went out the window as the white *chapeaux* filled the air, a very natural reaction to the hard-earned triumph on the fearsome slopes of Igls.

The time that it takes a flame to ignite gas had separated the leading teams. The Britons had so narrowly capped a wonderful week of consistent performance by finally beating off a two-pronged attack by the most famous Italian pair. What had been the slowest British time of the championship turned out to be by far the fastest of the final run. The doubters who had said GBI had no chance of winning because of a slow last run were proven drastically wrong.

The drama had been gripping. First the Englishmen had their two-run overnight lead snatched from them, just before the end of the third round, by a rip-roaring third run by the Italian second string. The most feared challengers of all,

Monti and Sorpaes, were waiting menacingly in third place. It left the straining British pair to do all they could in an all-or-nothing fourth round, to push as hard as possible, to take chances if necessary, in an attempt to get their noses in front. Seemingly they failed, returning their poorest performance when they needed their best. Despite Zardini's failure to capitalise on the situation, British supporters still feared the worst. But their fears were confounded.

After the Italian maestro gave Nash an elaborate continental kiss, Tony said, "Now let's celebrate. I've never been so thirsty. And the first drinks must be with the sporting Italians."

The pupils had beaten their tutors. As Dixon conceded, "The Italians taught us everything we know about the sport . . . We thought they would catch us after the third run. We had to sweat it out until Monti finished. It was all a bit nerve racking – we could not have won without all the help we got from them. They've been our teachers ever since I partnered up with Tony."

The great bond between bobsleighers was rather like that between National Hunt jockeys, racing drivers and boxers. Continually facing danger evokes great respect for one's peers. Certainly the Italians had been among the first to cluster around Nash and Dixon, shaking hands and smiling when the final heat was over. It was a tremendous climax to years of hard work for the British team, and the likes of Monti and Zardini were quick to acknowledge this.

Heat 4
1. Great Britain I: Nash/Dixon 1:05.88
2. Italy II: Zardini/Bonagura 1:06.05
3. Germany I: Wormann/Braun 1:06.24
4. United States I: McKillip/Lamy 1:06.25
5. Austria I: Thaler/Nairz 1:06.33

6. Italy I: Monti/Siorpaes 1:06.38
7. Canada II: V. Emery/Kirby 1:06.45
8. Canada I: J. Emery/Currie 1:06.63
9. United States II: McDonald/Pandolph 1:07.02
10. Austria II: F. Isser/Durnthaler 1:07.04
11. Sweden I: Lutteman/Freyberg 1:07.20
12. Romania II: Oancea/Cotacu 1:07.26
13. Switzerland I: Zoller/Zimmermann 1:07.38
14. Romania I: Panturu/Pasovschi 1:07.47
15. Argentina I: Tomasi/Rodriguez 1:07.72
16. Switzerland II: Kiesel/Lory 1:08.25
17. Germany II: Maurer/Grasegger 1:08.37
18. Great Britain II: McCowen/Hedges 1:08.95
19. Argentina II: Bordeu/Agote 1:10.26

As Tony reflects, "In any major sport you get your heroes and Monti was a hero; he could win anything. He used to be rough down the track and hit the sides and appear to make nonsense of the track. But every time he hit the sides he was making time; he just used to gain time from nowhere and how he did it, I wish to heavens I knew – I'd have been a better bobsleigher for it."

But even the miraculous Monti could not work his spell on ice that was becoming slush; his final run was his slowest, as GBI took the gold by a margin of 0.12 of a second from Zardini and Bonagura.

At the culmination of the run, according to Robin, "Everybody just hugged each other. It was a great moment. Monti looked as pleased as all our families. It is hard to describe how we felt about what he did for us. I don't know many other men who would have done what he did. I wouldn't have done it. Tony would and I'd have probably tried to stop him."

As Tony confesses, "Robin and I were just terribly lucky that for the last run of the Olympics we were near the beginning rather than the other end. My old girlfriend's draw would have affected us all the way through."

The British boblet win at Igls made history. Monti covered his disappointment to wholeheartedly congratulate Nash and Dixon, the first Brits to win an Olympic gold medal in bobsleighing. The renowned Curt Gowdy of ABC TV told Nash on camera that he had beaten "a great man" in Monti. As Tony and Eugenio shook hands in front of millions of television viewers, a smiling Nash said the Italian was "a very good friend of mine." Monti commented that he didn't drive well and that the course was slow, but also that he didn't win because Tony drove terrifically.

How hard must it have been for the man from Cortina? He had broken his own official record and could not have driven better on the day, as the chute slowly deteriorated around him. The friction between the steel runner and the ice was eroded beneath the unforgiving gaze of the clock.

(Given the deterioration of the chute, it was remarkable that the event presented no serious casualties. However, Mrs Joyce Hartigan, aged 43, from Plymouth, was taken to hospital seriously injured after a riderless sled struck her on the forehead.)

Nash and Dixon had been fortunate to get down the run before the thaw had taken its full toll on the track. As Tony admitted shortly after the competition, "There's no doubt that the change in conditions made the going much harder."

However, Mike Freeman, one of the members of the British bobsleigh squad who worked tirelessly over the two days at the start and in the garages, told how after the first day they had warmed rags to wrap the runners in on the radiators in the tiny café nearby and rubbed the blades for ten minutes before take-off. "This is the greatest moment in British bobsleighing ever!" was his unequivocal view.

Robin, who once said that that the competition was "no time for wives and families," though "race days were the exception," was hugged in celebration by his wife Rona. "Absolutely wizard, darling!" she told him. "But I'd like to give Eugenio a great big hug too."

She probably spoke for many when she spread her hands in an almost conciliatory gesture. "I cannot say I am sorry, and yet . . ."

Robin Dixon remembers how, shortly after Britain's win had been confirmed, he got a telephone call from his father: "the first thing he said is don't get drunk before you go on television tonight," he laughs, "it seemed like a long time to wait!"

As Tony Nash recalls of the post-competition celebrations, "There were several of our parents from both British teams out there. At 10am we were back at the hotel in Igls where they had been staying and, with the help of friends etc, the champagne began to flow; we sank 64 bottles! It was a start of a long series of festivities. I gather I had four baths[51] during the course of the day."

"We were trying to keep him clean," jokes Robin.

Tony tells of how he and Robin "were much sought after afterwards – it never stopped but we had this interview with David Coleman and we'd promised to go down to the studio."

"The state he was in," laughs Robin, "the only way we were going to get him down to David's studio to do anything was to keep him off the whiskey for a fair while but promise him one when he got there. That was the lure! Anyway, we got down there, very old fashioned stuff, black and white, David

---

51 These were attempts to counter the effects of copiously imbibing alcohol.

was sitting at the table and put one of us either side of him and he played the recording of our last run and put the commentary on it while we were there. We got rather animated. David was a brilliant commentator and sitting beside him it was really terrific. It was the first time I got excited about winning. I just realised we had won it, actually seeing it for the first time."

According to Tony, "there was a delayed reaction" to their victory. Come evening, Robin and Tony were still barely able to believe they had routed the world-champion Italians and crack teams from across the globe. Indeed, even the next day Dixon was asking, "Did we really win? I haven't woken up yet."

Looking back today, Robin continues, "When David Coleman had finished he brought up the bottle of whiskey and a glass as Tony's promised reward." The dram with Coleman was the last act in what was a long day of celebration.

As Tony recalls, "Winning meant going to about four prize-givings because the World Championship was part of the Olympics in 1964. We had a hell of a party after we'd won. Then we went down to the World Championship prize-giving. After that we moved on to a party the Burgermeister of Innsbruck had decided to throw."

Following the champagne-fuelled merriment immediately after their victory, Tony recorded the day thus;

2pm Official World Championship ceremony – more booze – bath

5pm Party given by the Mayor – more booze – bath

7 pm Presentation of medals (very moving)

10pm interview by David Coleman (BBC) and we told him we liked whiskey which was under the table – bath and very pissed

Whilst in the Army, Nash had made a rash statement that he would one day win the Winter Olympics. Although this seemed out of the question at the time, he promised he would never show his face in the mess again if he didn't succeed in his ambition. While it may have slipped his mind over the years, he still received many telegrams of congratulations from his former comrades in arms.

Nash and Dixon had scotched the myth that the Italians were unbeatable, and also that the builder of the Podar bobs – Ewaldo D'Andrea who, like Monti, hailed from Cortina d'Ampezzo – had ensured the best sleds would not be supplied to 'foreign competition'. (It was also whispered that D'Andrea refused to share the secret of the metal runners attached to Italian sleds.)

But Eugenio Monti, twice previously an Olympic runner-up, truly understood the Olympic ideal. His noble gesture could potentially have deprived him and his country of the Olympic title, and many believed this to be the case. Replying to a storm of disapproval from the Italian press, he declared, "Much has been said but Nash didn't win because I gave him the bolt. He won because he had the fastest run . . . because he was the best driver and deserved to win."

In 2009, Vic Emery recollects how Eugenio "only wanted to win if his opponents were at their best, anything else would have been second best and so a bit like an empty victory. If you were disadvantaged, even in the heat of competition he would help you out to make sure you were at your best – that is some legacy!"

As American Olympic swimmer John Naber, after winning four golds and one silver medal in Montreal in 1976, would say, "A true sportsman, who understands the Olympic ideal, wants to win against his best opponent on his best day." Monti not only wanted to race against the best but to compete on equal terms.

Nash and Dixon took Great Britain's only gold of the

Games home to England, a country without a single bob course. Italy's finest were left to make do with bronze and silver consolation.

As Mike Freeman later said of Monti, "Looking back, it was almost something we expected from him because he was such a nice guy . . . Even so, giving up the possible chance of a gold medal was an extraordinary thing to do."

At the time, when questioned about the Italian's chivalrous attitude, Nash replied, "We have always been very close to these Italians. We have trained together, had fun together, and battled with bitter rivalry for years. But Eugenio is a wonderful chap and we knew he would never let us down."

Many years later, he concludes, "On the day I drove better than him. I had the luck of the draw and the weather but we beat him and Zardini fair and square. However, the gesture with the bolt is a magical story of sportsmanship that should never be forgotten."

For Siorpaes, the man who removed the legendary bolt, it wasn't such a big deal. "I felt, 'Yes, so what?' But what a tale it has become!"

Monti was equally modest. "Contrary to what was said I don't think I did anything extraordinary. It would have been poor sportsmanship not to have offered assistance. I just told Dixon, 'When I get down I'll take out the bolt from my bobsled and give it to you.' I never thought any more of it." More defiantly, in the face of exasperated criticism from the Italian media he declared, "It was nothing. For these two Englishmen I would do anything. I love them like my brothers."

Today, perhaps fittingly, no one knows where the actual replacement bolt for the British sled came from. It's likely that one of the other teams had a spare and just handed it to a desperate mechanic working on GBI. It was the BBC's David

Above: Alpine heroes – Tony Nash (left) and Robin Dixon, St Moritz, approx. 1960/61.

Above: Secret weapon – pot scourers tied to rugby boots.

Left: Riding the 'Big Truck' – the four-man is always faster.

Below: Building the Grenoble run.

Right: From left –
GBI: Guy Renwick,
Robin Dixon, David
Lewis, Tony Nash;
GBII: Robin Seel,
Andrew Hedges,
Bill McCowen,
Tony Brooks (team
captain), Mike
Freeman, Martin
Boyle.

Left: We've won!
After the fourth
run, Franz
Kemzer (behind
Tony, right)
congratulates his
friends, while
Swiss driver Hans
Zoller cheers
(extreme right).

Right: Bronze
medallist Eugenio
Monti receives
congratulations at
the 1964 Winter
Olympics in
Innsbruck.

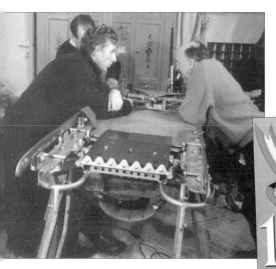

Below: Commemoration of the 20th anniversary of 'Monti's Bolt', the great sporting gesture between the Italian and British Olympic bobsleigh teams.

Above: Basement of the Hotel Eden in St Moritz – Dixon and Nash talking to the BBC.

Below: Tony returns to his engineering factory in Penn.

Left: Tony Nash (second from left) with Swiss champion Johnny Carietzel (on Tony's right) and Franz Kemser (far right).

Above: From left to right – Robin and Rona Dixon, Tony Nash.

Right: Tony with his mother's collection of championship trophies.

Above: Tony Nash (left) and Robin Dixon in St Moritz, 1965.

Above left: GBI – Nash finds the line.

Below: Nash lining up the front and back runners in St Moritz – "very technical", as he puts it.

Left: The triumphant British and Canadian gold medal teams – from left to right: John Emery, Douglas Anakin, Dixon, Nash, Peter Kirby and Vic Emery – at the rink where they were presented with their gold medals.

Above: Canadian Olympian Vic Emery (and friend).

Below: Robbin Widdows and Guy Renwick, crew on the four-man.

Below: The RAF were always to the fore but in the early 1960s they were no match for Nash and Dixon.

Above: The Canadian Olympic four-man team, winners of the gold medal for their event.

Above: Equipe Nash.

Below: Tony Nash meets Princess Alexandra at the Olympic Ball, 1964.

Inset: Nash (left) and Dixon – Olympic and World Champions, 1964, "we also won various small prizes thrown in," says Tony.

Coleman who propagated the version of events that has persisted for nearly half a century. As he interviewed Tony Nash following the event, he stated that Monti had saved them from disaster. Though we now know this to be untrue, as Robin Dixon says, "It was a typical Eugenio Monti spontaneous act. I took it for what it was and afterwards, as the world knows, we did do quite a lot to make a fuss of it because, gosh, it was a fantastic sporting gesture!"

As Monti's ex-wife, Linda Constantine, reflected some years later, "I think it was part of Eugenio's natural behaviour to be generous. His actions in 1964 were certainly not pre-planned by him in any way. I think the reason why he was so modest about it was because for him it was not out of character or an unusual thing to do."

TWO-MAN OLYMPIC BOBSLEIGH RESULT
Date: February 1, 1964. 21 bobsleds from 11 nations were on the runway. 19 received official scores. Two did not start in the third and fourth runs.

1. Great Britain I (Tony Nash/Robin Dixon) 4:21.90
2. Italy II (Sergio Zardini/Romano Bonagura) 4:22.02
3. Italy I (Eugenio Monti/Sergio Siorpaes) 4:22.63
4. Canada II (Vic Emery/Peter Kirby) 4:23.49
5. USA I (Lawrence McKillip/James Lamy) 4:24.60
6. Germany I (Franz Woermann/Hubert Braun) 4:24.70
7. USA II (Charles McDonald/Charles Pandolph) 4:25.00
8. Austria I (Erwin Thaler/Josef Nairz) 4:25.51
9. Austria II (Franz Isser/Reinhold Durnthaler) 4:28.09
10. Switzerland I (Hans Zoller/Robert Zimmermann) 4:28.15
11. Canada I (John Emery/Gordon Currie) 4:28.87
12. Sweden I (Kjell Lutteman/Heino Freyberg) 4:28.93
13. Romania I (Ion Panturu/Hariton Pasovschi) 4:29.10

14. Germany II (Hans Maurer/Rupert Grasegger) 4:29.77
15. Romania II (Alexandru Oancea/Constantin Cotacu) 4:30.25
16. Great Britain II (Bill McCowen/Andrew Hedges) 4:30.67
17. Switzerland II (Herbert Kiesel/Oskar Lory) 4:31.20
18. Argentina I (Héctor Tomasi/Fernando Rodríguez) 4:31.87
19. Argentina II (Roberto-Jose Bordeu, Hernan-Marcelo Agote) 4:40.19
– Belgium I (Jean de-Crawhez/Claude Englebert) DNF
– Sweden II (Jan-Erik Åkerström/Carl-Erik Eriksson) DNF

Former Olympic two-man winners – 1932: Stevens/Stevens (USA); 1936: Brown/Washbond (USA); 1948: Endridi/Waller (Switzerland); 1952: Ostler/Nieberl (Germany); 1956: Dalla Costa/Conti (Italy).

*   *   *

Even when it was officially announced that Great Britain had won, Nash and Dixon were still saying, "We can't believe it." As Tony Brooke, manager of the British team, described it after shaking hands all round in something of a daze, "It's a dream – I keep thinking I'm going to wake up any minute."

Brooke, then 51, farmed near Harrogate for ten months of the year but spent January and February acting as the British team's diplomat, social secretary, tactician and father-figure. He understood the value of close attention to detail, and even assigned a team member to make sure Tony's 'lucky gloves' would always be tucked under the front seat of the bob. What Brooke lacked in expensive equipment was more than made up for by efficient organisation, covering as many of the variables as possible.

As Tony Nash tells of the prelude to the medal awards ceremony, "Nothing in sport can be much better than winning an Olympic gold medal. That's just about as good as it gets, so you felt honoured and a sense of pride.

"The Olympic medal ceremony was in the evening, down in the ice-rink in Innsbruck. We arrived down there in good time but we couldn't find our way into the stadium. It was pretty much chaos because they'd brought in a load of police from all round Austria and they were a fairly officious bunch. We rushed around as time was drawing on and all of a sudden we found a gentleman limping along on sticks and we knew it was the Marquis of Exeter. We said, 'Excuse us, sir, how do we get into this place to get our medal?' He answered, 'Don't worry about it at all, dear boys. Follow me. You have come to get your medal and I'm giving it to you, so they can't start without us, can they?' There were some lovely people then," laughs Nash.

The roar from the 10,000 crowd in the Ice Stadium when Nash and Dixon took the medal podium was enormous, but the cheer for Zardini was almost as great. However, for Monti the applause grew from a relatively low volume over what seemed like minutes to gigantic applause, almost equalling the congratulations the gold medallists had commanded.

It seems that, even back then, there was some nervousness about the British capacity for celebrating. There had been a rather energetic scuffle immediately prior to the presentation ceremony, when around a dozen male and female members of Britain's Olympic team, wearing the red capes seen at the opening ceremony, were pushed and shoved around by attendants who tried to refuse admission to the Ice Stadium. Reporters helped some of them get inside, but they were ordered out again by the attendants who alleged they had not got the right passes. Some of the group jumped over barriers but were pushed back again by the attendants. One angry Briton was heard to yell, "This is the first medal we have won in 12 years and now you won't let us watch our winners receive it!"

Alpine skier Anna Asheshov, bobsleighers Robin Seel, Flying Officer Mike Freeman and the team doctor, Dennis Cussins, were amongst those caught up in the melee. But the group were eventually allowed to cheer their champions.

After the unfurling of the Union Jack in top place to the accompaniment of the red-jacketed Tyrolean band playing 'God Save the Queen', Robin and Tony were the guests of honour at a lavish dinner on behalf of the British Bobsleigh Club. It was the start of a long evening of dancing (mostly the twist) and toasting, as telegrams of congratulations poured into the Olympic headquarters at Innsbruck.

As Nash recalls, one of their supporters had become something of a mascot for the British team. "When we won it, Franz Kemser was more excited about it than anybody else. The night after the medal ceremony we went in a couple of cars to dinner at his Shutzenhaus in Partenkirken (with the Swiss and other friends), and as we drove up the drive there were fireworks all over the place. We had a barrel of beer and venison – I think he was as proud of us as anyone could be, a real sports friend."

We might frequently feel ourselves let down by the culture of modern sport that too often seems to be all about supremely selfish activity, artificially enhanced performances, a win-at-any-cost attitude and latterly, on occasion, outright criminality. With the incursion of big business into seemingly every avenue of competition, few athletes are involved merely for the love of the game. At the same time the money and fame the star performers can generate is beyond the comprehension of many of those who watch them.

As such, what happened on the bob run in Innsbruck in 1964 might seem somehow unreal, like a parable from a dim and distant time, rather than reflecting the actuality. However, at that time many top performers competed simply for the joy of what they were doing, showing a depth of personality that, for some, probably mattered more than the winning; a sporting spirit expressed to the utmost as one man reached across the divide of rivalry to help his competitors.

Tony Nash remembers the atmosphere of the time and something of how the British bobbers worked together. "In 1964 the whole team had done National Service. We all knew how to give and take and we were all chums. Our four-man team was made up of our pals and we didn't change them because, apart from anything else, they'd probably got money in the sled. Now, because of official money, you've got different people getting in behind you who you may not know or you may not get on with but they're good athletes.

"We were more like the Corinthians of former times. Everybody was amateur and everybody had a lot of fun. Okay, it was lovely to win – the Italians were the only ones being seriously sponsored, Italy had a ten percent tax on all football which went to minor sports, so they had some finance for development, experimenting and training."

Tony effectively sums up the difference between then and now. "It was more about fun in those days. We got a gold medal, that's lovely, no one can take it away from you, but there are other things to do in life."

Walking away from Igls might have felt like the end of an era for Nash, Dixon, Monti and perhaps bobsleighing in general. In a television interview, Tony was asked whether he would continue racing. "I don't know," he said, adding that he'd just spent £500 of his own cash and was wondering how long he could afford to pay to represent his country.

Apart from this, the Brits had little left to prove and were thinking about getting on with their lives. As Nash said at the time, "Money apart, we must spend three months every year achieving the necessary degree of training and we just can't afford the time . . . There's nothing left in the kitty."

This sparked something of a national debate about government funding, with one newspaper asking, "Is it right that gold medallists should have to beg, 'Bob a job for the bob' style? Should the Government finance our amateur sportsmen?"

Soon after GBI's victory in Austria, Dr Alan Thompson MP called for a government-backed 'Sports Development Council' to spend £5 million a year with the aim of stemming the loss of British prestige in international amateur sport. Thompson told the Young Socialists in his Dunfermline constituency, "While we applaud the great achievement of Tony Nash and Robin Dixon in winning a gold medal at the Winter Olympics, it is a sad state of affairs that these two champions only reached the top by spending hundreds of pounds of their own money.

"Our youth services are stunted by lack of finance and all too often they have to rely on dingy premises, third-rate equipment, and lack of outdoor facilities.

"Although the Government promised to spend £3 million in new building for youth services in the three-year period beginning 1960 this target is nowhere near fulfilment. We should accept the recommendations of the Wolfenden Report[52] and greatly increase expenditure on running tracks, sports fields, and swimming baths.

"We need a Sports Development Council that will be prepared to spend £5 million a year. On our young people!"

Although Dr Thompson was probably looking for a way to counter the moral panic about young people engendered by

---

52 The 1957 Wolfenden Committee on Sport.

the activities of mods and rockers around the coastal resorts of England in 1964, it seems Nash and Dixon had done something to kick-start the future[53] (although many of the same ideas continue to be debated today).

At the time, Tony Nash was diplomatic when asked about the public financing of sport: "In matters like these it is up to the public."

For all this, Grenoble, the venue for the next Winter Olympics in 1968, at that time had no bob run. It looked as if it might follow Squaw Valley in 1960 and dispense with bobsleighing, as many in the Olympic committees believed that the Games were getting too big and too expensive. This would mark the end of Eugenio Monti's golden ambitions.

Some may say that Monti paid a high price to maintain his principles, but after the two-man event the Innsbruck Games continued and the great Italian had another chance to go for gold in the four-man competition.

Robin Dixon tells of a visit his pilot paid to Italy later that year: "Tony went out in the summer – I couldn't go – and we gave him a beer mug with the broken bolt inscribed on it and a suitable message – I think Tony spent about three days delivering the thing," he laughs.

The tankard had a broken bolt depicted on it and the inscription:

To Eugenio. In Recognition of a Great Sportsman.

---

53 Following the election of a Labour government in 1964, Mr Denis (later Lord) Howell MP was made Minister with Special Responsibility for Sport. The following year the government decided, based on the Wolfenden Committee Report, "To establish a Sports Council to advise them on matters relating to the development of amateur sport and physical recreation services, and to foster cooperation among the statutory authorities and voluntary organisations concerned."

X

THE CANADIANS

As the other competitors besides Britain and Italy to enjoy major success at the 1964 Winter Olympics, it is worth mentioning the Canadians. Similarly to the Brits, the Canadians had been working their way through the ranks for several years and the Emery/Kirby team had proved themselves the best pair in both boblet heats on the second last day of trials. However, on the last day before the two-man event, as Emery would admit later, he had "held the reins too tight" on a very bumpy track and fallen back to 11th place following the two runs, after which no one gave them a chance. Their moment of glory seemed to have surely passed them by.

Dismissed by some sections of the press as 'rich ski bums' and 'playboys' who came to the Games simply to party, they were even rumoured to have entered the four-man bobsleigh race by pure fluke. Their country could not so much as boast a single bobsleigh track and there were certainly no coaching or specialist facilities. In fact there was not even an organisation to support them, or anything that came near to resembling a coordinated programme related to the sport.

However, their rise to the top was uncannily similar to that of the Brits, who regarded St Moritz as their home track and Eugenio Monti as their guru and mentor. The Canadians had flair and unbounded enthusiasm, and Emery's four-man team in particular was regarded by the bob fraternity as serious, smart competition.

Before it was announced that no sled competition would be held at Squaw Valley, the Canadian Olympic Committee had declined to send a bob team to the 1960 Games, declaring that there was no interest in the sport in Canada. Shortly before the 1964 Games it was only when Chuck Rathgeb, Director of the Canadian Olympic Association, fought their case that he persuaded the COA to enter the bobsleigh competition for the first time after he literally guaranteed the COA medal – promising that the Canadian bob squad would bring either a gold, silver or bronze home from the Games, whether four- or two-man. According to four-man team member Douglas Anakin, "They were worried we would just take up beds in the village."

Rathgeb, the owner of the Comstock Construction company in Canada, had a great interest in motor racing and was instrumental in what was perhaps his nation's bob squad's most crucial victory to date – just getting to the Games! If it wasn't for his push then the Canadians would not have sent a bob team to Austria. As Tony Nash says of the man who took up the role of the Canadian crew's manager and saviour, "He had a personal four-engine plane and was a barracuda and marlin fisherman, an altogether larger than life character, a smashing man – he kept the party spirit going."

"Every day was a celebration there," confirms Canadian

bobber John Emery. It was the Canadians' hedonistic reputation which led those who did not know them well to believe they didn't take their sport as seriously as they might. As such there were those who dismissed their motivation for coming to the Games as simply an opportunity to party. However, although they liked a good time, the tag 'playboys' was just a little exaggerated. The Canadian team were nicknamed 'the intellectual sled' by their rivals at Igls, and this probably said more about their collective personae.

Victor Emery, John Emery, Peter Kirby and Anakin were a group of determined winter sports experts who were not intimidated by their Olympian task, despite having no bob run in Canada. Like the British, they regarded St Moritz as their home track – although they also practised from time to time at Lake Placid, New York. Between bob seasons they played a variety of sports to keep fit. It was widely reported that they did push practices on dry land, though Vic Emery confirms, "We only did push-start practices on snow."

The Canadians' journey to Innsbruck had really started some eight years before the 1964 Games. Vic Emery was on a skiing tour of Europe and snowed under in St. Moritz, Switzerland. As Tony Nash acknowledges, "he decided to ski right across from St Moritz to Cortina."

Emery's 300-kilometre odyssey to Italy, with his belongings in a rucksack, was made in order to watch the 1956 Winter Olympics. The trek was no mere whim; according to Nash, "He used to do this long distance ski run from Montreal to Toronto which takes about three days. He took me out and you used to have to change your ski wax every so often."

Deep in the heart of Italy and having run out of snow, Emery was offered a lift in a truck transporting the British bobsleigh team to the Games. Vic travelled with the cargo in the back. He would later say this was the first time he had rode a sled, albeit more as a seat rather than a means of transport in itself, but it was the start of his commitment to the sport. He stayed with the Brits during the Games, "they put a rope out of the bedroom and got him up so he could sleep there," recalls Nash.

Emery – who during this period was introduced to the Cresta by Portago and Nelson, who would lose their lives in the Millie Mlgila motor race in 1957 ("we called Gunnar Nelson 'Gurnar' and Alfonso Portago 'Fons'," he recalls of their affectionate nicknames) – was won over by the dash and romance of bobsleighing after watching the contests at Cortina d'Ampezzo. There was no turning back for the Québecois skier. As he now says, "My first time down a bob run was right after the 1956 Olympics as number two in Portago's four-man sled in the Swiss Meisterschaft.[54] It was a loaned two-man sled from Portago that got me started in bobsleighing that same winter."

Vic swiftly passed on his newfound passion for bobsleighing to his older brother John,[55] who says his sibling came back from Europe exclaiming, "Hey, I've found us a great sport!"

Thus the history of Canadian bobsleighing may be said to have started. Vic was determined not only to take up bobsleighing but also to qualify for the World Championships. Along with John, Vic and Monty Gordon (who, like Vic, had become enamoured of the spirit of the cold runs), a year after his discovery of the sport at the 1956 Olympics he established the Laurentian Bobsleigh Association in Montréal, signing up friends and colleagues whose membership fees just about raised the finance to build a team that might compete on the international stage.

54 Championship.

55 Born 4 January 1932.

The Laurentian membership was a collection of fine athletes and many expert skiers, their number including boxers, wrestlers and exponents of track and field. According to one of them, Vic's rugged Olympic brakeman Peter Kirby, "The danger was part of the excitement."

The first Canadian entry into international bob competition took place at the 1959 World Championships in St Moritz, a run which Vic and Monty knew from 1956. They finished 13th in the four-man out of 16 sleds. But they did manage one win; an ad hoc Spanish-Canadian Cup when they sent their fourth man (Chuck Rathgeb) down the curling ice on a rock which cleared the house and gave them wins in curling and ice hockey against a loss in the bob to Portago's cousin, Vicente Sartorious.

When the 1960 Winter Olympics excluded bobsleighing Italy came to the fore with a World Championship tournament in Cortina, to which the Canadians were invited with an offer of half the air fare, loaned bobsleighs and substantially reduced charges for accommodation. The Italian experience was so amazing that the team of four committed to the purchase of four new sleds from Podar, a couple of two-man and two four-man vehicles, before returning to Canada. There they raised the $8,000 required from amongst themselves and a growing group of young athletes, keen to try out for an expanded team readying for the following winter's World Championships, slated for Lake Placid in 1961 – only two hours from Montreal.

At the New York track, practising for the four-man event, the front runners of Vic Emery's sled broke through the fragile ice of a thawing chute. It threw the three men behind him clear but the sled landed on top of Emery, smashing his face into the ice and injuring a leg. A week later, when Eugenio Monti visited Montreal, the great man pronounced that

Emery's nose was now so like his own that it was an omen that Emery would become a champion one day.

The team benefited from the coaching and guidance of Monti, determining henceforth to work towards becoming their country's first representatives in Olympic bobsleigh. Undaunted by less than encouraging initial results, each year the Montréalais brothers and their team-mates competed in the World Championships and gradually gained valuable experience before moving up the field.

Vic, attending the Harvard Business School at the time, sat out the 1962 World Championships, where Monty Gordon drove the four-man to a fourth place finish, winning the Commonwealth Gold at St Moritz.

That same year, the Canadians' club was affiliated to the Canadian Amateur Athletic Union. This increased the club's visibility and opened the path for the team to represent Canada in future Winter Olympics. The Canadians were on a roll, and the 1963 pre-Olympic trials in Igls for the two pilot positions were hotly contested amongst the two Emery brothers and Monty Gordon, before Gordon was carted off to the hospital with a slit throat after crashing out of the *Hexenkessel*.

The Canadians got to the 1964 Winter Games without corporate or government sponsorship. Having to pay their own way, the brave and innovative crew looked to challenge the mighty Italian team, the indomitable Brits and the strong Austrian crew on their home ice.

As Vic Emery says, "Making it to Innsbruck was the first step up the ladder of our ambitions. As we were consistently improving at St Moritz and Cortina, only the inner sanctum of bobbers recognised the potential threat we represented before arriving at the Olympic venue. By then I had thought about a lighter way to drive since the prior winter, and we were amongst the best in many of our runs."

Having achieved their goal of making it to the Olympics, the men wearing the maple leaf over their hearts were setting their sights higher. Canada had no traditions of bobsleighing in an age when even the best in the sport could suffer serious injuries, risking possible death as the bobs flew off the bends of the rough natural runs, unprotected by even the most minimal safety features. The sport had more of a reputation for killing its practitioners than for achieving international glory.

Added to this, the make up of Emery's squad of 1964 went against any conventional wisdom. Before the mid-1950's a useful bob crew were more hefty than swift; more weight was seen to provide more momentum down the run. But, subsequent to the 1956 weight limitations on sleds, the better teams fully grasped the advantage that a fast start might provide and the Canadians were athletes who could produce a competitive start.

John Emery, a practising plastic surgeon, had been a notable track-and-field performer in college; he had also excelled in boxing and skiing. Before bobsledding, Peter Kirby[56] had been a great skier. He was the Canadian Junior Alpine Skiing Champion in 1953 and a member of the Canadian Fédération Internationale de Ski (FIS) team that went to the World Championships in 1954. In 1956 he captained Dartmouth University's ski team.

Doug Anakin, from Chatham, Ontario, was a classmate of John Emery at Queen's University. An intercollegiate wrestling champion, after graduation Anakin had taught high school and coached around Ontario. He then went to London to teach, but also took opportunities to ski in the winter and climb mountains for most of the summer in Austria. He also taught school in Windsor and skiing in Michigan.

56 Born 17 December 1931.

In 1959 Doug returned to Europe to ski with his former university friends John and Vic Emery, who were bobsleighing in St Moritz. Doug got involved with Canadian Purvis McDougal and became one of first lugers to represent Canada internationally. He and Vic were to be a driving force in the development of luge competition in Canada. By 1962 he was teaching at Mount Royal High School in Montreal, where he also coached football, wrestling and skiing. During the winter of 1963 he competed in bobsled and luge in Austria and Lake Placid. In 1964, Doug joined the bobsleigh team in Cortina for training and then went to Innsbruck, Austria to compete in both bob and luge.

Victor Emery, like Kirby, first saw the light of day in Montreal, Quebec. An all-round sportsman, he took part in swimming, wrestling and skiing for the University of Western Ontario as an undergraduate. He and Anakin introduced luging to Canada in the early 1960's when he was still ski racing in the winter and Finn dinghy racing in the summer, while serving as general sales manager of United Aircraft of Canada. Prior to that he had sold and flown airplane charters after a few years as a pilot in the Royal Canadian Navy Reserves, including flying off his country's only aircraft carrier. Emery's background in skiing, combined with aerobatic flying in the navy, would make him comfortable with the unusual positions inherent in hurtling down a bob track.

According to brakeman Kirby, who helped developed one of the best starts in the sport during his era, "We knew we were getting better. Amongst ourselves we thought we had a good chance to get a medal."

By the start of the four-man competition the best four of the Canadian contingent were making starts only marginally slower than the Austrian Thaler and the Italian Monti, who they would have to beat sled for sled after gravity took over.

The Canadians, perhaps more than any other top team, were forced to improvise in terms of their preparation. It proved to be the mother of innovation. Anakin's background in coaching grid iron football fed into the team's start technique. They were comparatively new to bobsleighing, but their collective experience in other sports, together with skiing and driving on icy roads back in Canada, provided them with an almost innate feel for the run. According to Anakin, "We could kind of sit back and look at what was the best way to do things, we didn't have to follow along like robots."

Taking their annual holidays just prior to the Games, the Canadian team and their manager travelled to Europe to get some much-needed practice on the European runs. As Peter Kirby said around that time, "for the first time in the last three years we have been able to train as much as the other competitors and we always felt that given enough training time we could do fairly well."

However, the trip cost each of them around $800 each, a considerable amount of money at the time; alongside giving up work for several weeks, it showed how bobsledding was not a sport for poor men – although some cynics had it that the main requirements were relatively low intelligence and the strength to push close to a third of a ton of metal (in the case of the four-man machine) over a cliff. However, the men who crossed the Atlantic were a bright bunch, successful in their individual fields, with personal histories that showed them to be capable of focused achievement.

Eight years after Vic's first sparks of interest in bobsleighing, the brothers from Montréal, plus Kirby and

Anakin,[57] formed a resolute team to make an assault on the greatest prize their sport could offer.

However, the unfavourable weather in the Austrian Alps foiled their practice plans. The Canucks managed just four four-man practice runs on the Igls course before competing in that event. The Austrians had been sliding there for several days before the other countries were admitted for official training. But the run had been improved from the previous year and all the teams were still intact when the competition started a day early, out of fear that warming weather was on its way.

Within the close fraternity of bobsleigh racing, the Canadians were recognised as a promising crew. Vic Emery and Kirby – who had formed the Canadian team in the two-man event, with Vic as the driver – had done well to finish fourth. As such, they proved themselves able to match the best of the Europeans, who now included Great Britain. Some experts were beginning to argue that the good-looking Canadians had an outside chance of a podium place.

The Canadian team were not afraid to give bold views on tactics and preparation that some saw as lacking in substance. But theirs was an able team, capable of a high level of disciplined performance.

Historically the Olympic four-man event had been shared between North America and Central Europe; the USA had won the event in 1928, 1932 and 1948; Germany had claimed gold in 1952, while Switzerland had been victorious in 1924, 1936 and 1956. But for most people involved, it was a safe bet that 1964's gold medal would never cross an ocean.

---

57 At over 33 years old, the senior member of the Canadian bobsleigh squad.

XI

GREAT EXPECTATIONS

Tony Nash recalls something of the background to the four-man competition in Innsbruck:

"The four-man event in 1964 took place a week after we won the gold medal.[58] They brought the event forward a day as the ice was going soft. I was also in the four-man bob in 1964. I was the driver when we came fourth in the four-man in the 1963 World Championships, which was as good as anyone from Britain had done for a long time. At first I was in the middle, but when Henry Taylor stood down I took over driving the four-man as well as the two-man."

The makeup of the British fours was not decided until almost the last minute. All that was assured was that Tony Nash would pilot the British number one sled. Along with David Lewis, Guy Renwick and Dixon, they had finished fourth in the previous year's World Championships and it

58 5 February 1964.

seemed likely that these men would once more be the crew of GBI.

In Britain, following the success of Nash and Dixon in the two-man event, expectations were high for the four-man competition. The media were speculating about a British 'double' on the bob run.

However, the continuing thaw, which had brought too much water down on the tracks at Igls, caused the last two runs of the men's and women's single luge events to be postponed. With no appreciable change expected in the mildest first week in February experienced in Innsbruck for 58 years, it looked as if the start of the four-man bobsleigh might also be delayed.

On the Monday before the scheduled start of the competition, hours of sunshine and temperatures of over 40 degrees[59] left the bobsleigh track at Igls unsuitable even for practice. The British team manager Tony Brooke commented worriedly that, although everyone was in the same boat in terms of being prevented from practising, "our three four-man bob teams all have points they want to sharpen up. Our chief rivals, the Italians, Germans and Austrians, all get a good deal more four-man racing than we do."

However, the enforced rest caused by the curtailment of practice allowed Robin Dixon the chance to recover from bruising sustained in the two-man competition. There was also a chance for a little 'rest and recuperation', as Tony Nash recalls:

"We found the time to sober up and have the odd photo taken. The Argentineans thought they'd have a barbeque. So we all went down there but in the middle of it there was a phone call saying, 'Get your sleds up to the run because it's coming in freezing tonight and you'll be on the ice tomorrow

59 Fahrenheit.

morning,' and they'd want all the bobsleighs weighed – this was in the middle of the party – so the wine barrels were put on the roof of the lorry, the bobsleigh was put on the back with the barbeque going full steam and all the girlfriends. The organisers couldn't believe it when we turned up!" laughs Tony. "That's the sort of thing that went on."

With no further chance for experimenting, the British team manager, Tony Brooke, decided that the make-up of the GB bobs would be left until the last possible minute and crewed according to the state of the course on whatever day the competition commenced. Whether it was hard or slushy would influence selection. But Brooke confirmed that the injured Robin Dixon would definitely be fit in time to ride in Nash's sled; however, it was not certain whether he would be brakeman. At that point it was rumoured that Andrew Hedges would be chosen to ride on the back of the sled and that Wing Commander Evans would steer GBII.[60]

The responsibility weighed heavily with Brooke. There is a popular misconception that the two bobbers placed in the middle of a four-man crew are no more use than two sacks of potatoes, yet at best all four team members need to synchronise with rhythmic understanding, which can be as essential in bobsleighing as it is in rowing. The weight-transference technique of crew members can often prove profitably skilful.

Meanwhile, workmen were covering the bob track with sheets of plastic in an effort to protect the melting ice from the sun at Igls. An article in a glossy West German magazine, published in English and devoting all its space to the Winter Olympics, paralleled the slightly surreal atmosphere at this

60 The future Air Chief Marshal Sir David George Evans GCB, CBE, RAF – senior commander in the Royal Air Force – was born and educated in Canada. Following his retirement from the RAF, Evans was a military adviser to British Aerospace.

heated winter festival. Something about the laboured Teutonic humour mirrored the unreal feeling within the no-man's-land of the Ice Village:

"Even if the fraternisation magic of the Games is not nearly as strong as our Olympians may assert or wish this mighty sports festival warms the human climate.

"It no longer has the power to interrupt or even prevent wars, as it had in antiquity.

"But even countries without diplomatic relations can, so to speak, thaw out a little through the handshakes of their athletes."

On the Tuesday before the four-man competition, conditions were not suiting the British. The form of both crews was disappointing and the chance of emulating the success in the two-man event seemed, at best, slim. GBII was faster than its sister sled.

For the two runs Bill McCowan drove an aggregate time of 2.10.88. Nash piloted the first string team to 2.11.36. But with Italy I making 2.07.86 under Monti, and neither British team making the first six of the 19 teams, it seemed there was too much of a gap to be made up. In the end, Tony and Robin were teamed with David Lewis and Guy Renwick in GBI; Dixon was brakeman.

Because of warm weather softening the run, the four-man event was brought forward a day, with the first two of the four runs held on Wednesday. Austrian soldiers had worked through the night to repair damage to the chute from training that took place the day before.

According to Canadian four-man pilot Vic Emery, "In retrospect, the two-man event had been a four-sled contest in which we went from first to fourth, and so perhaps we could call ourselves part of the 'inner sanctum' of the sport. We had won the first heat of the two-man championship by a big margin and, despite a mediocre third run, were able to hold onto fourth place in that event on a deteriorating track when we were the last sled to go down. But the performance overall confirmed to me that we were ready for the four-man event."

For Tony Nash, they came to the four-man event with something of an advantage. "The Canadians were good in 1963 and came to the Games without new sleds, which proved unwittingly to be the right sleds – the 1964 model was not as good as the 1963-64 bobs."

The Igls course hardened up by the start of the competition, with a number of earlier teams breaking the 1.04 mark. USAII returned a time of 1.03.92 on their first run. Five minutes later, Austria I zoomed down the 1,051 metre run in 1.03.67. Then the Italians, piloted by Monti, surged into the lead in 1.03.43. This was not as fast as his unofficial record on the last day of practice (1.02.99), but he was leading the pack until Canada I, piloted by Vic Emery – with Anakin, John Emery and Pete Kirby behind – equalled Monti's unofficial record. Bill McCowen guided GBII – with Andrew Hedges, Robin Widdows and Robin Seel – to a 1.04.49 finish.

The Canadians had cornered superbly, taking each turn at the ideal point, and in their first run achieved what would be the fastest time of the day, 1.02.99. They took the final major turn so fast that they almost went over the top, exiting hard into a side wall which set them on two runners before humping the sled down while slamming into the side-walls on the final straight. In spite of the hard hits on the finishing straight, the result was a record-setting run, producing a secure lead and excited media reports across the globe.

But the twisting tunnel of ice at Igls had taken its toll. A quarter of an hour prior to Canada I's second run, as Vic Emery recalls, "I walked up the run, as I would normally do between heats, and got to the top to see our sled was upside down being worked on. But then I realised it was being more than just worked on, it was being pulled apart – Eugenio's mechanics were trying to de-seize our axle."

If the axle, strained by the near miss at the bottom of the run, was not repaired in time for Emery's second run then his team would be disqualified. However, Monti and his mechanics came to the rescue and the axle was freed in time.

When the bob was repaired for the second run, the Canadians were second best in the heat behind Franz Schelle, the world champion of 1962. Like Woermann, who had competed in the two-man event, Schelle was in the trucking business and coated his runners with a secret lubricant that turned out to be brake fluid.

Zardini was in sixth place but still well in the running for a medal, just 1.24 behind the leaders. Nash's time in the first heat was 1.04.56. GBI was in 16th place, lagging behind GBII in 13th (in a field of 18) after the first day. Tony was two and a half seconds adrift of the surprise leaders, Canada I, who with their two-run aggregate time of 2.06.81 now had to be taken seriously. But Monti was less than 0.7 of a second behind.

There was some suggestion that Nash was handicapped by starting last, a point at which the course may have been more difficult, but the Canadians were 15th to go down and did not seem to be harmed by being at the foot of the draw. But to get a second medal, one of the British bobs would need to record the two fastest times the following morning.

The track had continued to deteriorate, as in the mild weather the ice turned to a chilly mire in parts. Nash protested against the resumption of the race after the first run, complaining he was hindered by a huge patch of slush which appeared in the final straight. "They are bloody crazy to have that second run today. These soft spots are extremely dangerous."

Although others agreed with the British pilot, the organisers decided to go ahead with the second run after emergency repair work. The plan was that, if weather conditions permitted, the third run would be held the next day and the final run on Friday.

According to the consensus in the British press, the heavier machine did not respond to the delicacy of Nash's handling in the same way as the livelier two-man bob had. However, this did not explain how, in the space of one season, the four-man first string had tumbled from a top-four crew to also-rans.

The next day did not start well for the British, when McCowen and Co. narrowly escaped crashing on the third run of the competition. GBII almost shot over the top of the run as it sped round the last big curve before the finish, and brakeman Andrew Hedges claimed the jolt almost threw him off the bob.

On finishing, a hole in the ice-wall of the track was isolated as the cause; the Brits complained they were not warned about the hazard before starting their run. McCowan brought the sled home in 1.05.53, his slowest time of the competition, bringing GBII's aggregate time for the three runs up to 3.14.70 for 15th place. GBI clocked 1.04.64, giving a total time of 3.14.27 and slotting the first-string Britons into 12th spot with the last run to be held the following day, Friday 8 February.

Italy I achieved the fastest time of the day, 1.03.59, but that was only good enough for fourth place. Sergio Zardini, pilot of the Italian number one bob, had arrived at the start without his special racing shoes, but two British bobbers sent their shoes to the run and he was able to start on time.

As if the competition wasn't eventful enough for the

Canadians, the night before the third heat Vic Emery suffered a reaction to a tetanus injection, breaking out in hives overnight and developing a constricted throat. He dragged himself from his sick bed to complete the heat, but his brother quickly got him to a nearby hospital where he was admitted.

Canada I made 1.03.64, the second best of the third run, making a total of 3.10.45 for the three runs to put themselves in pole position and provide a 0.91 of a second advantage over Austria I. But they were being chased by the Italians, with Monti in Italy II, and the Germans had grabbed the best time in the third run. Canada II, Dave Hobart,[61] Gordon Lamont, Gordon Curry and Chris Ondaatje were in tenth place.

Looking forward to the final run, Peter Kirby was optimistic but also conscious that the competition was far from over. He told the media that the Italians could never be discounted as they were able to produce terrific runs; although Monti was just over a second behind his crew, Kirby warned that he'd beaten the Canadians by more than that previously, voicing his further concerns:

"The Austrians are very fast, they are lying in second place and they can do the same thing. Thaler[62] is driving very well in the four-man . . . and he has the fastest team behind him with a tenth of a second lead over us at the 50-metre timing point. Eugenio's team is second fastest there, approximately a 20th of a second ahead of us and so we have our work cut out to pass them on the way down."

On day two, following the third and only heat that day, for a while the temperature rose again. This vindicated the decision to extend the event to a third day, by which time dropping temperatures were forecasted. During the night, a dusting of

61 At 28 years and one day exactly, the baby of the Canadian team.

62 Erwin Thaler, the Austrian pilot.

snow fell around the slopes of the Patscherkofel, giving the authentic feeling of a winter Games. The night temperatures refroze the track and the program was able to continue.

By the morning it was cold enough for a fire to be lit close to the finishing line of the bobsleigh run, around which the newspaper men could shiver. As the start time approached, holding their cameras steady and scribbling with pencils in the numbing chill was becoming something of a task.

Before the final run, Kirby commented that he considered his team's lead to be "a very good one although it's always possible to blow it of course, we blew a fair lead in the two-man, but it wasn't as good a lead as this one, if we do crack up we haven't got a chance but with a half decent run we'll do all right."

The next day a crowd of 30,000 snaked along the track. More Austrians than had been usual up to this point were present to coax Erwin Thaler to guide his currently second placed crew of Adolf Koxeder, Josef Nairz and Reinhold Durnthaler to a famous local victory.

Vic Emery somehow heaved himself out of hospital to the track for the final heat. As he recollects, "It may have worked to our advantage . . . Maybe because I was so concerned with just getting to the run as opposed to how well we might do, that might have taken the pressure off me."

Looking forward to what would be their do-or-die moment, Kirby reflected that he couldn't detect any problems with the driving of the sled as Vic had been doing very well, particularly in the straights where he avoided hits, "that's an advantage that he has over the Italians at the moment. They're rattling down the straights with quite a few hits and that's time consuming."

Sticking his neck out, Peter told the world, "I think we'll come up with the gold medal."

It was true that the Canadians were so far ahead that only a disaster would keep them from the gold medal. But the unpredictable state of the track, together with the desire of the indigenous Austrians and the hunger of the Italians, all cast doubt on the ability of the relatively raw Canadians to hold their form and their nerve.

But Anakin, Kirby and the Emery brothers proved equal to the task and took to the course brilliantly, racing to victory with a steely self-confidence to give Canada the laurels at her first Olympic bobsleigh competition. When the Canucks came to a stop, after leading throughout the competition, they had won what was to be their nation's only gold of the 1964 games. They completed that last 14-bend run in 1.04.01, the fastest of the heat, giving themselves an overall time of 4.14.46. Austria won silver, a long 1.02 behind with 4.15.48.

Monti, going out last on the deteriorating run, made a brave effort to catch the Canadian bob but was unable to pick up the necessary fractions of a second. He finished in 1.04.08, the second fastest run of the day, giving him and his crew their second bobsleigh bronze of the Games. Although Monti was faster than Thaler in the fourth run, his team lost out to Austria I by 0.12 of a second. Once more Monti was denied a gold medal, but he came away from the games with perhaps more glory than if he had won.

The best British bob finished well down the field. As Robin Dixon remembers, "of course the newspapers at home were full of 'Nash, Dixon and team failed to win the four-man.'" He smiles at the memory. "The headline was 'Nash and Dixon Fail' – we were suddenly expected to get gold in both events."

After winning the title, 30-year-old Vic Emery said: "We have the Italians to thank for our victory, as did the British in the two-man event. They helped us tremendously in the practice runs, giving us invaluable advice and without their mechanical assistance neither the Brits nor ourselves would have been able to continue in the competition."

Emery was also gracious enough to acknowledge the help and advice given by the British squad. However, as Tony Nash concedes, "The Canadians were a very fit team. Vic Emery rode it very well."

The Canadian crew said the gold medal had cost them £17,850 in their five-year build-up for the Olympics. Though most of the money came out of their own pockets, they agreed it was worth every cent.

With the Olympic title went the World Championship, the first ever victories in these events for the Canadians. GBI could not get beyond 12th place, McCowen's crew were just behind.

Those who had stayed with the bobsleighing throughout detected a warmth and friendliness among the competitors not evident amongst any other international group at the Games. After the event, celebrating at the Sport Hotel in Igls, Emery pulled Nash onto his chair above the milling crowd, yelling, "This is a great Commonwealth occasion!" It was a sincere gesture with nothing sententious about it.

The Emery brothers, alongside the other Canadians, had almost taken over the large, timbered Sport Hotel during the day (with some help from the British). After their victory an enormous barrel of wine was produced in the reception room, and a great throng of bobbers and elegantly dressed wives and girlfriends helped celebrate the success. The Canadian manager Chuck Rathgeb circulated among them, inquiring, "Is everyone enjoying themselves?"

The Canadian quartet had made remarkable progress since the World Championships the previous year, when they were eighth. Emery attributed their improvement to organisation and riding behind Eugenio. Taking a hint from the Italians and the motor racing circuit, they had removed from the crew all serious responsibility for maintenance of the bobs by employing a mechanic. Their athleticism had also given them the third fastest start in the four-man competition. Above all, they were pleased to compete on a level playing field where the better crews raced on Podars and all, barring the Austrians, ultimately had the same number of practice runs on the Igls track.

Britain's performance raised some questions though. Nash confessed to having a better feel for the lighter two-man bob than the four-man vehicle, likening it to the difference between a sports car and a six-cylinder saloon. But he felt that the British bobs should have been in the top four or five.

Still, sentiment overrode recriminations and regrets about the competition itself. At that point it looked pretty certain that Monti had raced in his last international event, feeling drawn to retirement as he was. Zardini, who was about to become a naturalised Canadian, would certainly never compete for Italy again, having invested in a hotel in Montreal. While he would not be able to race for Canada under the qualification rules of the time, it looked likely he would compete at Lake Placid sufficiently often to give further impetus to North American bobsleighing.

The Italians had not expected their supremacy to be challenged by the Canadians, which was understandable. But for all this, it was the Canadian number one bob that tore down the track to set an Olympic record in the first run of the four-man competition to the astonishment of both other competitors and spectators, carving out a half-second lead on the rest of the field. Peter Kirby, Canada's brakeman at the 1964 Olympics, gave an insight into the team's performance:

"To come down with a good time you just can't afford to hit the sides. You lose a considerable amount of time when you hit. You don't use the breaks in a racing run, only when you are breaking in a new driver or when a driver is getting used to a new course."

Such a result was unprecedented from a team that, for most observers, were newcomers to competition at Olympic standard. It was a harbinger of things to come. Like many of their rivals, the Canadians had been schooled in 'bobcraft' by Eugenio Monti and it was his action in 1964 that kept the maple leaf in the competition. For perhaps one last time, the Italian driver was out to win his first Olympic gold, but once again he wanted to compete on equal terms with the best. It was also he who had ordered his men to fix the beleaguered Canadian sled. A battered undercarriage had dangerously compromised the steering of the Canadian bob, so Monti had instructed the Italians to do what they could to repair the damage.

According to Sergio Siorpaes, if called upon by anyone in competition he would help – although he had his limits: "Maybe not the Swiss because they were a bit nasty. But with the Spanish, the British, the Americans or whoever else, if they said, 'Sergio there's something not working can you take a look?' it was natural to go and fix it – run a check."

Emery, looking back, still feels gratitude toward the Italians in general, and Eugenio in particular, for doing what they could "to allow us to get to that point." As he told the television cameras at the time: "We certainly owe it to the Italians. They taught us everything we knew and it's going back a long time and if there's one chap who I wouldn't mind being beaten by it's Eugenio Monti and I hope he won't retire because he certainly deserves more than he got in these championships."

Now, many years later, he says, "On reflection I suppose Monti was a little bit sad that he got the bronzes, but he took it as you would expect him to take it, absolutely pleased for us, seemingly happy to get his medals."

The Canadian victory over the red-hot Italians and the

disciplined Austrians was an outstanding achievement. As the coach of the US team said, it was "the greatest upset in bobsledding history".

John Emery described the victory party as, "Lots of fun and laughter; dancing, running down the streets and spraying champagne."

(According to Peter Kirby, in attendance were four very attractive members of the Norwegian ski team, captained by Liv Jagge. Vic Emery and Liv would become reacquainted later in life; they now live together in London and Oslo.)

Doug Anakin had been scheduled to compete in the luge event in Innsbruck but, with the bobsleigh events in mind, he pulled out of that competition, not wanting to risk injury.

There are those that continue to insist that the Canadian win of 1964 was the product of poor conditions and good luck on their part. But Vic Emery earned much praise from his fellow competitors for his skill in directing the bob through the course's sharp turns and challenging straights. His crew triumphed because of their skill and his personal fortitude, eclipsing the best quartets in the sport with an extraordinary, commendable performance. Looking back, Vic sums up the situation:

"In the three to four years [1963 to 1966] that we were on top of our game, Tony consistently showed that he was a better boblet than bob pilot, and I was the reverse. The lighter hand thing helped me almost break through in the skittish boblet competitions, where one has to give the sled its head but keep the reins collected as in horse riding. The same is true in the four-man, except that monster is like a runaway truck, going faster than the boblet and requiring considerable handling exiting the big curves. I was more comfortable in the big 'zug', as we called it, and our starts were competitive – I don't think Tony's were quite so competitive in the four-man."

Which is not to say that there is a hierarchy of driving skill between the two and four-man vehicles; the four-man goes faster but its weight provides stability denied to the boblet. While the differences between competing in the larger and smaller bobs are not quite the same as the divide separating F1 and Monster Truck Racing, for instance, they are as related and as different to one another as Tasar and six-metre class racing in sailing.

At the medal award ceremony, following the only playing of 'O Canada' at the Innsbruck Games in the hockey arena, the Canadians nearly slipped over as they left the medal podium – having negotiated their way around a potentially fatal course practically without mishap. The four happy North Americans had reached the heights of their sport against all the odds.

Olympic four-man bobsleigh results – 18 sleds from 11 nations were entered. 17 received complete scores. One did not start in the third and fourth runs.

FINAL	TIME	DRIVER	BRAKEMAN			HEAT 1	HEAT 2	HEAT 3	HEAT 4
1. Canada I	4:14.46	Victor Emery	Peter Kirby	Douglas Anakin	John Emery	1:02.99 1	1:03.82 2	1:03.64 2	1:04.01 1
2. Austria I	4:15.48	Erwin Thaler	Adolf Koxeder	Josef Nairz	Reinhold Durnthaler	1:03.67 3	1:03.94 3	1:03.74 3	1:04.13 3
3. Italy II	4:15.60	Eugenio Monti	Sergio Siorpaes	Benito Rigoni	Gildo Siorpaes	1:03.43 2	1:04.07 5	1:04.02 4	1:04.08 2
4. Italy I	4:15.89	Sergio Zardini	Romano Bonagura	Sergio Mocellini	Ferruccio Dalla-Torre	1:03.95 6	1:04.10 6	1:03.59 1	1:04.25 4
5. Germany I	4:16.19	Franz Schelle	Otto Gobel	Ludwig Siebert	Josef Sterff	1:04.21 7	1:03.50 1	1:04.15 5	1:04.33 6
6. USA I	4:17.23	William-D. Hickey	Charles-W. Pandolph	Reginald-J. Benham	William-F. Dundon	1:03.90 4	1:04.11 7	1:04.43 6	1:04.79 11
7. Austria II	4:17.73	Paul Aste	Hans Stoll	Herbert Gruber	Andreas Arnold	1:04.65 14	1:04.40 9	1:04.43 6	1:04.25 4
8. Switzerland II	4:18.12	Herbert Kiesel	Oskar Lory	Bernhard Wild	Hansrodi Beugger	1:04.33 9	1:04.54 13	1:04.65 10	1:04.60 8
9. Germany II	4:18.68	Franz Wörmann	Hubert Braun	Anton Wackerle	Rupert Grasegger	1:04.47 10	1:04.42 10	1:05.25 14	1:04.54 7
10. Switzerland I	4:19.05	Hans Zoller	Robert Zimmermann	Hans Kleinpeter	Fritz Lüdi	1:04.83 16	1:04.52 12	1:04.97 11	1:04.73 9
11. Sweden I	4:19.24	Kjell Holmström	Carl-Erik Eriksson	Valter-Eric Aronsson	Kjell-Evert Luttemann	1:04.26 8	1:04.04 4	1:04.56 8	1:06.38 16
12. GB I	4:19.40	Antony Nash	Robin Dixon	Guy Renwick	Walter-David Lewis	1:04.56 12	1:05.07 16	1:04.64 9	1:05.13 12
13. GB II	4:19.43	Will. Mccowen	Andrew Hedges	Robin Widdows	Robin-Edward Seel	1:04.49 11	1:04.68 14	1:05.53 15	1:04.73 9
14. Canada II	4:19.78	Gordon Lamont	Gordon Currie	Christopher Ondaatje	David-Gordon Hobart	1:04.63 13	1:04.43 11	1:05.06 13	1:05.66 14
15. Romania I	4:19.80	Ion Panturu	Hariton Pasovschi	Gheorghe Maftei	Constantin Cotacu	1:04.70 15	1:04.89 15	1:05.05 12	1:05.16 13
16. Argentina I	4:25.51	Hector-Julio Tomasi	Jurado-Fern. Rodriguez	Carlos Tomasi	Hernan Agote	1:05.74 17	1:06.08 18	1:07.07 17	1:06.62 17
17. Belgium I	4:25.84	Jean De-Crawhez	Camille Lienart	Thierry De-Borchgrave	Charly Bouvy	1:07.46 18	1:05.56 17	1:06.51 16	1:06.31 15

The Canadians later presented Monti with a tankard inscribed, *To Eugenio, in recognition of a great sportsman. Canada bob.* The glass bottom of the flagon has a picture of a hanging man entitled *The Last Drop* – something the Italian maestro would have appreciated.

XII

HOMEWARD BOUND

On Sunday 9 February, 48 hours after the four-man event, Tony Nash rang his home to say he was on his way to St. Mortiz. He was intending to enter further competitions that might include the German championships, and after that was going to stop off in Paris for a day or two.

"The line was so bad I could hardly hear a word he was saying," complained his father. "He rang off saying he would ring again when the line was better."

By Monday Tony had still not telephoned again. "I expect he's been too busy," said his mother, who had received a phone message from her son via a close friend.

The Nash family had been inundated with messages of congratulation from all parts of the world, the phone hardly remaining silent since their son's glorious 1 February victory in the two-man event. Immediately after the gold run, understandably, Mr and Mrs Nash could hardly find the words to express their pride. "I can't believe it," his father had told the world's media, "I think it's marvellous."

"Thrilled . . ." was all Tony's mother could say.

By mid-February, Nash and Dixon had left Innsbruck and arrived back at St Moritz. On the 12th they won the St. Moritz International Boblet Derby in a field of 18 teams from Britain, Austria, Canada, Italy, Germany and Switzerland, including names like Kirby and Thaler in their ranks.

The British pair's first run of 1.17.32 was the best of the day, and set a new fastest time of the season on the St Moritz Olympic bob run. Nash and Dixon finished the derby by winning by a significant margin.

It seems the more relaxed atmosphere of St Moritz was causing Tony to have second thoughts about continuing with his sporting career. As he told the press: "I'll compete again unless I get married and right now I haven't even got a girlfriend."

However, back home in England he continued to make sporting history, albeit on a more minor scale, when the committee of Chiltern Rugby Football Club passed a resolution to break the oldest unwritten law of the Rugby Union: *That no person, military or otherwise, shall wear medals of any description in the clubhouse.* The club had sent their reserve team hooker a telegram of congratulation when he and his brakeman won their gold medal in Innsbruck, implicity urging Nash to come to the club wearing it.

Olympic two-man pilot gold medallist Pierre Lueders had once warned: "The thing I found over my career is the Olympics stir up emotions in an athlete that have never been stirred up before. And that's something you have to be careful of."

The Games are the pinnacle of any athlete's career, but this situation was probably exaggerated almost half a century ago, before the advent of professional athletics. Where was one to go after becoming an Olympic champion?

In the case of Nash and Dixon it had been almost 'zero to

hero' literally overnight. As Britain could not boast a single bobsleigh run, their victory was compared by one Fleet Street commentator to a competitor from an arid desert nation winning a gold medal for swimming. Many people didn't know the first thing about bobsleighing and not a few thought the two Brits had won the 'tobogganing' – sliding down a hill on something slightly better than a tin tray. For all this, the home of conquering heroes was determined to celebrate their victory.

It's hard to describe how little was known of bobsleighing in Britain. The men who came home from Innsbruck in 1964 were not subjected to the kind of exhaustive media hype they would probably have to contend with today, but there was a natural wave of affection. People expressed a response pitched somewhere between genteel national pride and respectful enthusiasm, tempered with polite appreciation and gratitude. Above all, the welcome home for 'our' Olympians was genuinely affectionate, as this piece drawn from a local newspaper in Surrey at the time reflects:

"At the Bell House Hotel, Beaconsfield, on Saturday evening [following Nash and Dixon's win] a special toast was devoted to these two young men. The occasion was when 170 local Catholics and friends held a dinner and dance, and Sqd.-Ldr. H. P. McGrath proposing a toast to 'Our Guests' referred to the Winter Olympics and this spectacular triumph for Great Britain. He concluded by stating that he felt certain that the guests would be delighted to forgo their toast, but not their welcome, and join with all present in a Toast to the Gold Medal Winners."

Licensee Jim Lennard and the regulars at Tony's local had sent a telegram of congratulations to Austria from "all at the Red Lion and at Little Missenden", and were determined to stage a worthy welcome for the homecoming hero. "They will be 'putting out the flags' when Tony returns home," predicted Jim. In the Red Lion, situated a few hundred yards down the road from the Nash family home, they would also hang the steering wheel that Tony removed from the winning bob in favour of guiding it with ropes.

Soon after the British victory, it was agreed by Little Missenden Parish Council to send a letter of congratulation to Tony. Local papers were at pains to point out that the Olympic gold was not the first medal to be bestowed on the Nash family, as Tony's father, formerly a managing director of Chesham Breweries, "once won a gold medal for brewing against competition from all over the country."

This sense of national pride is almost ineffable. Nash and Dixon seemed to bring a breath of fresh air to a country still stained with the aftermath of post-war austerity. With the benefit of hindsight, it seems to have been the start of the most hopeful era of the 20th century, as located in Philip Larkin's 1967 poem, 'Annus Mirabilis', "Between the end of the Chatterley ban and the Beatles' first LP."

Tony Nash recalls the post-competition atmosphere: "We were in the Olympic village, where there were other winners and competitors, and that was lovely. But we didn't quite understand just how isolated we were from the press and the reaction of the public. We didn't realise the impact the win had made in Britain."

Coming home, he gradually became conscious of what their achievement meant to their countrymen. "Land Rover very kindly lent us some forward control Land Rovers and the whole team came back together. As we came back into London everybody was waving and cheering. We got to the Australian in Sloane Square and had a few beers. That's where the team broke up and we all went home. Then it all started over again.

"Immediately after getting back from the Olympics we really didn't have much time to ourselves, we were being wined and dined all over the place."

For all this, Robin was able to avoid the limelight. "I missed out on all the jollity after we got home. That was not necessarily a bad outcome. My general condition was probably in better shape than it might have been otherwise.

"The other members of the team had a year's fun working on getting fat," laughs Robin. "I got back to Britain and had to go back to work for the Army. I believed that I was going to Cyprus to join up with the Guards Independent Company, doing United Nations work with the Blue Berets, but I got a signal to report to Hereford, to 22's depot. I was immediately sent off on duty for a tour of Borneo and was in the Far East for the rest of 1964. So while Tony was having a ball I was in the jungle." He smiles at the contrast. "I returned to Britain just in time to travel back to St Moritz for the World Championships."

On a Wednesday in late February, in a tiny Surrey village that was fast becoming famous, large flags and banners fluttered in the mild morning breeze. Behind this colourful façade there was a feeling of great excitement in Little Missenden – the whole population was waiting to welcome back Tony Nash.

Among the most excited people were the children at the village school. While Tony had been thrilling spectators with his electrifying bursts of speed, the children had sat composing letters of congratulation to their local hero. One read:

Dear Tony
I have 57 photos of the Beatles but I think you are even more FAB. I am proud to live in the same village –
Andrew Smith

Another, written by nine-year-old Graham How of Mantle Farm Cottages, was received while Tony was still in Innsbruck:

It must have been very thrilling and exciting to have travelled down the track at such a fast speed. It must also have been very scaring.

We are very proud that you have won the Gold Medal, and very proud to live in the same village.

The following reply was received:

Dear Graham,

Thank you very much for your letter of congratulations on behalf of yourself and the children at the village school.

It was a great triumph for us to bring the Gold Medal back to England and even more so to Little Missenden.

Robin Dixon and I hope that keen sports fans like yourself will one day grow up and do the same as we have done, so we hope that you will all have fun and work hard.

The Headmistress of the school, Mrs. M. L. Laws, said: "The children were so excited when they heard that Mr Nash had won the Gold Medal. They followed his progress throughout the whole of the Games and were really thrilled when he finally won."

Preparations for Tony's homecoming were in train from the time the British two-man team were crowned Olympic and World Champions. The Rev. Francis C. C. Roberts, vicar of Little Missenden, organised the welcoming celebrations:

"We naturally want to do something – this sort of thing doesn't happen every year, but a lot will depend on which day he gets back. I am waiting to hear from his father. Someone ought to do it. The church has been here for a thousand years and is the focal point of the village . . . The celebration will have to be absolutely spontaneous. I can't visualise anything except an informal get-together."

One scheme put to him by villagers was to drive the winning bobsleigh through the village on a lorry, but the vicar was thinking in terms of an evening event, claiming, "Tony is such a shy, humble young man that anything special would embarrass him."

American actress Patricia Neal, who only the previous year had won an Academy Award as Best Actress for her performance in *Hud* (alongside Paul Newman), lived at Great Missenden at that time and attended the local church. She told how she was so thrilled to read about the local man's exploits that she rushed home to tell everyone. "There were disbelieving shouts of 'No!' from my husband[63] and my sister-in-law," she said.

Speedway champion Ron How, then 34, ran the Crown public house and was Tony's next-door neighbour. "I am very proud indeed to think that a local boy should get an Olympic Gold Medal," he commented. Ron had fought his way to ninth place in the 1963 World Speedway Championships (finishing ahead of the great Peter Craven, the World Champion of the previous year) and was one of many at a cricket club dance in the village who toasted Tony on the evening of his and Robin's historic win.

It was about 8pm when Tony was officially welcomed home at a special party held in the village hall. He arrived with his family and was immediately pounced upon by autograph hunters who swelled an estimated attendance of

---

63 Legendary writer Roald Dahl.

over 200 people from the village's 90 households – the entire population, in fact. This was the first time ever that every man, woman and child had congregated in one place at the same time. "Everyone was there. It was a wonderful success," the Rev. Roberts noted

After the majority of the villagers had given their personal congratulations to Tony, the Reverend Vicar officially opened the proceedings with the introduction of film footage supplied by the BBC of one of the Olympic bob runs. It gave a second chance to those who'd missed a short close-up of their local hero on the television coverage.

Wearing his medal, Tony continued to sign scores of autographs before the Rev. Roberts asked him to mount the stage to be presented with a silver plate from the villagers, suitably bearing the Olympic insignia, engraved with the words: *With our grateful thanks for the achievement at Innsbruck*. Tony was also presented with a book on antique glass, as at the time he was a collector.

Called upon to say a few words, he thanked everybody concerned, typically and graciously concluding, "I want to thank my parents, for all the cooperation they have given me, and the Vicar who has done so much in arranging this party. He has been the mastermind behind it all."

After the cheers had died down, the Rev. Roberts mentioned that he had received a message from David Coleman of the BBC *Sportsview* team, who had covered the Olympics but was unable to be present at the gathering, congratulating Tony on his success. The Rev. Roberts pointed out to any "television addicts" that if they tuned in at 6.10pm the following day they would see the "historic occasion" repeated on the BBC's *Town and Around*.

In full view of everyone, Tony then held up the handsome Olympic medal and, before placing it around his neck, gave a proud victory sign. As he left the stage the village hall echoed with the sound of 200 voices cheering, followed by a resounding chorus of 'For He's a Jolly Good Fellow' and the traditional three cheers.

On 18 February, just ten hours after his return from Austria, Tony, surrounded by cups, medals, photographs and telegrams[64] in the sitting room of his family's picturesque converted mill home beside the River Misbourne, at Mill House, Little Missenden, announced that, providing funding could be arranged, he and Robin Dixon would race on.

"I will obviously need financial aid, but I will certainly have a crack at retaining the World Championship cup next year."[65]

It was while still in Austria, having expressed doubts in a television interview about being able to carry on competing due to the financial challenge, that Tony had received a personal call from England. The sales promotion manager of tobacco company W. D. & H. O. Wills had seen the interview and offered financial help. This was a landmark for amateur and Olympic sport, the beginning of the end of the era when international champions virtually had to pay to represent their country.

Tony still considered Eugenio Monti the finest bobsleigh driver in the world, but felt he and Robin had a good chance of retaining their world crown as the next championships were due to be held at St. Moritz – in effect their 'home ice'. If all went well, he and his brakeman would also seriously consider being part of the British Olympic team for Grenoble.

---

64 At one point so many telegrams had been sent from the Amersham area that the operators were not even bothering to ask for the Innsbruck address.

65 As World Champions, Nash and Dixon were automatic qualifiers for the next World Championships.

The Olympic committee had previously granted the British bobsleigh team of 16 £870 for Innsbruck, which was hardly enough for their training expenses during their three-week stay in the Olympic Village. Taking everything into account, Tony's ambition to gain the gold medal came with a personal cost far in excess of half the entire team's basic allowance, while other team members also carried substantial costs out of their own pockets.

A week after Tony's homecoming from the Games he returned to his family's engineering factory, T. and A. Nash (Penn) Ltd at St. John's Road, Tylers Green. He was welcomed by 60 or so members of the staff who had followed his progress during the Olympics, his first day back being a welter of handshakes and backslaps. Later, on 7 March, a 'victory dance' and social evening was held at Tylers Green Village Hall, at which Tony was the guest of honour. But, all this aside, the victory celebrations can now be seen as the start of a new epoch in British and international sport.

XIII

IN DEFENCE OF
THE CROWN

Following the Innsbruck Games, when asked if he would continue racing, Eugenio Monti replied, "I have already thought about retiring because I am getting old and it is best to retire. I will manage my ski lifts in Cortina." The great man was not to compete at all in 1965, not even in the World Championships in Switzerland.

After Robin Dixon had spent most of the summer ocean racing, a sport he had recently taken up, British prospects for that coming winter seemed good. According to Tony Nash, St Moritz was slower than Igls because there were "more small tricky bends".

At the time, Robin also reflected, "I want to be honest and say that if I started losing now, I wouldn't enjoy it terribly. After all, the more you do it, the less thrill you get from the actual sensation. Now, what thrills me is the competition."

Almost immediately on reaching St Moritz, the British started practising for the British championships, the first ever, and the Wills Boblet Goblet. Ten pairs were expected to compete on 15 January. A British driver had to be chosen to replace Bill McCowen in GBII, so it was expected that the competition would be healthy.

The two-man world event was scheduled for 23-24 January and the four-man a week later. Nash had one new member to join Dixon and Renwick in his four-man bob, Robin Widdows, who raced in the second sled during the Innsbruck Olympics.

It was understood that the Austrians would be strong competition and, of course, the Canadians were always a threat. The Americans and Swiss seemed capable of producing surprises as both had newly designed sleds. Two years previously, a US Air Force general with a yen for bobsleighing had suggested to General Motors executives that it was time to end the Podar monopoly.

The new GM sleds resembled the Podars about as much as a conventional family saloon did a sports car. For years, the best competition bobs had been crafted by an Italian blacksmith named Evaldo D'Andrea, who produced around 20 handcrafted, slipper-shaped Podar bobs a year, at prices ranging from about £500 (for a two-man machine) to £700 (for a four-man model). These machines were practical and modest in comparison to their American counterparts. But, in trial runs at Lake Placid in January, one of the two-man sleds beat the best time of a heavier four-man Podar and the four-man GM was even quicker. At St Moritz the European bobbers nicknamed the US two-man sled 'the Ghost', because its rubber-seated runners merely whispered over the ice, while the Podars clattered and clanked.

The burly US team had used their new vehicles the previous year and were expected to refine their machines further. Their sleds, at a design and manufacturing cost of £25,000, included such refinements as shock absorbers and sportscar-style direct steering. The Americans, bedecked with Olympic badges and equipped like college footballers with helmets seemingly inspired by astronauts, contrasted dramatically with Nash, Dixon and their helpers, who turned up for practice in ancient crewneck pullovers like a bunch of weekend gardeners plucked from the Home Counties.

Tony Nash scorned needless mechanical modifications and, as such, the British kept refinements to the minimum. Although impeccably prepared, their vehicles could not boast the same sophistication as the 'GM Specials'. The US team were also equipped with two-way radios, used by linkmen placed at each of the 16 bends down the run. The Brits' response was to take photos with Tony Holloway's Polaroid camera on the vital bends, so that Nash could study the lines taken by his rivals on the way back to the top. Always reserved in the heat of competition, usually he handed these images back without saying a word. It wasn't until days after the competition was over, at the Kulm Hotel over lunch, that he was effusive about "those fabulous pictures".

Nash and Dixon also had one significant advantage; they were champions and they had a particular aura on the great Swiss chute. All over the Alps the locals, from hotel porters to medical doctors, knew about the latest exploits of the British pair.

At this time, Guy Renwick, the bulwark of the Nash team, declared, "Tony is probably our most outstanding and complete world champion, though you wouldn't think so to read the British newspapers. We make precious little noise about it."

This is perhaps a little surprising. The *Dan Dare/Paul Temple* ethos of the two Englishmen should have appealed to mid-1960's Britain. Nash, the speed-obsessed lad who turned to the bob runs after promising his racing driver father not to risk his neck in fast cars, and Dixon, the debonair, aristocratic SAS Guards officer, together had the qualities of mythical heroes of an earlier era. They were the tradition of the Great British amateur, the Corinthian ethic of fair play personified. Akin to Ian Fleming's rather than Cubby Broccoli's Bond, they formed their words more like George Sanders than Sean Connery. Their victories appeared to be merely part of the course of their lives, rather than providing the meaning of life – although in actuality, Nash, Dixon and the entire British team were ultra-organised with a characteristic military precision. Nor was there any pretence of being a one- or two-man band; without the *Equipe Nash* there would have been no gold medal and no golden era of British bobsleighing.

Ambling slowly down the mile-long track before each of his four runs, Nash examined the icy surface centimetre by centimetre, looking for any new crack or bump that could cut a precious hundredth of a second from GBI's time, calculating the height at which he would take each of the corners. Of course, Tony knew the run well enough, but conditions change with weather, time of day and relative use. According to him, you could never really *know* a track but you could learn to anticipate its demands better. This would translate to the feel of the course when he was driving, handling the runner ropes with the light but firm hands of a jockey.

As he recalls, "In 1965, at St Moritz, we were favourites to retain the World Championship.[66] The Italians had strength in depth, much more than any other country at the time, but Monti and Zardini, their two best really, were out. We were really on our home track and as such were favourites."

---

66 The Olympics and the World Championships had been combined in 1964, as in most Olympic years.

Characteristically, the Brits appeared laidback as they came to the start. Other teams arrived at the top of the run with crash-helmets on; Robin strolled up in an antique blue beret while Tony was adorned with a fur hat a number of sizes too big. They might have been a couple of pals attending the event on a whim whilst on a leisurely winter break.

As the competition started it was snowing slightly, but it had snowed continuously during the night which suggested that no records would be broken. British team manager Tony Brooke said he thought the run was slower than it was on the Thursday during the final training runs. However, Dixon and Nash made two runs on Saturday, as Tony recalls:

"The third run of the championships was our first on the second day and we led the rest by over a second, which was an enormous advantage."

Britain's Olympic gold medallists were leading by four tenths of a second after the first run. Nash and Dixon had zipped through the initial heat at 1.18.49, the GBI boblet streaking down the icy run, rounding its steeply-banked corners smoothly, to throw down the gauntlet to the rest of the world.

Canada I, crewed by Vic Emery and Mike Young, was the last of the 18 bobs from ten countries to pelt down the chute; it clocked the second best time with 1.18.89. Rinaldo Ruatti and Enrica De Lorenzo of Italy lay in third place with 1.19.11. As described by Emery, he had started the competition with the worst physical disadvantage:

"We were coming close to Tony in the two-man when we crashed, as did a lot of other sleds, about four days before the event, putting me in the hospital for two days with separated shoulders and a gash through to the bone from wrist to elbow. In fact, after missing two days we only got in the last day of practice before the two-man event, and even then turned over momentarily onto our side on one of our runs."

In contrast, Nash recalls how, with a second run of 1.18.96, "We were pretty much well ahead after the first day." Overnight, Nash and Dixon held a respectable although not unassailable lead of a third of a second over Ruatti and de Lorenzo.

There was bright sunshine on Sunday 24 January 1965.[67] After walking around the course, the Britons felt sure there would be some fast times. Suddenly, the first day's lead they had carved out looked decidedly thinner than just a few hours earlier. The 0.33 of a second gave the top end of the field something to aim at, rather than cushioning the Brit pair.

Starting at number seven on the second day, Nash and Dixon tore down the track, plunging straight into the chute, ripping into the 180-degree Horseshoe Corner, swinging high on its sheer wall and dropping surely to the narrow, slotted straight to pick up extra speed. Their time for the run was a course record of 1.16.94, but the Brits were not finished yet.

Looking back, Robin says, "We were confident that we could win as long as we stayed on the ice. Other teams were advising us to take it slowly, keep it safe because we had already got it in the bag. We agreed that would have not have been the best strategy."

Nash concurs with his former brakeman. "Being overcautious would have meant we would not have been running our own race. The second day was cold, frosty and sunny, an absolutely lovely St Moritz day, and that suited us down to the ground. We broke the track record on the third run down and on the fourth run we took it again."

On their last run, Tony and Robin sliced another 0.3 seconds off their own record. The Italians, hitting the wall with a resounding smack near the top, had ruined their

---

67 "Winston Churchill died on 24 January, and I'll never forget we wore black armbands and all of the flags of every nation went to half-mast," recalls Tony Nash.

chances on the first run of the second day, taking 1.19.46 to get down. The Britons thus had only to play it safe on the last run.

Dixon, pushing at the top, prudently did board the bob a couple of paces earlier than he might otherwise have done. But, according to him, "We took no notice of the pretty unhelpful advice about taking it easy. That wasn't the way we did things. It was one of the biggest winning margins ever recorded. I think the final run was perhaps the most hair raising I'd had in bob racing. On at least three occasions we were on two runners; we were at the absolute limit. I can recall exactly where the runners were lifting."

Vic Emery recalls the situation going into the final run: "Our best heat relatively speaking, given the draw, was our third, when we went back into second place. We were in second place in the two-man event until the last heat, when I pulled too hard at the start and painfully tore one of my separations, which distracted us into the side wall momentarily and slowed us down until gravity got us going again. We fell back to third."

The Brits ran to a resounding triumph over the 1,620-metre course. Their aggregate time was 3.27 seconds faster than the runners up – a record margin for a World Championship and a result equivalent, in bobsleighing terms, to lapping the field.

Nash and Dixon's new record of 1.16.91 on the snaky course was a massive achievement in a competition that supposedly didn't require such all-out commitment. The idea was not just to win, but to fight for excellence to the very last metre of track. Nash and Dixon didn't really understand the notion of coasting to victory.

St Moritz was particularly suited to the fearless Nash, who loved a fast course. At 3,303 metres above sea level and protected from the sun, the run was fast and deteriorated little with wear. This was just as well as Canada II, which went down immediately in front of the Brits on the final run, unshipped its riders before the notorious 'Devil's Dyke' and wound its own crazy path down to the bottom. (Happily, neither of the Canadians was hurt.) Usually this would have damaged the run, but although Tony complained of the bumpy ride afterwards, their final run was the best of the championship. Hot on the heels of the Canadian accident, the Englishmen's stirling performance almost defied logic.

The superb driving of Nash and the efficiency of brakeman Dixon were obvious as the pair won their second successive championship. It was watched on television by millions of viewers, proving at a stroke that their success at Innsbruck was no fluke. In the context of a sport where every hundredth of a second may be a vital loss or gain, the pair had shown themselves to be exemplary champions.

RESULTS (18 SLEDS FROM NINE COUNTRIES TOOK PART IN THE CHAMPIONSHIP – THREE FAILED TO FINISH)

1. Nash/Dixon (GB) 1.18.49/1.18.96/1.16.94/ 1.16.91 Total: 5.11.30.

2. Ruatti/de Lorenzo (Italy) 1.19.11/1.18.67/1.19.46/1.17.33 Total: 5.14.57

3. V. Emery/Young (Canada) 1.18.89/1.19.03/1.18.73/1.18.34. Total: 5.14.99

4. Caviezel/Birk (Switzerland) 1.19.67/1.19.20/1.18.19/l.18.29. Total: 5.15.35

5. Woermann/Braun (Germany) 1.21.11/1.19.06/1.19.0l/1.18.60. Total: 5.16:78

6. Blockey/Freeman (GB) 1.20.42/1.19.62/1.18.32/1.18.50 Total: 5.16.86

During the championships an incident nearly occurred when the British found out another team had 'borrowed' some of their gear. But such episodes were few and far between. Bobsleighing remained the most sporting of any sport at an international level. Nash, one of nature's diplomats, was full of praise afterwards for the camaraderie that existed within the British camp, which, he emphasised, played such a big part in the success he and Dixon had spearheaded.

"Congratulations on repeat of last year's triumph," ran a telegram to Dixon the following Monday from the Chairman of Woking Council, Mr. V. G. Pearmund. It spoke for millions of newly converted bobsleigh fans.

One team that had seemed most likely to challenge Nash and Dixon had, in the end, proven to be no threat at all. The Americans had all kinds of trouble with their sleds. These 'secret weapons' (at $70,000 for the pair) really didn't get off the ground. The GM sled was too fast for its own good; on a practice run, driver Larry McKillip hit a rut and lost control coming out of 'Shamrock Corner', and smashed full force into the retaining wall. The bob's frame was hopelessly bent and McKillip badly bruised an arm. The solution seemed clear: slow down. But that didn't work, either.

James Hickey piloted the four-man GM sled into Devil's Dyke so sluggishly that it could not hold the wall. It dropped like a stone from the face of the curve, damaging runners in the process. As a final indignity, the US crew wound up using an old Podar sled for the two-man race. Steersman McKillip leapt in feet-first and put one leg right through the steering wheel. At that point he decided retreat was the best option and quit.

Swiss two-time world champion Fraz Kapus declared, "Forget the crashes. When those Americans get themselves straightened out, they will definitely be the fastest in the world." But several of their fellow competitors seemed much more 'straightened out' at the time.

With GBII, ridden by Blockley and Freeman, in the first six and an imposing crew for the four-man championships the following weekend, Britain seemed to be on the cusp of dominating the sport in the way that Italy had in the first half of the 1960s.

Having produced the sportsmen, the next natural step for Britain was to manufacture a homemade sled and end the dependence on Italian machines. The bob that won the championship had been a new one from the Podar factory at Cortina, at a cost of £450 from the newly acquired sponsorship.

*   *   *

GBI, steered by Nash, drew starting place number 13 for the opening run of the world four-man competition on 30 January. The day after the British two-man victory of 25 January, Dixon had been injured during practice when the four-man sled he was riding hit one of the big ice corners of the St. Moritz World Championship run at around 100kph. The brakeman was thrown against the ice but managed to stay on the sled. Later, he was treated for a badly bruised shoulder and face abrasions. The crew achieved 1.20.22 on their second run, but it was Canada and Austria that made the fastest times, both clocking 1.19.92.[68]

Fifteen bobs from nine countries took part in the two-day event. Over the 1,620 metre-run they would all take a vertical drop of 143 metres (nearly 470 feet), and ride 16 precipitously banked curves. GBII was drawn to go down tenth in the opening run.

Emery and Kirby were keen to show that their Olympic

---

68 Once up to speed the four-man is typically five percent faster than a boblet.

victory was deserved. As John Emery and Douglas Anakin were unable to join them, they recruited Gerald Presley and Vic's cousin, Michael Young, for their World Championship title campaign. As Vic says, "In 1965, both the British and the Canadians were out to prove a point and defend our crowns, which we each did by substantial margins. By the start of the four-man event I had full function following my injuries in the two-man competition and we won handily."

The British number one bob, including Dixon in its crew after it was decided he was fit to compete, was in second place after the first run on the Saturday. With Nash going all out, GBI narrowly escaped disaster when the sled smashed against a side wall at Shamrock and the bob's cowling was cracked. But it was Canada I, steered by Vic Emery, which led at the halfway stage with an aggregate time for the two runs of 2.38.52; the 16 steeply-banked curves were negotiated first at 1.19.43 and then 1.19.09, providing a 1.35 second bolster between them and West Germany II, piloted by Toni Pensberger (aggregate time 2.39.87).

Italy I, driven by Nevlo De Zordo, was in third place with 2.39.91, while GBI made fourth with 2.39.94. GBII, manned by Royal Air Force flight lieutenants with John Blockey steering, was lying at 14th with a total time of 2.43.46.

The Canadians proved their point by winning three of their four runs at the Championships, claiming the top prize a clear two seconds faster than the Italian runners-up, who were fractionally ahead of the American four piloted by Fred Fortune. GBI, although finishing seventh, was less than a second behind the runners-up. The British second-string bob (John Blockey, Michael Kirby, John Morrison and brakeman Michael Freeman) came 12th. Nash's crew clocked their two slowest times of the championships on the second day. As he said afterwards, "We cannot always win."

Leading aggregate times:
1. Canada I 5:17.78
2. Italy I 5:19.82
3. USAI 5:19.83
4. Germany II 5:20.32
5. Italy II 5:20.54
6. Switzerland I. 5:20.77
7. GBI 5:20.80.

The gold medal was significant for Vic Emery. As he puts it, "You're not real champions unless you can do it a second time." He had certainly shown himself and his team-mates to be worthy of World Championship status, and paved the way for the development of a national bobsledding programme in Canada.

Emery and Young had also won the bronze medal in the two-man event – quite a feat considering Emery was suffering from the injuries he had sustained earlier. The Emery brothers, Kirby and Anakin had already been inducted into Canada's Sports Hall of Fame in 1964, following their Olympic triumph, while Presley and Young joined them in 1965. "We had a serious party after that," says Tony Nash, "the Canadians liked a good time."

Nash won the Helen Vlora at St Moritz on 3 February, with Tony Holloway as brakeman. They clocked 2.40.51 for their two runs. Dixon, who switched to driving with Frank Usher, finished sixth:

1. Nash/Holloway (GB) 1.20.21/1 20.30 – 2 40.51
2. Evelyn/Widdows (GB) 1.20.70/1 20.60) – 2 41.30
3. Severino/Collins (USA) 1.24.71/1.24.05 – 2 48.76
4. Said (US)/Julitia (Switzerland) 1.28.00/1.21.40 – 2 49.40
5. Stadler/Morger (Switzerland) 1.27.62/1.28.32 – 2 55.94
6. Dixon/Usher (GB) 1.29.50/1.27 07 – 2.56.37

On 4 February, Nash and Dixon won the highly regarded President's prize race for two-man bobs in St Moritz, with an aggregate of 2.37.69 over the two-run competition. They recorded 1.19.40 on their first run and their second run of 1.18.29 was the fastest of the day.

Their closest challengers were the British pairing of Patrick Evelyn and Robin Widdows, who were 3.19 seconds slower with a total time of 2.40.88 (1.21.14/1.19.74).

Other placings:
Brook/Lesser (GB) 2.44.49
Said (US)/Julita (Switzerland) 2.45.42
Severino/Collins (US)   2.47.53
McGrath/Patterson (US) 2.50.56
Held (Switzerland)/Sauer (Germany) 2.56.48

That same week, on the Cresta Run, Nash and Dixon recorded 1.24.93 on their best run. Swapping places in the bob, they went down the run in 1.33.94 and 1.33.22. Tony Brooke, the British team manager, said there "was no significance in the switch. They were just trying it out – getting a bit of practice . . . As far as two-man bobbing goes you can learn some lessons this way."

On 7 February Nash teamed up with Frank Usher for the St. Moritz Boblet Derby. Their total time was nearly four seconds faster than the runners-up, Evelyn and Widdows of Britain. After the two Saturday runs Nash and Usher had only a narrow lead, clocking 2.39.58; Evelyn/Widdows had achieved an aggregate time of 2.39.78, the latter pair having the quickest time of the day with 1.19.04.

In the first run on the Sunday, however, the leaders took a firmer grip on the event, going down in 1.17.88; Evelyn and Widdows managed 1.19.03. During this heat, Dixon – taking over the driver's seat – and Holloway crashed at the 'Snake' bend, the third corner at St Moritz, when Robin's steering rope snapped. Holloway was seriously hurt. The nine-foot bob, weighing about the equivalent of half a Mini Cooper, shot up the righthand side of the icy banking, screeching like a banshee before going over the top and crashing into a tree that stood a dozen yards from the trackside. Holloway was put on a stretcher and carried down to a car, with Dixon helped along at his side.

Both men were taken to hospital at Samedan, near to St Moritz. A doctor later confirmed that 26-year-old Holloway's left arm was broken and there was also a suspected fractured shoulder, a back injury, a deep leg wound and several smaller injuries, though his condition under the circumstances was said to be good. Dixon had a flesh wound in his right thigh and suffered shock, but was allowed to return to his hotel after having stitches in his leg. He said later that he was "perfectly all right".

Nash and Usher made sure of victory with a final run of 1.18.16, for a total of 5.15.62; Evelyn and Widdows finished with 5.19.11. In third place were the American pair Dick Severino and Larry Collins, who took 5.23.63.

Boblet Derby:
Nash/Usher (GB) 5.15.62
Evelyn/Widdows (GB) 5.19.2
Severino/Collins (USA) 5.23.63

It was on the Saturday of this event that the St. Moritz Bobsleigh Club announced it had been decided to name two corners of the St Moritz-Celerina Olympic Bobrun after Nash and Dixon, in recognition of their being the only two members to win an Olympic gold medal. The corners, previously unnamed, were between 'Sunny Corner' and 'Horseshoe'.

After the race, Nash took Beatle John Lennon – who was on holiday in the area with his then wife Cynthia – down the St Moritz run. Prince Michael of Kent was also going up and down the Cresta Run at the time.

In the spring of 1965, the newly formed international sporting committee for fair play officially recognised Eugenio Monti. For his selfless sporting actions during the 1964 Winter Olympics, Monti was awarded the first *Comité Internationale des Trophées du Fair Play Pierre de Coubertin* in Paris. The award, named after the founder of the modern Olympic Games, is one of the noblest honours that can be bestowed upon an Olympic athlete.

XIV

"THERE ARE RISKS AND SO YOU ACCEPT THEM . . ."

Eugenio Monti did not compete in 1965, but when the World Championship returned to Cortina in 1966 he made a comeback after friends suggested he owed this much to the local community. However, peer pressure was not the only motivation. Monti still had a passion for the competition, and of course the motivation to make that elusive Olympic gold his own.

According to Vic Emery, "In 1966, Tony and I both recognised Cortina as our biggest challenge yet – the toughest course and the Italian's home track. Compounding this was the first-time use of lights, not very effective under the bridge between Belvedere and Bandion curves."

Monti drove the Italian bob to victory in the two-man event, but the championships of that year were dominated by the death of West Germany's Toni Pensberger. "It was something that occurred in bobsleighing," reflects Tony Nash, "we usually had two or three deaths a year."

He looks back less sombrely on the '66 contest itself: "In 1966 we went back to Cortina and, of course, the Italians were on home ground, literally for Monti and Siorpaes, who knew every inch of the course like the backs of their hands, and won. We came in behind Gaspari and Cavallini for the bronze, which was as good as we might have expected there."

It had certainly been predicted beforehand that it would be hard for Robin and Tony in Cortina d'Ampezzo. The Brits had ridden the track less than a dozen times before the championships and the Italians knew it better than anyone, in particular Monti.

For Vic Emery, "Tony did well to earn third behind the Italians." But the British team could probably not have been much better organised in competition. Led by Guy Renwick, the team of Tony Lessor, Frank Usher and Eddie Nelson worked hard with Nash and Dixon, absorbing any relevant information that Blockey, Freeman and their RAF colleagues could muster. Understanding that they had just four days to acclimatise to the course and learning from the Americans' strategies of the previous year, they used walkie-talkies and stationed men at key points on the course in an attempt to learn from their rivals about the way the chute worked.

It was quickly realised that Monti was going higher than most on many of the turns, once or twice nearly touching the protective boards. At that time he had a huge wound on his forehead held together by 30 stitches, having hit a hole in the course on his second comeback practice run and flipped the bob.

Before the official practice started, he admitted to thinking he was getting too old for the sport; then, shortly after, piloting a sled so advanced in design to be close to two seconds faster than any other in the competition,[69] he set a

69 Both Italy I and II were advanced design bobs.

new track record. At 38, his hair thinning, he remained a quiet, modest person, an ethos punctuated by the faintly morose expression he adopted in concentration.

Before a run, Monti went through a series of breathing exercises that, in another era, might have been interpreted along with the rest of his attitude as Zen-like. On the track the respect he had commanded for many years was heightened by his peers' understanding of him as a man who'd put more into his sport than he'd taken out of it. No one regretted his comeback or begrudged any potential success he might achieve.

Gaspari and Cavallini had formed the crew of Italy I only because Monti preferred the number two tag. Gaspari was ambitious and bold enough to go for broke on the last run; he required a relatively ordinary time, something better than 1.20 to ensure the runner-up spot. In the end they took second place with an aggregate of 5.10.09; Monti was 2.57 seconds in front of them and 2.66 seconds ahead of Nash and Dixon. Canada came home in seventh, having recognised too late that Mike Young was heavier than Pete Kirby on the brakes; the front runners were also floating slightly, reducing Vic Emery's ability to control the sled's trajectory.

However, Gaspari's previous record did not suggest he was in the same league as Tony and Robin, in a sport wherein performances were generally consistent. Sometimes people did win bobsleigh events out of the blue, maybe as a result of a fortunate draw or a change in conditions, but for the most part experience mattered. If participants rose through the ranks, they did so in the main slowly.

On past form Gaspari would have been regarded as doing well if he'd reached fifth place, or more probably the lower half of the top ten. If two seconds a run were added to his times to allow for the superior sled[70] he would have come eighth, just in front of the RAF duo of John Blockey and Michael Freeman; that would have been about par for the course. The same formula would have put Monti in second place, behind Nash. But all along, Tony had believed that Monti would win, even in the traditional Podar.

However, the Italians had made no secret of their technical work to advance the bobsleigh. Initially, they had used an articulated sled at St Moritz the previous year, although Gaspari's failure to make much of a mark there might have lulled other participants, including the Brits, into a false sense of security. But the Italian success of 1966 would have motivated a desperate worldwide attempt to catch up in time for the Grenoble Games.

It was clear that further refinements had been made by the time Monti arrived back on the scene; indeed, he had been part of their development. The Italians had taken the basic Podar and split the chassis frame just in front of the pilot's seat – at the thinnest point in the sled's structure. A muscular coil spring with shock absorbers acted as a dampener each side; at the same time the bob was made faster and more stable, as the runners were more inclined to stay on the ice while those of the conventional sleds were, in comparative terms, bouncing along.

At the time the four-man bob was seen to be too heavy for the same modification, but as this competition was abandoned in 1966 there was no evidence to suggest what kind of result it might produce. However, it was clear that, if Great Britain were to remain a contender on the bob runs, there was no other choice but to redouble efforts to produce a sled to allow the likes of Nash and Dixon to compete with the Italians.

70 Which seems about right in terms of the superiority of the new design.

Tony was committed to time-testing and experimentation, but simulated conditions had proved unsatisfactory. In practice at Cortina, Blockey and Freeman had used runners developed by part-time researchers at RAF Farnborough; they had the slowest time of any run by any nation (1.28). Having hardly got over the finishing line, resources were strained to get them winched up the run-out slope. A genuinely concerned German pressman asked if Blockey was inebriated. According to the RAF man, the blades had more bow, which gave less contact with the ice and thus potentially more speed. The modified runners had provided good results on hard ice in simulated conditions, but even on a course as fast and hard as Cortina was at night, the sled just churned up the track. This obviated the need for experimentation to be undertaken in 'real-life' conditions (as the Italians had done for well over a year).

If Nash and Dixon were to race a British vehicle at the 1968 Olympics, everyone concerned knew that the development needed to start immediately; two years of development work was in fact less than minimal in terms of improving on what the Italians had done and the Americans and Swiss had started as long ago as 1964. The blades were obviously the most underdeveloped facet of bobsleigh design, but the fact was there was not much scientific knowledge about how runners acted on snow and ice.

The British were not short of riders with potential; this was helped by the Army's decision to attempt to run a crew. John Lewis and Tony Woodward, and Prince Michael of Kent and Rory Cochrane-Dyet, were paired up for the European Championship at Garmisch-Partenkirchen. They were under firm instructions to brake until they were accustomed to the run, and it was a shame that the final two heats had to be cancelled due to a softening track, depriving them of valuable practice.

However, for Tony during the 1966 World Championships, winning and losing paled into insignificance during the four-man competition. "The whole thing was overshadowed by the death of Toni Pensberger in the four-man event, which was abandoned after his crash. Pensberger and the German team were given the gold medal posthumously."

Looking back over 40 years later, Vic Emery paints a picture of the hazardous nature of the run: "In the four-man we were doing well after the second heat, when the event was cancelled due to the track breaking up and Pensberger's death. In the first heat we had the fastest time to the Belvedere mid-point, when I instinctively knew – thundering under the bridge into Bandion – that we were literally going too fast for the run. And so I let the sled run up onto the boards above the ice before cranking it down, only to hit a side wall so hard that both reins were jerked out of my hands and we ricocheted past a contra curve and a following straight before I got a hand on one rein in front of the handle and the other in the handle,[71] managing to awkwardly get through the remainder of the course in 11th place.

"We slalomed through the ferns marking the ruts in the ice on our second heat, improving to third overall behind the Italians. There were about three sleds to go when the race was cancelled. Pensburger had been second to us at Belvedere, on our first run, but he seemingly tried to get off Bandion below the boards, flying sideways out of the run into the trees. (You can't get off a curve before you're well on it.)"

In those days bobsleighers were obliged to confront their mortality on a regular basis and in February, just weeks after Pensberger's fatal accident, an Italian was killed in an even more horrific tragedy at Lake Placid during the International Diamond Trophy.

71 The reins had handles attached to them.

It was bitter cold, 40 below freezing, on the Mont Van Hoevenberg course, making the run so hard and slick that the runners on the bobsleighs could not bite into the ice, tending instead to slide sideways on the turns. When asked about the Lake Placid track, Monti had once said: "It is not a difficult track, but it is a dangerous track because it is wider than the European tracks – it is much wider on the straights."

Conditions were particularly bad going into 'Zig Zag', where a wooden superstructure had been erected to prevent the bobs from flying completely over the rim of the course. At the start of the four-man event an American bob overturned and two of the crew were hurt. This prompted the wife of Lake Placid's own Joe McKillip, who was to drive the next sled down, to approach her husband and plead: "Don't go. Please don't go." Joe dropped out and the 34-year-old Sergio Zardini took his place.

The Zig curve at Lake Placid was where Zardini would lose his life. The crash came as he entered the notorious 13th bend. He had plummeted into the turn at close to 130kph and the bob literally took off on its side, throwing its four passengers head-first into the wooden lip of Zag (turn 14) and hurling them onto the track. Zardini's helmet had come off during the smash in Zig and his head was left unprotected. The empty sled rattled on to cross the finishing line as rescuers did what they could to help its crew. One had a concussion and a broken cheekbone; another was severely bruised; a third was amazingly unhurt. But Zardini, the team's driver, was dead; his head had been crushed by the wooden safety rail.

Immediately after the accident, Bob McGonegal, 'the Voice of the Bob Run', announced over the loudspeakers that the track was closed. Spectators and competitors left in a daze.

According to Tony Nash, "We had motor racing helmets, the Italians went for cycling helmets and they weren't up to the mark. In Lake Placid in 1966, unfortunately, Sergio Zardini's bob tipped up into the ridge and his helmet came off and that was awful.[72] We all went to his funeral."

One of those in the bob was Michael Young; he had been in the Canadian four-man team which won the World Championships the previous year. Suffering facial injuries, Sergio's 22-year-old number three man was rushed to the hospital in Lake Placid and subsequently flown to a hospital in Montreal, to undergo extensive reconstruction and plastic surgery. The future FIBT president, Robert H. Storey, was also involved in the crash.

Young returned to bobsledding for a couple of seasons before emigrating to the United States in 1975, settling in Denver, Colorado. He later moved to Dallas, Texas where he became a business consultant. He had no memory of the crash, but in that fraction of a second the sport had lost one of its greatest exponents. Zardini had been an unassuming, considerate and highly respected athlete.

Two years earlier, after the Games in Innsbruck, the diminutive and dapper Zardini had emigrated to Canada from Italy, where he and Eugenio Monti had dominated their sport. He had been the four-man world champion driver in 1963 and won the Diamond Trophy for two years running. The day before he died, on the same course, he also piloted a two-man bob to victory in the North American National AAU Championships.[73]

On hearing of his friend Zardini's death, Monti said, "This is always the kind of news you hope is not true. I was very upset when I heard . . ."

Sergio Siorpaes reflected: "You know there are risks . . . you accept them when you race . . . but you must imagine nothing

72 The Italian was practically decapitated.

73 American Athletic Union.

can happen to you . . . if you start thinking that something might happen to you then you can't perform . . ."

Such events beg the recurring question as to why men place themselves in such danger. But, as Siorpaes explained, "There's a great satisfaction once you've done it. . . that gives you immense joy . . ."

XV

GOING DOWNHILL

After the disappointment of 1966, efforts were made to develop a British bob that would enable Nash and Dixon to defend their most important title, the Olympic gold, at Grenoble in 1968. But before this there was a chance to try out the track that would host the bobsleigh competition at the coming Games in France.

By 1967 preparation for the Olympics was well underway, but, as Tony says, problems were envisaged long before even the first practice runs on the new track built especially for the Games:

"The French built this track at Alpe d'Huez for the Grenoble Olympics. It cost over five and a half million francs – an incredible amount of money at the time. But its south-facing aspect meant that it got more sun than the south of France! It was dismantled after the Games. It had been built in what was basically a sun bowl; it's one of the sunniest spots around Grenoble. They didn't want bobsleighing, but they had told the Olympic committee that they would have a track so they built it – it got put there purely because they'd got the money to build the road up there; they weren't ever going to hold bobsleighing events there again. They wanted to open up the area as a ski resort and the only way they could get the finance was to build a bob track up there. It was very dangerous, a disaster area. In the 1967 World Championships we all crashed! Monti was back trying to get ready to get an Olympic gold in 1968 – the only thing he had never won."

Vic Emery's impressions of the track were not good: "In the autumn of 1966, because I was by then married with a baby on the way, I went to Grenoble to look over the track being built there. I was so alarmed by what I saw that, after making no headway with the contractors, I contacted the FIBT about the need for drastic changes to the entrances into some corners and was again stonewalled, saying all could be corrected with snow and ice. I didn't agree and contacted Tony, Eugenio and others about my findings, with the view to a pressure boycott which didn't materialise. And so a number of my bob colleagues competed in 1967 and were injured, Siorpaes included, on a track that wasn't used from the top, didn't hold a four-man race at all and was substantially rebuilt the following summer.

"In fairness to my growing family and survival, we declined 1967 as a team."

The French were going full throttle for their first Games since 1924, whacking out a cool $200 million at Grenoble.[74] They originally had the ambition to make the bob track at Alpe d'Huez the finest in the world. Italian Architect Luciano Galli, who designed the course at Cervinia, then

74 To put this in some perspective, the production cost of the 1964 Beatles film *A Hard Day's Night* was around $500,000. *The Boat that Rocked*, a 2009 film made with similar production values, cost more than $45m.

considered as one of the best, had been commissioned to map out the new run high on the shoulder coming down from the Col de Poutran.

Galli produced an undulating concrete chute, snaking round a drop 459 feet, spiralling through a warren of half a dozen near-hairpin bends and four gruesomely rapid curves. Its chunky concrete boundaries soared to a height of 15 feet on the bends. The whole thing cost a massive $800,000. All in all, prior to any snowfall, its lethal appearance suggested it would not take much of an error to inflict pain on even the most talented.

On completion, the track got in an awful state during practice; the British decided not to allow their second pair to risk their necks on it. The architect had wanted to bring in specialised labour to lay the carefully cut and shaped segments of the course, but the French authorities overruled him and further decreed that every segment should be of the same material and texture so that it could be mass produced; it would then be forced into place by bulldozer. Finally, the builders managed to overdo the saline content of the concrete, so that the sun's heat was absorbed and retained.

No other alpine chute faced the south. Ostensibly, this was done because the ski runs took up all the other slopes, but no one seemed to have been conscious that the course would be bathed in bright sunshine all day. Alpe d'Huez was thought to be the sunniest ski resort in the world, and for weeks through the usually cold, grey January this was confirmed; it received 12? hours of sun each day! In such conditions, at times the run looked like a flowing brook. However, as the sun went down and temperatures plummeted, the ice hardened but not enough to provide an adequate surface. At the 1967 World Championships, held as a precursor to the Olympics, after early use the first part of the track had the appearance of being ploughed. So it was decided to start the runs 500 metres below this point, at the 1,000-metre mark and, if required, to limit the championships to one, two or three runs instead of the usual four.

The start was postponed for two days to allow work to be carried out. The starting times were altered from 6:30pm to 6am, so that the course might be hosed all night to build up the ice that the day's sun had washed down the chute. What resembled the longest shower curtain in the world[75] lined the course in an effort to protect it from the sun, but it had little effect; the ice was not bonding adequately with the concrete walls. To make matters worse, serious construction faults were exposed after practice was resumed; the inruns and outruns were inexplicably defective. At the time, 45-year-old US veteran Fred Fortune saw the danger. The 1948 Olympic bronze medallist commented before the start of the competition:

"It's dangerous because of the flat spots on the inrun and outrun. The throats between the curves are supposed to blend in and throw a sled from one curve to the other, but here you come off a curve and hit this flat area and you go flying into the next curve."

The Swiss Chef de Mission, Gaudenz Gartmann, who had observed the construction of the course, commented: "Plans for the course were perfect, but mysteriously, somewhere between the architect's plans and the finished run, something went wrong. On the curves the spaces have been changed and the whole thing is off enough to make it a monster."

Danger was a constant in the bobsleighing of the mid-1960s. Robin Dixon recalls, "When we first started the sleds we were on then were much slower than modern sleds, even

---

75 This attempt to minimise erosion of the track was continually frustrated, as local inhabitants got into the habit of taking these screens to make spinnakers for their yachts.

than the sled we used later. In the first year or so I wasn't really scared but later I did get a bit scared occasionally."

As Tony Nash says, "You were always aware of the dangers. Everyone of course thought about the possibility of getting killed or injured but in those days it was just one of those things that happened. But if you had sanity on your side you didn't fool around, it kept the odds on your side.

"Robin had an accident when he took up driving for the Commonwealth Championships for Northern Ireland. But his brakeman wasn't fit and we had a job keeping him alive. He got a tree right across his two kidneys and he wasn't very well at all. Robin was in bed after the accident in the hotel and I went up to see him. I took him a bottle of whiskey. He said, 'These bloody pills the Swiss doctor has given me – I can't even swallow them with a glass of whiskey!' I had a look at the pills and they were suppositories," laughs Tony. "Thick bloody Guardsman! Because the Swiss always give suppositories!"

Bobsleighers accepted danger. US Olympian brakeman Philip 'Bear' Duprey was not unusual in preparing himself at the start of a run by buckling on a padded leather girdle as a kidney protector and donning thick leather elbow guards. Although few bobbers were idiot suicide jocks, however, it was not in the nature of top international riders to approach competition cautiously. When asked about the possibility that he might use a sled's anchors on a particularly hazardous run, Lake Placid-born Duprey replied: "Hit the brake? We're here to race. I wouldn't think of it . . . all I have to do is hang on for the ride."

Robin once argued that courage is much less important when riding a bob than self-confidence, reckless courage being a positive disadvantage. He saw "the courage of a competitor" as being chief amongst the requirements of crew members, but this type of bravery had a distinctive professional hue. As he recalls, "After our crash of 1962 in Garmisch, it would have been very easy for Tony to say, 'We had a prang yesterday, do you mind if we take it easy today?' But he said, 'We're going to go flat out.'"

Being too careful – like being too rash – can kill you, according to Vic Emery. "To be safe in most speed sports one has to be sensibly aggressive. Competitors on the defensive are much more prone to accident."

The professional in any field acts on the basis of evidence rather than raw emotion or feeling, and bobsleighers are no different in this respect. According to Manfred Stengl, who won the gold medal in the luge doubles event at the 1964 Winter Olympics in Innsbruck and a bronze in the four-man bobsleigh at the 1975 FIBT World Championships in Cervinia, Italy, "First you sense what the ice can do, its limits and possibilities. But what at first one might take as instinct you find is confirmed by facts. Sometimes you just pick up things unconsciously, but looking for the reason for your feelings allows you to perform better."

Seemingly in an effort to save the day, the French Minister of Sport, Francois Missoffe, took a ride down the chute. A tall, angular man, Missoffe strapped on a helmet with an expression straddling resolution and concern. Members of the French four-man crew cushioned him between themselves and their pilot. Looking a little pale, after his ride he announced, "It is a splendid run . . . On the Vercors curve you go up very, very high. I started out looking ahead, over the driver's shoulder. But when I saw that one coming, I just closed my eyes. It is the first time I am ever inside a bobsled. Next I am going to parachute into the snow. It is a new sport for French skiers!"

With the minister's words echoing over the mountaintops, it was decided to continue with the event. However, Robin

Dixon, recalling the state of the track, says, "Honestly, we didn't think we had better than a 50-50 chance of reaching the bottom; Tony and I knew when we saw the state of that run that it was a disaster waiting to happen. But when you happen to be in the position we were in, you've got to go. And that doesn't take courage, because you're scared. It's like standing in the door of an aeroplane; it takes a lot more courage not to jump."

Bobsleighing, like most winter sports, is usually better undertaken in the light of day. In fact one would be slightly insane to think that darkness might add to the quality of performance. However, at Alpe d'Huez, because of the potential damage the sun might have caused (although the course was too soft and badly rutted) the heats were scheduled for before dawn – when the ice was at its hardest. This produced a Dantesque vision. The serpentine track gleamed in the sallow saffron of the sodium vapour illumination, intended to enhance depth perception. The shadows they cast distorted reality. Participants and spectators appeared cursed by an epidemic of jaundice, while the mountainous prospect that surrounded the run disappeared beyond the frayed edges of the gloom.

As Nash complained at the time: "This is a plaything . . . We are trying to get this meet stopped. If not stopped, we want to call it merely an international meet, not a World Championship. Running a sloppy course for 1,000 metres does not prove anything.

"It could be a fabulous course, but the entrances and exits are flat and throw the sleds off line at the most crucial points. Remember, a two-man bob is exerting 40 tons per square inch of pressure on the ice and using only a small portion of its runner. The slightest mistake in course design can throw it off."

Locals were later to call the event that took place high in the Grandes Rousses, the rooftop of France, *un massacre*.

At the end of the first run, Monti and Siorpaes were leading Austria's Erwin Thaler and Reinhold Durnthaler. Nash and Dixon lay seventh, 0.66 of a second off the leader.

That next day the ice, under the early morning lights, lay scintillating sickly, mashed and furrowed. Monti crashed, sending up a plume of wet ice shards and chiselling a fresh scar close to the finish line. As he later recalled: "I had a beautiful run until that curve. Then I hit that bump, and the sled went wild."

The mishap was to put an end to the career of Monti's brakeman. It was around 6:30am when, travelling at just under 100kph in cold blackness, Monti climbed the glassy vertical wall of the Vercors turn. The sled was a faint smear of colour against the sinister illumination. Without warning the bob flipped over. Sergio Siorpaes was flung out like a toy soldier as his driver went careering down the run on the top of his helmet, his arms doing what they could to protect his face. The sled tumbled again, flinging Monti half out of it, but gravity continued to both trap him and drag him along the ice. The bob eventually bounced to a halt as it jammed into the channel a few feet short of the finish line.

For one protracted moment a threatening silence dropped like a rock over the spectators. Something between shock and anticipation ruled those elongated seconds. But as a small mob ran in the direction of the bob's landing place, Eugenio began to direct the oncoming medics back up the run to where his brakeman lay, a casualty of a cruel Alpe d'Huez track. As Siorpaes described it: "The sled flew in the air . . . we turned upside down and went crashing against the curb – we were tumbling down the track and my [left] arm was broken."

As Robin Dixon remembers, "Coming out of the last

corner, Monti crashed. His brakeman lost the full use of his arm for life. Then it was our turn to go down. I knew exactly what had happened but there was nothing you could do about it. We did the same thing. That was the only time I was carried off a run in my life. I was unable to ride again that year."

Before Nash and Dixon came roaring off Vercors, many could already see what was to come. Another plume of ice erupted as the GB sled bucked off its riders. Trundling over the ruts, the bob appeared to disintegrate at the finish − vomiting up its rear runners and banging between the walls of the chute; the Brits finished with not much between them and the ice.

With one run left, although he was assured of a medal, American rider Howard Clifton remarked, "Who cares about the medal? All right, so we won a medal. All we want right now is for everybody to get off this hill alive. Pray for this last sled."

In 2009, Tony Nash ruefully recalls, "The French didn't know a lot about bobsleighing and didn't appear to care too much either."

In the end, Austria's Erwin Thaler and Reinhold Dumthaler took a rather meaningless victory away from France. The silver medal went to Italy's Nevio De Zordo and Edoardo de Martin, with the USA's Howard Clifton and James Crall third.

There was an effort to start the four-man competition and an Italian sled did make it down the course, but, despite the desperate pleas of French officials for competitors to continue practising, the event was abandoned. The warm temperatures on the track caused the ice to melt to such an extent that it made the competition impossible.

An aura of bad luck seemed to hang over the track that was destined a year later to be the Olympic run. Initially, snow had filled it up in places. Then it was shrouded in fog before being softened by the sun. No one had been able to get sufficient practice, even if they rose from warm beds at 4:15am. Monti's assessment of the track was character-istically succinct: "It is not very well made. I will be glad when it is over."

The track became more rutted and bumpier, necessitating that French soldiers were assigned to maintain the course. They spent much of their time trying to conceal the ruts with a mixture of snow and ice, like vanilla frosting. During a rare trial Monti struck one of the grooves and was sent flying down the run, landing on a single blade, barely managing to keep control of the bob. As he walked back up the course he quietly commented, "I didn't see that rut. It was hidden."

Monti asked a soldier for his shovel and smashed it into the wall, chipping the frosting away. As he walked on he mumbled, "It's fixed!"

It was clear that a great deal of work would need to be undertaken way up on the Col de Poutran before the Olympics, and many were asking how could it be made ready on time.

Franz Kapus, a 59-year-old bobsleighing expert from Zurich who broke his back in a spectacular accident at Cortina in 1954, was placed in charge of the run. A four-man world champion in 1955 and Olympic champion in 1956, Kapus argued that the entire course was an $800,000 blunder. He claimed the cement chute needed to be demolished and rebuilt with earthen walls, in order that the ruts could be repaired with shovels. "The best thing to do with it is to break it up and put it into trucks and drive it back down to Grenoble."

America's Olympic and three-time World Champion bronze medallist Fred Fortune agreed, saying that the best idea would be to "dynamite it and start all over again. We tried shaving the ice down to eliminate the humps and we hit solid concrete. Blasting is the only answer." The course had to be entirely rebuilt over the summer, but it was never to lose its reputation amongst bobsleighers as the planet's largest white elephant and the most hated bob run in history.

After losing his brakeman, Monti was obliged to build a new crew and new tactics to take on competitors who were gradually closing the gap in terms of skill and technical know-how. The push was becoming more crucial, so Eugenio recruited young men with size and speed. Roberto Zandonella, like Monti, was a committed athlete whose voracious thrill-seeking had led him to bobsleighing. Uncharacteristically, Monti also enlisted a complete outsider, Luciano de Paolis. De Paolis was in the military and regarded being chosen by the great man as a tribute in itself.

The new crew were schooled by the master in his credo of hard work. This, together with the ceaseless emphasis on the importance of preparation, spending many hours buffing the steel runners with lamb's wool and sandpaper, moulded them into a team. According to Zandonella, "The skate would become like a mirror, smooth and blindingly shining . . . in order to increase our speed. Eugenio would sleep with those runners so they wouldn't be damaged or snatched."

Speed and slickness were incorporated into their new technical innovations, anything and everything to make the bob go faster. Monti kept his retired brakeman close and together they innovated the wearing of leather shoes with steel nails in the soles. Siorpaes has described how the Italian bobmen had extensive discussions about what they could do to improve their performance. Monti's consistent response was, "Do *something*!", urging his team to experiment creatively.

In response, Siorpaes came up with a retractable push-bar and mounted it. As soon as they had completed the initial push and were moving fast they could retract it, making the bob more aerodynamic and getting rid of a potential hazard in the event of a crash. This innovation enabled the Italians to gain several hundredths of a second on each run.[76]

By now, Monti had decided that the 1968 Olympics in Grenoble would be his swansong in competition, and the world of bobsleighing looked towards the Italian Alps with anticipation.

---

76 This wasn't the first collapsible push-bar, but it was the first fully retractable one.

XVI

DEVELOPMENT

Despite the disastrous World Championships of 1967, Tony Nash continued to work for a design breakthrough. "We wanted to build on the success. Because I had the engineering background it was the only thing I did at school, mechanical drawing; I knew a bit more about it than other people competing in the sport. We tried desperately to make a British bob but we never had the time or the ice to do it. We tried to build a new bob with Alex Moulton, which came out in 1966."

Dr Alexander Eric Moulton CBE was a British engineer and inventor in his mid-forties. The great-grandson of rubber pioneer Stephen Moulton, he specialised in suspension design. Alex had worked in the family business, George Spencer Moulton & Co. Ltd, founded by his great-grandfather following the Second World War, where his specialist project was rubber suspension systems.

Towards the end of the 1950's, after Moulton's had been

acquired by the Avon Rubber Company, Alex started Moulton Developments Ltd, a new suspension design company, as well as working on the British Motor Corporation's new car design, the Mini, which was the brainchild of Moulton's friend, Sir Alec Issigonis. The combination of small wheels and conical rubber springs was one of numerous pioneering innovations that Issigonis was to realise, resulting in the Mini's revolutionary compact dimensions.

The other famous design concept Alex was responsible for was the 'Moulton bicycle', once more deploying rubber suspension and relatively small wheels. Alex Moulton Bicycles continues to be based in Bradford-on-Avon, Wiltshire.

Tony recalls the bobsleigh design that Moulton collaborated on with Issigonis. "The great thing was to keep the runners on the ice and we were trying to use a version of the Mini suspension. From there we went to Farnborough, where we did a lot of testing with various pieces of metal on the ice.[77] I was working with Miss Shilling."

Beatrice 'Tilly' Shilling OBE, PhD, MSc, CEng, was the daughter of a butcher and an aeronautical engineer, best known for inventing the 'Miss Shilling orifice', a relatively simple mechanism designed to prevent engine cut-out in the first Spitfire and Hurricane fighter planes during the Battle of Britain. As Tony puts it, "Spitfires used to lose fuel. She came up with this very small but ingenious thing that she'd invented to get over that problem. She had them made privately because of the time it would take to go though government procedures, which would have been about two years, and sent

---

77 This was at the Royal Aircraft Establishment (RAE), a research centre formerly part of the Ministry of Defence (MOD) in Hampshire. In 1988 it was renamed the Royal Aerospace Establishment before merging, in 1991, with other research establishments to become the Defence Research Agency.

them out to all the squadrons with the instructions on how to fit it."

Some historians argue that her work on this fuel valve – based, rather poetically, on the workings of a human heart valve – was a vital factor in the RAF's victory over the Luftwaffe, preventing Nazi Germany from fully inflicting on Britain the Blitzkrieg strategy which had conquered Europe.

Beatrice dismissed any hint of the idea that, as a woman, she might not be an intellectual match to any man in the scientific or technical realm. Once described as "a flaming pathfinder of women's lib", she was also a well-known racing motorcyclist in the 1930's on the famous Brooklands track. Riding on a Manx Norton 500, she was awarded the Gold Star for lapping the circuit at more than 100mph.

Married to George Naylor, a bomber pilot with 625 Squadron RAF, Shilling worked for the RAE up to the middle of the 1960's. She held a doctorate from the University of Surrey in chemical engineering, and was a member of the Institution of Mechanical Engineers and the Women's Engineering Society. She passed away in 1990, aged 81, a mostly unsung heroine of the victory over Nazism.

Nash recalls his first encounter with Beatrice. "I was given the introduction, went down to Farnborough, went up to her office, sat down. She hollered, 'Excuse me, old boy. Just hang on a minute – I've got to go through these part two orders – splendid!' She took me down to the officers' club. She said, 'I used to get up to 100 down here!' – it was a 30-mile limit! 'Those were the days!' I asked, 'What was that in, Miss Shilling?' She replied, '"In", my boy? "On" my motorcycle!'

"She wanted to find out about loading on corners. We had this recorder in the sled and it built up anything up to eight Gs going through a hole in the ice, on the apex of a corner."

An untrained person would be pretty uncomfortable at

three Gs,[78] although pilots are often trained up to five Gs. People have gone up to ten Gs or so, some more, but only for very short periods as it is often very dangerous and destructive.

"It was much more than she had anticipated. She then had a look at steels. We wanted to find what produced the least coefficient of friction.[79] She wanted me to fire different steels across an ice rink with a 2.2 blank behind them to see which steel went further – then she wanted me to go out to Nova Scotia and try it on the ice out there," chuckles Tony, "but we didn't get round to that. She was fascinating – a very interesting woman.

"Also with Miss Shilling we were playing about with suspension. We were looking at whether we could absorb the small defects in the course. Which there were then, but you don't get them on the modern courses because they're shaven. In the old days you used to bounce like hell – the work we were doing was trying to absorb that bounce, to create a sort of shock absorber. The Americans had done it and were successful enough to win the four-man at the 1959 World Championships at St Moritz. They had worked on ideas developed in the space projects. An astronaut got General Motors to build and develop a sled for him – I can't remember his name – it was very flexible and had its runners encased in rubber vertically, like the underground trains. I tried to make it; we wanted to place the runners on rubber, something like you've got now on the undercarriages of underground trains

78 'Gs' refers to 'g-force', a unit measuring the inertial stress on a body rapidly accelerating, measured in multiples of the sea-level acceleration due to gravity on Earth. Three Gs therefore is a gravitational force three times more powerful than that usually experienced at sea-level acceleration.

79 This is the ratio of the force that maintains contact between an object and a surface and the frictional force that resists the motion of the object.

– metal sitting in a rubber block. We were trying to get the runners to take up the absorption in these rubber blocks. It wasn't successful and we had very little training time. Soon as you were on the ice you were fighting for your place on the team. We never had time to really do it.

"We had built a de Haverland bob and had learnt from that – the team leader was Henry Taylor – but there were things wrong with it. It had the appearance of an aircraft, it was beautiful looking, that was in 1960-61. It was too heavy on the front end and too long – if the nose is longer you hit the tape going slower than if it's shorter. It was a fraction but it made a difference. It had design faults in it that we stupidly should have anticipated, but we never got there."

Tony was never able to get where he wanted to go with bobsleigh design, even though he persevered long after his retirement. "We tried to build a bob up at AEC,[80] I think they built the tanks, near Leeds, about 1976. They did it through their apprentices, we went up there and jollied them along, and I tested that and it went all over the place. But by that time I'd given up bobsleighing, although I came out of retirement to test it because other people didn't have the time.

"None of our modifications worked, except maybe trying to make the runners work a bit better – they were bolted at either end and in the centre there's a rubber pad. This was on the Italian sleds. This rubber pad takes up the absorption of the runner. When we were experimenting with the rubber blocks, we stuffed rubber in the centre so we had to press down to get the bolt in. So the rubber was powerful in the centre which made the runners bowed all the time as opposed to flattening out when it was going down."

It says much for Nash and Dixon that what they were

---

80 Associated Equipment Company; they also manufactured buses and commercial vehicles.

unable to accomplish in terms of design was more than made up for by their remarkably close empathy as racing partners. As Vic Emery says of the responsibilities of a bobsleigh pilot, "As a driver you can win the race, you can lose the race or you can get everyone killed. It's not quite the same for everyone else."

When asked about the qualities required to make a great competitor in bobsleighing, Robin laughs. "Blind, thick and unimaginative? For a start it took a lot of courage and incredible dedication. A driver needs to be capable of shutting everything else out and of terrific concentration. Tony had all of those qualities. To be a brakeman you need to be strong and a good sprinter – the start is critical. You need to be able to focus and understand what the driver's doing, you have to be a team player. In those days I was also Tony's critic."

The latter point was an important factor in the Brits' success. Tony makes it clear that this critical analysis was a key to being able to improve subsequent performances. "Almost as soon as we finished a run Robin would be critical. That was vital because as a driver you didn't recall what went on behind and he could remember; he was able to tell me where we might have improved. So I'd walk back up the track and try to work out how we could do better. At the same time Robin was keeping himself warm and supple. It was necessary to have complete confidence in the other bloke on and off the track. But the other two team members were also vital. They were there to receive the sled back at the top of the track, get it turned over and make it right for the next heat.

"Damned if I know what makes for a good partnership between a brakeman and a driver. We all got on well together because we all shot and sailed. One of my team had a speedboat, we were always doing something and we met up in London and, by and large, went out with the same girlfriends.

It was the latter days of debs[81] and there were dances to go to where we used to meet each other.

"Some of us were motor racing, some were sailing. People knew one another. You used your nous quite a lot – we'd learnt to take orders. We were friends and you don't really get that so much now in modern bobsleighing; you're put there because you're best, as opposed to being a chum."

Robin gives the background to the pair's camaraderie. "We lived together for weeks, months on end. We'd drive ourselves thousands of miles in that Land Rover with the trailer, moving from track to track, from event to event. We'd share the same hotel room day in, day out, week in, week out."

At five foot seven (170 cms) and weighing 201 lbs (91 kgs), Tony Nash was physically suited to his pilot's role, but his essential aptitude was innate. As he says, "I don't know where my talent for driving came from. The seat of my pants? We were all reasonably fit. We were reasonably coordinated. We had a sense of self-preservation rather than 'spatial awareness'," laughs Tony.

"A lot of the courses at that time were built by hand. They didn't have the sort of nice curves you get on modern-day tracks. There was no sense of conformity between them. You had to drive it more intuitively; you had to improvise more than anything else. You tended to react before something actually happened; impose yourself on the situation rather than just be taken by what was happening. If you wanted to take a bend you pre-empted the outcome before you actually got into the turn. Today they would call that 'visualisation'. But it was more educated guesswork. I always reckon a

---

81 'Debs', or 'débutantes', were young women usually from aristocratic or upper-class families who, having reached the age of maturity (usually 21), were introduced to high society at a formal presentation known as their 'début'. The best connected were presented at 'court' (a formal reception presided over by the sovereign) at the start of the 'social season'.

motorcycle racer would be a first class bobsleigh driver. I never did it – because that was the other thing I promised never to do, ride a motorcycle – but my guess is that motorcycling would be the nearest thing to practising bobsleighing."

XVII

GRENOBLE

The Frenchman Jean-Claude Killy – who managed a grand slam by winning the downhill, giant slalom and special slalom events – and American figure skater Peggy Fleming were destined to be the star names of the 1968 Winter Olympics, who would go down in history. The site for the X Olympic Winter Games had been decided on 28 January 1964, one day before the beginning of the events at Innsbruck. It took three votes to reach the result. Those of the first round of voting were divided in the following way: Grenoble (France) 15, Calgary (Canada) 12, Lahti (Finland) 11, Sapporo (Japan) six, Oslo (Norway) four and Lake Placid (USA) three. The second vote determined the final three places: Calgary 19, Grenoble 18 and Lahti 14. There were 51 members on the International Olympic Committee,[82] and Calgary's narrow lead necessitated that another vote be

82 There are now 205.

taken. This time Grenoble won with 27 votes against Calgary's 24.

Grenoble is the capital of the French Department of Isere and had been the favourite from the beginning. Calgary was only ever an outside chance, but because of the narrow margin it was expected that Canada would host the Games in 1972. (Of course they went to Sapporo, and the Canadians had to wait until 1988 for the Games to be staged in Calgary.) The fact that, four months earlier, the French city of Lyon had competed for the summer Games at a session in Baden-Baden and lost to Mexico City was also a probable factor in the voting.

Grenoble, like Innsbruck, is a university town. But unlike the Tyrolean capital, which had a population of 106,000, Grenoble was decidedly larger, with 185,000 inhabitants. Like Innsbruck, it was also a big tourist area.

The distances from the city to the alpine competitions, located at an altitude of nearly 3,000 metres, would vary between 20 and 45 miles. The distance to the Nordic competitions,[83] which were staged on the hilly plateau of Vercors, was about 30 miles. The same was true for the bobsleigh events. As great as the achievement of hosting the X Olympic Winter Games might have been, the worries about the preparations and the financing started from the point of the award. The President of the Organising Committee for the VII Olympic Winter Games at Cortina d'Ampezzo, Comte Paolo Thaon di Revel, warned about this trend when he said, "We have to avoid being manoeuvred into the distressing position of the sorcerer's apprentice, who was capable of summoning help to carry water with his magic formula, but could not remember the formula which would have made it

83 The Olympic Nordic sports are the biathlon, cross-country skiing, Nordic combined and ski jumping.

possible for him to stop the onrushing flood of excess water."

These words were spoken more than half a century ago. The 'Olympic flood' continues to rise. It will be interesting to watch how the 'sorcerer's apprentice' will cope with the forthcoming winter Games in Vancouver, and then the summer Olympics in London.

In the bobsleighing, Robin Dixon believed that Eugenio Monti was the favourite for the gold medal. For him the Italians had massive technical advantages, while the man from Cortina had ten world champion titles to his credit. Monti's approach was by this time essentially professional but noble, while Dixon and Nash remained, due to factors of opportunity and finance, gallant amateurs, albeit of a thorough and dedicated calibre. One noticeable vacuum was created by the absence of the usual faces (apart from Mike Young) in the Canadian team. As Vic Emery recalls, "With most of my team married and wives resisting, there was no appetite to rebuild and so I went to Grenoble as Canada's *Chef de Mission adjoint* [the assistant to the *Chef de Mission*[84]], a role to which I adjusted uneasily from that of a competitor."

It seems that the Englishmen got into the swing of the Games from the start; according to Tony, "We went to the opening but again I can't remember the closing."

It was understood that the Olympic track would not, by championship standards, be a fast one; Dixon expected to reach speeds close to 130kph – swift enough, one might think, but at some parts of Lake Placid the Brits had hit well over 30kph faster.

Time was catching up with the Nash and Dixon class of

84 The *Chef de Mission*'s primary role is to be a spokesperson and provide overall leadership for an Olympic team, as well as to support and promote the team by creating an on-site environment for athletes and coaches conducive to optimal performance.

athletes. International sport was, in effect, depreciating the human element as technical and design innovations cancelled out much of the innate difference in terms of participants' skill, but if fight and determination meant anything then the Brits would make their presence felt. As Robin put it at the time, "I don't think we ought to make any excuses. We shall do what we can. I'm all for making the odd excuse afterwards, if we're beaten by superior machinery. I'm not convinced that we shall be."

He had boxed and played soccer for Eton, he was more than accomplished on a squash court and knew what it was to win in sport. Indeed, he drew an analogy between bobsleighing and squash: "when you are winning and on top, you have sufficient confidence to try all sorts of refinements which you would otherwise avoid."

Both Dixon and Nash disliked the inclination towards making the sport a set of tests between engineers, with the driver and brakeman becoming minor factors. Robin believed that, if Monti had got his way, everyone would have raced in the same Italian-styled sled, making it a competition of men against men that would draw the best from all. But the world had turned, and 1968 would probably be the last time the Corinthian spirit would truly manifest in the Winter Games.

Compact and strong, Nash, as a driver, fulfilled Dixon's penchant for packing in low above the steering mechanism. Though the precise contribution of the brakeman is hard to measure or define, it was incontrovertible that Tony raced faster when Robin was his tail gunner. All their experiments at St Moritz had confirmed this. Once, in a four-man sled, Dixon wanted to drop out because he was taking such a hammering at the back of the four-man bob. Nash pleaded with him to reconsider, even if it meant occupying the comparatively comfortable and unexacting place of number two. As Tony said: "I don't care where you ride; you've got to ride in the sled, because they [the rest of the crew] can't tell me anything."

Nash was referring to the relationship between the two men, not besmirching the rest of his team – his comment was about communication, and the fact that Dixon knew how to convey the right kind of information to the highly self-critical Nash. After each run they performed an elaborate post-mortem, and the next run was always better informed.

By official French invitation, Dixon, Nash and Monti too had already practised on the course at Alpe d'Huez before 7 February. According to Tony, "They'd got the Olympic venue and they hosted the bobsleighing, so they turned to the Austrians to sort their problems out and help them save face. The Austrians had been experimenting with artificially icing tracks, so Alpe d'Huez became the first run to have artificially iced corners for the Olympic Games, but it was only partially iced.

"From the start it was spoilt for us a bit," confirms Nash, "because we had ordered new sleds but were told by the Italians that they hadn't received our order. So we had to do without and face what was advanced technology with the new articulation. The new sleds had all sorts of improvements. A generous American let us loan his sled but it wasn't what we were expecting to use. The Italians were damn sure they wouldn't give us a new one.

"Alp d'Huez had seen an awful lot of snow; around three or four metres on the hillside where the bob track was situated. There were literally igloos under the snow with the crowd standing on top looking down onto the track! Even a slight breeze blew snow onto the track. At one stage it just filled up. One day we spent 19 hours on the track with all the other teams stuffed into a cramped hut at the top of the run. Tempers became slightly frayed."

Monti had never been better prepared for a big competition. His first Games, now so long ago, had obliged him to compete using an inferior bob, but in Grenoble his Italian team was at the cutting edge of bobsleighing innovation; the new telescopic push bar being just the most obvious accoutrement. According to Zandonella, "We covered the sled. This just made people more curious. Other competitors were inquisitive. There was a cartoon in one of the local newspapers depicting de Paolis and our brakemen encircling our sled with guns to defend our big secrets." The Italian veteran smiles at the memory.

Although having some advantages in terms of equipment, the 40-year-old and his rookie brakeman were not seen as an unbeatable combination. At the time the 25-year-old de Paolis was a pack of nerves. "Before the start I was very conscious that I was representing Italy, a relatively small country. I felt I had to demonstrate to the rest of the world that we could be strong."

The situation was probably not helped by knowing how much Monti wanted to win. "Genio called me 'Romalito', as I came from Rome. He told me, 'Romalito, for a single Olympic gold medal I would give all my other medals.'"

In the two-man event Monti took the early lead, but the fundamentally-flawed track meant that nothing was certain. Defending champion Robin Dixon recalls how the weather was not doing anyone any favours. "We were playing water polo outdoors in the swimming pool, just heated by the sunshine, so it wasn't surprising that there was nothing less than a trout stream coming down the bob run."

In those sloppy conditions, Monti, whose hands would be busy guiding the bob, ordered his relatively inexperienced brakeman to strip off his driver's goggles for him if visibility became an issue. At the time, the young Roman was worried that if he did remove Monti's goggles he might break the older man's concentration and, as a consequence, "everybody would kill me!"

In an attempt to avoid the obvious damage done by the daytime heat, the organisers started the second day of competition before dawn. In the third run Monti and de Paolis were overtaken by the West German pair Pepi Bader and Horst Floth. However, in the last heat Monti piloted the Italian bob to a track record. It seemed that Eugenio's Olympic jinx had been lifted, but fate had robbed him of the outright victory he desired. As Tony Nash explains, "He tied for first place with the Germans; their combined times were equal! But there was a paragraph in the rules that stipulated that in such an event the bob with the quickest individual run would be deemed the winner; Monti had the fastest individual run so he got the gold medal at last."

With the Olympic title going to Italy, Eugenio's 16-year wait was over. "It was incredible at the end of the four rounds," commented Monti, "my sled and the German sled were exactly tied to the 100th of a second – the gold medal would be won by a technicality, the team with the fastest heat in the four rounds. Fortunately, our last round was the fastest round of the two days. It was a glorious moment. I had won my first gold medal."

As Robin Dixon remembers, "We hated losing the title, but the consolation was that Eugenio had won. We knew he was always going to win sometime and we thought it was great. Tony and I were very happy for him."

At the medal ceremony, Monti lightheartedly turned to the Germans to ask if he should step up onto the victor's rostrum. According to de Paolis, he also said, "Why don't they give a gold medal to those poor guys, as we have the same time as them?" (His brakeman replied, "It's okay, better only for us.")

It's a lesser known fact that, during the two-man competition, Monti and his mechanics once more came to the aid of a British bob when GB II, crewed by John Blockey and Mike Freeman, ran into technical problems. Although, unlike Innsbruck, this would not have any potential effect on the race outcome, it was nevertheless another amazingly generous gesture. Having finally achieved his ambition, there was no more popular champion amongst his fellow competitors than Monti.

Although the last Saturday of the Games started out biting cold, by the start of the four-man competition the weather threatened to make the event impossible and it became a two-run affair.

During the pre-Olympic competition the year before Monti had crashed heavily, taking the final bend on his helmet. For a good distance the bob was as good as on top of him. Perhaps with that in mind, the Italian master studied the run more closely than all his rivals combined. Rather than hitch a truck ride back to the top of the course following each practice run, Monti climbed slowly back up to the top alongside the track. Soon, spectators came to recognise the man in the red knitted cap and old scraped lucky blue parka as the greatest figure in bobsleighing. The Italian's surgically refashioned face, camouflaging the map of his experience on the bob tracks, scanned every inch of the ice. Each curve and bump was consigned to memory.

The problematic conditions in Grenoble also meant that many athletes had more time on their hands. Romance also blossomed between a female Olympic volunteer and a competing athlete. This was doubtless not the first time such a thing had happened in Olympic history, but in 1968 the media presence at the Winter Games had never been greater; the eyes of the world were on the French Alps.

The French authorities disapprovingly agreed to expel the volunteer. When this came to the attention of Eugenio Monti, he organised a strike by his fellow bobsleighers. Not one of them broke the line, despite the threat of possible sanctions from their various Olympic Committees. Due to Monti's leadership qualities and chivalry, the bobbers won the day when the volunteer was reinstated; romance had defeated bureaucracy

*   *   *

The Italians' diligence paid off as they beat Austria I by 0.09 of a second. Monti claimed a second gold, the only non-German to claim the bobsleigh 'double' at any single Olympic Games. After his victory, he received Italy's highest civilian honour – *Commendatore* of the Italian Republic.

It is perhaps a shame that only a relatively few sportspeople finish their competitive life at the peak of their endeavours. In any decade a mere handful will walk away at the pinnacle of their achievement, as with Monti's grand finale.

Roberto Zandonella tells how, "As the national anthem started at the Olympics, a shiver ran down my spine . . . now when I hear it I get this great feeling, knowing I've been part of the life of someone who was at the highest level of achievement, who was responsible for some extraordinary historical events."

After his double-gold triumph, Monti confessed, "I was going to quit. The only reason I came back into competition two years ago was to get the thing I wanted most, an Olympic gold medal. Now I can stop. At 40 it is too old for the bob."

After the Games, the chief Olympic press officer, Paul Blanc, told the world, "The organisation of the Olympics, the time, planning and money that goes into them, is much bigger than the actual event. The thing has grown all out of size. It is no longer possible to do it on the intimate, less-troubled, carefree Squaw Valley scale. Those days will never return.

"But if we had it to do all over again, I suppose we would do everything the same. Except that we would never put that bobsled run at Alpe d'Huez. I don't know where, but not there."

Of course, the Games would continue to grow. The 2006 Olympics would make 1968 look like a ski party. Back then, however, Robin Dixon had no regrets about the decision to carry on with his sport after Innsbruck.

"We continued to have a lot of fun. It was great in 1965 and 1966. And while 1967 was a downer, we didn't do badly in 1968, getting into the first half dozen; we were fifth and we had a reasonable result in the four-man."[85]

But, of course, there were other distractions, as Tony Nash acknowledges. "Serious sport has changed a great deal. When we were at Lake Placid, when we weren't involved in competition, people used to call out your name, get to know you and have a chat.

"In those days it was our money we were spending and St Moritz was St Moritz. So we could only afford to eat as cheaply as possible. But we were a good gang, which meant we had loads of fun. We would go down to the station as you could get a cheap meal there, and all the girls would come down. The party would start from there," Tony laughs.

"Monti was incredibly lucky, but the Games of 1968 were something of a disaster for us. We had intended to pack it in after the previous Olympics, but with the sponsorship from Wills tobacco and one or two others we decided to carry on to Grenoble."

85 GBI was eighth in a field of 19, the mere 1.45 seconds between them and the winning Italians being a fair way in bobsleighing terms – but if they had gone 0.81 of a second faster over the four heats they would have been on the podium.

Before the competition started, Nash and Dixon had decided that – after defending their title at Alpe d'Huez, which at points had been a nigh-on impossible, potentially fatal run – they would retire from bobsleighing. Nash was 31; Dixon was a year older, having recently taken a job as public relations officer at Kodak and admitting that racing was harming his career. They had tried to lay the ground for the future, not only in terms of trying to produce a British bobsleigh but in attempting to build the foundations for the sport to become a national tradition.

Tony recalls, "We used some of the sponsorship money to sort something out to get young people out to St Moritz and introduce them to the sport, but it didn't work out."

Reflecting on Nash and Dixon's move away from the sport, Vic Emery says, "All credit to Tony and Robin for continuing to race against the odds through 1968. In the same way that we felt our 1965 victories were a bit empty without Monti and Zardini, I am sure Monti would have felt similarly had both of our teams retired." Looking back on how they upheld the story of Monti contributing his bolt, Emery reflects, "Certainly, their marvellous tit for tat gesture honoured the greatest bobsledder of our era."

With the retirement of Tony Nash, Robin Dixon and Eugenio Monti, and Britain's failure to either produce a bobsleigh or a pair to emulate Nash and Dixon, it was clearly the end of an era.

XVIII

REMEMBER EUGENIO

There can be few sensations that compare with riding a bobsleigh down a fast, demanding run, navigating its towering walls of whiteness, its psychotic maze of twists and turns. Over a fortnight in March 1969, men from all over the world came together once more to determine who the sport's champions were at Lake Placid, upstate New York, whose run was to prove itself the fastest in the world. The course that wound down Mount Van Hoevenberg – with its three major curves, each with a little sister – took participants through a drop of 165 metres over its one full mile, at an average gradient of 10.2 degrees. This was a demanding run.

The track had been improved in recent years, the latest modification being an extended push-off area so that competitors were able to get a good sprint behind their sleds at the off. The old course's two-man record had been 1.08.84; for the four-man it had stood at 1.06.92. Times like these would became commonplace during the practice sessions alone in 1969, suggesting the most open championship for years.

For four years the World Championship had been plagued with problems. The weather had intervened in 1966, 1967 and 1968, and a whole four-run championship had not taken place since 1965 at St. Moritz. However, in 1969, in the Adirondack High Peaks, conditions were cold enough for the men of 13 nations who had come to try their skill and courage under the gaze of Whiteface Mountain. The Italians came as the European four-man titleholders, with their coach, Eugenio Monti, complaining of how coaching was 'terrible' and telling how he really wanted to get on a sled himself. "It is easy to ride the sled down," he declared. "Anyone can do that. It is not so easy to ride it down and win."

The two-man competition quickly demonstrated the demands that the course would make of the competitors. As a Japanese bob flew high into a curve, the brakeman's helmet struck the guardrail so hard he was immediately knocked unconscious. The pair slammed through a fence, devastating their sled while breaking bones and collecting bruises.

At the conclusion of the first day of the two-man competition, America were leading the field. However, the US ended up in fourth place behind the Italians, Gianfranco Gaspari and Mario Armano. The tough Romanians clinched the silver medal, leaving Nevio de Sordo and Adriano Frassinelli to take the championship home to Italy. Armano, the winning pair's brakeman, shrugged slightly as he commented, "We are to bobsledding what the USA is to basketball."

In the four-man practice, the US driver, retired Air Force jet pilot Les Fenner, had a bad crash, but their next run produced an all-time record for the course of 1.04.00. At the end of the first day, Fenner and his fellow Americans were in pole position, their two runs providing a total time of

2.10.50. The Swiss, who also experienced a major shunt during practice, were close on their tail with 2.10.69. Fred Fortune's USAII shared third place with the Germans, just in front of the Italians.

The morning of the second day (a Sunday) saw 7,000 spectators lining the run to witness one of the finest bobsleigh competitions in years. The Swiss produced a 1.04.73 third run which Fenner (at 1.05.36) could not match. But the Germans seemed to rise to the challenge and sped home in 1.04.76, their best time of the competition. It was then the turn of the Italians, Gaspari, Sergio Pompanin, Zandonella and Armano. They crossed the finishing line in 1.04.62, setting up a dramatic final heat As the Swiss pilot, Jean Wicki, commented, "We are leading with 3.15.42, but not by much . . ."

With less than a quarter of the course left to run, the Swiss looked like champions. They thundered through 'Shady', a lethal shovel of a turn, setting up their attack on 'Zig-Zag', which they hit full on. Suddenly the bob was on its side and the crew could do no more than hang on, perhaps offering up a short prayer. After Wicki (who'd sustained a broken rib), his crew and the Swiss sled were pulled out of the chute, the pilot explained that he'd stuck a runnel. " . . . For a few seconds I still thought I could get it upright again." But with the sled's cowling shattered, suspension smashed and runner detached, Wicki admitted, "that was the end – we were out of it."

The Italians soared down in a majestic 1.05.59. The American answer was a nail-biting 1.05.58. But the stoic Germans did even better – 1.05.13 brought Wolfgang Zimmerer victory.[86] Monti's Italy were runners-up[87] and the

86 With an aggregate time of 4.20.7.

87 4.21.20.

US bob took the bronze.[88] Wicki confessed that his crew, although knowing the Germans were in third place going into the final run, had neglected to watch Zimmerer's team. "We were just looking for the Italians."

The 47-year old veteran Fred Fortune, who had piloted the USA into fourth place, mused on how bobsleighing was a 'tough game' and that an initial mistake might mean the loss of a championship. "It is as easy as that. Trouble is, you're going so damn fast you're not sure where you made the mistake."

Lake Placid in 1969 marked the end of Monti's involvement with bobsleigh competition. But Eugenio could hardly be said to have retired after he left the sport. He turned his energies to developing his ski business and started a family. According to Marino Zardini, they changed the name of their ski-lift from 'Monti-Zardini' to 'Olympia' and emblazoned the Olympic rings on the hoarding above the foot of the ski-lift.

After his time in bobsleighing, Monti continued to live in Cortina. He married his American girlfriend, Linda, and they had two children. He left his sport with a glowing reputation as a respected and well-liked character. Tony Nash's opinion of him was typical, seeing Eugenio as, "A frightfully excellent chap; marvellous guy! He was just a lovely mountain man. He had spent all his life in the mountains. He was a world class skier who, after a huge setback, came back to be the best at what he did."

Monti's skill, experience and sportsmanship made him the obvious choice to become Italian team manager after his retirement in 1968. Apart from his achievements as an Olympian, between 1956 and 1968 he had won 11 world

88 4.21.44.

titles, together with three silver and two bronze World Championship medals.

However, in the long term his health was not to hold. As Robin Dixon notes, "Sadly, he developed Parkinson's, and after a while his wife left him."

According to Monti's daughter, Amanda, it was extremely hard for an active and independent person like her father to find himself unable to do what he wanted. Rather than assisting others, as had been his lifelong habit, he was suddenly obliged to ask others for help.

Following the couple's divorce, Linda returned to America with Amanda in 1993. Their son stayed with his father, but, three years later, 23 year-old Alec, who had a long-term problem with substance abuse and depression, died of an overdose. On 24 February 1996 he was found dead in a hotel in Auronzo, 120 kms north of Venice.

The men who had helped Nash and Dixon shape the future of their Winter Olympic sport were gradually being taken by time and history. Hubert Martineau died in Westminster on 11 September 1976, aged 85; Franz Kemser passed away in 1986, at 75. Following a serious racing accident at Aintree, Henry Taylor was invited to join Ford's works rallying team.[89] His later life experience has some parallels with Monti's, according to Tony Nash. "Henry Taylor lives in the south of France. He's got Alzheimer's now. He's never been right since his accident. So he went down there – he was very successful, he started looking after people's motorboats in the south of France. About three miles inland he stacked them up, kept

---

89 Taylor became Ford-UK's competitions manager in 1965. Under his auspices Lotus-Cortina became a winning rally car, with great names like Roger Clark, Bengt Soderstrom and Ove Andersson joining the team. When Ford's Advanced Vehicle Operations (AVO) was set up in 1969, Taylor took charge of their various high-performance engine programmes. Finally, he left Ford in the early 1970's to run a thriving boatyard on the French Riviera.

them for the winter in an old barn or something. He could do that very cheaply." But his twilight years would not end nearly as tragically as the great Italian maestro of the chutes. For on the morning of 30 November 2003, Eugenio Monti shot himself in the temple with a revolver and died the next day at Belluno, aged 75.

According to Marino Zardini, his friend, alone and helpless, could go on no longer. This was not for lack of courage, "but because he no longer had the will to live like that."

Amanda believes that her dad and his compatriots in bobsleighing had shared something special. As Robin Dixon says of his friend, "Despite Monti's idiosyncrasies he was always loved. He was always there for people. He was brilliant at what he did. He's a legend and he'll remain a legend."

Eugenio Monti's name endures as a celebration of what it means to be an Olympic hero – an epithet all too often misused to mark out an athlete who has done no more than win an event. His supreme conviviality and humanity overrode the competition and rivalry. He had no use of gain that he didn't earn; he didn't want to just sit at the top of the heap, getting there by hook or by crook, but to be unquestionably *the best* in what he did, without taking advantage of any temporary handicaps. Instead, he sought to help stricken rivals in whatever way he could, in his own words, "So that if I won, I won fairly."

The bobsleigh track that Monti competed on for years in Cortina was renamed in his honour, following his 2003 death. Turn 19 at Cesana Pariol, the site of the 2006 Winter Olympic bobsleighing, luge and skeleton[90] competitions in Turin, is

90 'Skeleton' involves hurtling headfirst down an ice track at something close to 130kph on a piece of metal half the length of your body. It is a fast-moving sliding sport during which athletes experience forces up to, but not exceeding, 5Gs (the FIBT's imposed limit). Sliders ('skeletoneers') are not allowed any steering or braking mechanisms – steering is managed by

now *Rosso Volante* – 'flying red', the nickname he was known by in Italy

Monti was the motivation and inspiration behind Italy's successes in bobsleighing and the sport's greatest exponent. His spirit endures today and continues to inform the sport. No one in the long history of this difficult and dangerous pursuit has so much exemplified the ideals of true sportsmanship by combining fierce competitiveness with an overriding passion for fair play; Eugenio personifies the glory and humane spirit of the Olympian ideal.

He is buried at the centre of his beloved mountain village of Cortina, the alpine paradise where he raised his family.

Eugenio Monti, his crews and his peers formed a long-gone brotherhood of ice and steel, which made a habit of cheating death. He remains alive in the memories of those he touched, like Marino Zardini, who witnessed his friend's resolute work ethic, Tony Nash, who knew his amazing generosity, and Robin Dixon, who asked him for help at a time of crisis because he understood precisely how Eugenio would answer. Vic Emery, Canadian entrepreneur and adventurer, has spoken of his debt to the man. And of course there was brakeman Sergio,[91] Monti's mechanic, who never left Cortina or Eugenio's side.

Monti's actions at the 1964 Olympics continue to resonate today, perhaps because we need his example so badly. We live in a time of winner-takes-all, an era of infighting even between team-mates. It seems competition has literally become all-

slight shifts of the athlete's body on the sled and by dragging the feet. The sport originated as a spin-off from the popular British sport of Cresta sledding in St Moritz. While sliders use similar equipment to Cresta riders, the two sports are different; skeleton shares a track with bobsleighers and lugers, while Cresta sledding can use only Cresta tracks and riders wear skates on their feet to help steer or brake the sled.

91 After his bobsleigh career, Sergio became an instructor with Ski Cortina.

against-all and notions of fairness or justice have more or less died. Sportsmen and women often appear to be willing to cheat by way of drugs, faking injury, conning referees or falsely incriminating their colleagues to the extent of expulsion; victory must be had seemingly at any cost, even human integrity.

In such a sick milieu, we need reminders of the noble potential of sport as embodied in Eugenio Monti. The code by which he lived his sporting life is now hard even to imagine; it is difficult to envisage a modern athlete supplying a close rival with the equipment that might grant them the power to win. Strangely, by modern standards, it was his willingness to lose that has earned Monti a prominent place in Olympic history.

At the World Championships in Koenigssee, Germany, in 2004, the International Bobsleigh and Skeleton Federation, FIBT, honoured the memory of Eugenio Monti. For the diminutive Italian was one of the most successful sportsmen ever to take to the ice. When you watch the next international footballer fall to the ground, holding his face in feigned agony as the ball brushes his left thigh, please remember Eugenio.

EUGENIO MONTI'S RECORD

Olympics
Gold medal in the two-man, 1968.
Gold medal in the four-man, 1968.
Silver medal in the two-man, 1956.
Silver medal in the four-man, 1956.
Bronze medal in the two-man, 1964.
Bronze medal in the four-man, 1964.

FIBT World Championships

Gold medal in the two-man, 1957, 1958, 1959, 1960, 1961, 1963 and 1966.
Gold medal in the four-man, 1960 and 1961.
Silver medal in the four-man, 1957.

XIX

'WITH GLOWING HEARTS WE SEE THEE RISE . . .'[92]

The original Canadian Olympic team of the Emery brothers, Douglas Anakin and Peter Kirby retired from competition in 1967. Vic returned to the business world in Canada. As Tony Nash says of his former Canadian rivals and now valued friends, "John Emery is a plastic surgeon. Vic comes over quite a lot – he was married first to the daughter of a big shareholder in the Savoy. She was very, very beautiful – he pinched her off of another bobsleigher. He was employed by the Savoy in some capacity but it didn't seem to tax him too much. He moves around. He's up to everything. He pops up from time to time."

All of the Innsbruck four-man gold medallists have lived extraordinary lives. In 1964 they were awarded places in the Canadian Sports Hall of Fame; the Canadian Olympic Hall of Fame came six years later.

92 From 'O Canada' – the Canadian national anthem.

Peter Kirby still lives in Quebec. A geologist and businessman, he retired to the place where he grew up near the famed Mont Tremblant Ski Resort.

John Emery became a leading plastic surgeon and now operates out of the Emery Medical Center in Sonoma, California. He has also launched his own range of wines from his ranch in Sonoma. For many years he remained an active athlete; he and his brother Vic ran the Boston Marathon together in 1979 in just over three hours, and the next year John competed in the world's first Iron-Man Triathlon in Hawaii.

After the Olympics, Doug Anakin continued bobsleighing through to the World Championships in 1966, after which he promoted luging both as a coach and as a track designer. Doug looked after a group of Canadian athletes at the 1972 Olympics in Munich, and coached the Canadian luge team at the Winter Olympics in Sapporo, Japan, that same year.

During his 35 years of teaching, Doug taught and coached for 19 years at John Abbott College in Montreal before retiring in 1990. He had also for a while owned a sporting goods store. In recognition of his service to the school, his commitment to his community and his passion for outdoor activities, the school established the Doug Anakin Scholarship for Outdoor Pursuits, which is presented annually to a student who best demonstrates the dignity and determination that Doug has embodied.

Today, Doug is retired and living in Windermere, British Columbia with his wife Mary Jean, a Nova Scotian, whom he met in Montreal and married in 1964. They have two daughters, both schoolteachers, and four grandchildren who share their grandparents' love of snow, water and hiking trails. Doug has also been inducted into Chatham's Sports Hall of Fame.

In the spring of 2005, Vic Emery wrote a journal for the

website www.whitenightsride.org.uk, when he and seven others motorbiked over 120,000 kms across Russia in support of that country's Charities Aid Foundation for the underprivileged, equipped with 1150cc BMW off-road touring bikes and an X-3 Chase car.

Always an adventurer, in his 77th year Vic remains an avid cross-country skier (in the top five in his age group in the World Masters). He divides his time between London and Oslo. In his working life he has been involved in a diverse and fascinating business career, occasionally involved in commentating on Canadian and US television for bobsleighing and cross-country skiing competitions.

The Canadians of the 1960's were trailblazers for bobsleighing in their country and created a legacy on which the future was to build. Without those early years, culminating in the successes of 1964 and 1965, it is doubtful if Canada would have become the bobsledding power it is, let alone be competing in the sport at all.

After the mid-1960s, Canada had a difficult time competing in bobsleigh competitions as skill levels rose and the design of bobs developed. At the same time the competitive season grew longer, making it hard for strictly amateur competitors to make headway in the sport. Without appropriate practice facilities, Canadian athletes suffered. The bobsleigh track from the 1988 Calgary Games would finally provide Canadian athletes with a means to become competitive and pave the way for nearly 20 years of success from the early 1990's.

All this started with the team of 1964; without them, it is doubtful Canada would have become the power in winter sports that it is.

XX

"TONY DOESN'T LISTEN TO THE ANSWER PHONE"

In their individual ways, Nash and Dixon remained of great value to British bobsleighing, passing on the benefit of their experience to others in the sport. Tony went on to be a powerful influence on its resurgence, not only inspiring others with his steering skill but also as a keen brain behind national technical developments in the sport he loved. Robin has been a constant in the sport in terms of its organisation and development at national and international levels. Together, the two men's contributions are immeasurable. But at the same time, both Robin and Tony are aware of how much they gained from the sport.

In 2009, Tony Nash says, "We were very fortunate to have achieved what we did at that time. We are getting long in the tooth and everybody turns round and says, 'Well of course, it's not like it was in my day' – but, taking it relatively, I think we would still be competitive. The current generation are probably more athletic than we were – we were 'Corinthian'," he laughs self-effacingly. "But we went out and we were competitive and we won and we were British!

"The whole ball park has changed so much – the modern public wants to see the best in the world. I know I do. I know nothing about golf whatsoever, but I'll sit down and watch Tiger Woods and think, 'That all looks pretty easy, I'd better go out and have a crack!' That's what people want to watch, the best doing their best, and now athletes get money for every sport."

After their retirement in 1968, that same year, they were each awarded the MBE. Tony recalls the award ceremony at Buckingham Palace. "We were doing a rehearsal with one of the equerries, and of course Robin, being in the Guards, knew the equerry and this chap said, 'Go in and you turn left,' and so on; Robin went in and got it wrong by what's called the 'Guard's standard'.[93] The equerry hooted with laughter."

In 1966 Tony married his first wife, Sue, a skier in the British 'B' team, and after he gave up competition he decided to change direction. "Just after we finished bobsleighing we came down to Devon and bought a farm." Tony and Sue's daughter, Annabel, was born in 1969 and son James came along two years later. Annabel now has two children, a girl and a boy; James has got two girls and a boy. "Annabel is involved in carriage driving with a company that puts on the Windsor Horse Show – just done Olympia in London." She also came close to selection for the luge for the 1992 Winter Olympics in Albertville. However, as her father explains, "It was decided that Britain would enter two men for the luge instead. It was disappointing for her, although she still did help cover the Olympics from Paris for Sky television."

93 The guard's standard is a particular style of deportment within official ceremonial contexts.

After inheriting his uncle's engineering company,[94] Tony sold it in 1982. Seven years later, his first marriage ended. But he has remained active and connected with life, now living in the West Country.

"I had a little business down here in Devon and put James into it, but he really didn't like it – he's done up a house or two. I've got a timber yard the other side of Tiverton which I've had since 1989 – it's been very successful, but God knows what this year's going to bring. I know very little about it, but it's well managed.

"I met Pam three or four weeks after my ex departed – she is a former BA air hostess. Her sister met me at a wedding, she said, 'My sister has just come back into Somerset with a divorce – you'd better meet her.' That was that. We married in 1992 and as soon as we got married we sort of retired. We went to New Zealand, where we fell in with all the family[95] on honeymoon – £34 return!" Tony exclaims playfully. "I sold the farm and was half-thinking of moving to New Zealand and setting up down there, but I love England – I don't think I could have stayed down there. Everything I love is back here.

"But ex-wife and bank manager didn't add up, so moved to present location in 1996."[96]

The Olympian pilot has literally returned to his roots, revelling in the rural idyll. "I loved farming when I first came down here – I'm much more a hands-on sort of person than a committee man. I've left that to Robin and he's very good at it."

For all this, Tony continues to take an interest in sport. However, he'd "rather watch paint dry" than be a spectator

94 Amongst other things, the company made valves and cigarette machines.

95 Tony has extensive family in New Zealand, including some Maori connections.

96 The Nash home is a large, traditional rural house with stables and a big garden in Devon.

to his wife Pam's achievements in the world dressage (she is an accomplished exponent of this discipline), even though she warned him before they married that he'd have to marry both her and her horse. But Tony continues to apply the Corinthian ethics he was weaned on as a competitor.

"My little timber firm [Pennymoor Timber] supports young people rather than old people within a ten-mile radius – it's logical to support the young farmers because of my connections with hunting. I support the pony club and we paid for the under-12 football club kit. They asked me where I wanted the company name on their shirts, I said, 'You're not going to put a company name on a child's shirt, that's awful.' That's taking commercialism to the extreme. I'm not going to do that with a 12-year-old!"

Robin and Tony are still in touch. In fact, according to Pam, her husband and his former brakeman are "like brothers".

"I still meet up with Robin, but I've given up shooting now, which is where we used to meet quite a lot at various venues. Now I just pick up the dogs behind, so these days I've lost the 'infighting' – who's doing what to whom and so on and who's died – I now hear it all a bit second-hand. I haven't shot for four or five years now – just pick up.

"Robin is still President of the Bobsleigh Association. We went back to St Moritz on the 50th anniversary of us meeting up. We are very close – Robin likes the public scene, he loves being in the organising world, but there's nothing I would hate more! I know quite a lot about nature and that's what I love. I love birds and I love fishing, I was master of fox hounds down here for ten years and I loved that. I'd much sooner go out and mess about in the garden."[97]

Tony has managed to keep in touch with the Olympic

---

[97] Tony has cultivated about two acres of his arboretum, turning it into a little paradise.

Games. He was asked to be *Chef de Mission* for the 1976 Winter Olympics[98] and recalls being advised to "watch the skating mothers". This protective and ambitious contingent would apparently stop at nothing in their attempts to get into the Olympic Village and stay as close to their offspring as possible. This was apparently an issue at both the 1964 and 1968 Games. "You had to be pretty careful with all those determined 35-to-45-year-old women ready to literally do anything to get in," Tony laughs. He also attended the Winter Olympics in 2002, at Salt Lake City. "I went there because a film about Monti was being made, and they wanted to do interviews with those who knew him. It was intended to be shown at the Turin Winter Olympics of 2006. I was just amazed at the amount of back-up the various teams had: physios, psychologists and sports scientists were all over the place!" Robin also arranged for Tony to attend to the British championships in 2008.

Asked if there was anything he'd change in his life, Tony says, "Not now! There are lots of things I wish to God I had done when I was younger. A considerable number of women!" he laughs. "It's all lovely in hindsight. What you know now you wish to God you'd have known when you were 18 or 19. I've made a complete arse of myself at times. Certainly joining Lloyd's was a disaster area, which I did when I sold the farm and lost a load of money that really put me back on my heels.[99] I would have loved to have had a bit more money to buy old cars. I love old cars. But I'm too old and fat to get under the damn things now! But I'm reasonably satisfied."

98 He was obliged to withdraw from the role upon being stricken by jaundice prior to the Games.

99 Lloyd's of London were embroiled in a huge investment scandal in the late 1980's, hitting those who had invested as 'names'. Many sports stars – including former British and European heavyweight boxing champion Henry Cooper – were badly hit, seeing much of the wealth they had accumulated during their careers disappear almost overnight.

Tony, who isn't a great fan of "the mindless stuff on television", is now an enthusiastic stamp collector/dealer and seems surprised that his fame as an Olympian lives on. He laughs as he shares what he sees as an amusing, almost magical anecdote. "A few years ago I got a postcard from the organisers of a bobsleighing event in Canada. It was addressed to 'Tony Nash, Olympic Gold Medallist, England' and it got to me!"

Dixon and Nash were nearly emulated at the Nagano Games in 1998, when Corporals Dean Ward and Sean Olsson of the Parachute Regiment (2 Para), along with Courtney Rumbolt and Paul Attwood, comprised the bronze medal four-man bob team.

Robin Dixon points out that, since he and Tony brought home the gold medal, "The services have taken it up in a big way. Recent Olympics have seen servicemen in first place overnight, and if you are first place halfway through you are right up there. There has been quite a history of bobbers from the services or ex-services that have been front-runners."

However, it's been the women who have led the way in the 21st century, with Nicole Minichiello and Jackie Davies gaining silver in 2005 and, in 2009, Minichiello striking gold with Gillian Cooke. For all this, Nash and Dixon remain the historic pinnacle of British bobsleighing. Perhaps this was partly the consequence of the way Tony and Robin organised themselves and their team; this appears to be Robin's underlying sentiment when he reflects on the way some of the current crews are brought together.

"The way military teams are organised now certainly wouldn't have suited us – they have a pool of brakemen and a pool of drivers and they have people that tell them what to do, when to do it and where to go . . . I don't think I would have wanted to be involved with that. We were very competitive, that was part of our personalities, but we played it straight and we made a lot of good friends."

Asked how he would want the sporting world to remember him, Tony Nash replies, "I'd like to be thought of as somebody who was a great competitor who was lucky enough to be in the right place at the right time on the right day."

The camaraderie between Nash and Dixon endures. Both have many stories about the times they spent in one another's company since their days on the icy runs of the world.

"I went to Cork to meet Robin to sail in a boat that had been brought back from Spain. We were going to go off round the south of Ireland together – stayed in the Royal Cork Yacht Club, formed 1721, oldest in the world – we got out of Cork and Robin said, 'There's something wrong here – well, I've never seen a noble lord bail so quickly in my life,'" laughs Tony. "We had water up to our ears! We put in to Kinsail – suitably it was May Day, the boat hadn't been sorted after his trip all the way from Spain, so that was the end of my trip – I came home. I haven't seen the south of Ireland yet; he's got another boat and was going round Scotland last year.

"Robin's a lovely fellow and I get along with him. When we were out in Switzerland he used to have various girlfriends and we always used to get him out of bother – he didn't know how to leave them. 'Darling I love you!'" Tony smiles wistfully at the memory.

Tony Nash continues to enjoy sailing, but insists he has no wish anymore to travel far. However, in 2009 he appears to still have a remarkable energy and a zest for life.

"I don't know where the energy comes from. I think it's all gone now," he laughs again. "I've never driven fast cars but I've had one or two old cars; we've taken them on the occasional beer rally around Europe and had some fun. I have a great gang of chums that I've known since coming down here. I see the bobsleighing friends and the guys I sort of grew up with or partied with now and again."

It seems that the one-time bobsleigh pilot has a life in which he can still fulfil his passions; as Robin says, "Tony doesn't listen to the answer phone." In a world which continually draws us towards the wants and demands of somebody else, pushing us away from our own enthusiasms, heartfelt wishes and personal interests, it seems Tony Nash has a strategy for the defence of self.

XXI

"MY LIFE IS FULL OF ACCIDENTS"

Robin Dixon returned from the Olympics to undertake three and a half years active service in the Far East, as part of the SAS 'G' Squadron and as a company commander in Germany. Finding it increasingly difficult to maintain control over his career path, he decided it was time to move on.

"I asked if I could be second in command of 'G' Squadron, which meant going down from a major to a captain, but I was only a temporary major anyway. I was told, 'It's time for you to do some proper soldiering,' which meant wearing a pink coat and marching on and off guard at Buckingham Palace. I put in my resignation and six months later I was out."

In comparison to army life, London seemed "pretty dull". But then Robin met the managing director of Kodak, "who was both a sailing man and a skier", while staying in the same hotel at St Moritz. As Robin tells it, "He hired me as his PR guy."

But Robin "got fed up with Kodak, and my parents thought if I wanted to come home and contribute there, which

261

they thought I should, then that was the time to do it. So I set about trying to get a job."

In 1971 Robin joined the Northern Irish business Redland Tile and Brick Ltd. He was to build it up into a multimillion pound subsidiary and become managing director. "Like so many times in my life, I ran into a friend, this time at a party. He was head of the brick division in Redlands and he said they were looking for someone to run operations in Northern Ireland.

"It was only a small business at that time. I just wanted to do things and to make things happen. I wanted to grow the business or leave. But after a while I didn't really want to leave. I wanted to stay in Ireland and the way to stay in Ireland was to persuade those in the boardroom to let me spend money and get on and use it properly, which I think I did very well."

According to Robin, "Business and sports success are linked into the type of person that you are. But what I think I am is probably not what other people think I am. I've always been very competitive. I'm a loner, not a total loner, not reclusive, but I like small teams of one or two other people. I have been a maverick, kicked over the traces, but I'm not a maverick by nature – although I can be if the situation gets to me to that extent. I like to win and I don't care too much how.

"That probably comes from my father's mother.[100] She was an international hockey player for Ireland. She was also a good golf and tennis player. She was a very competitive woman and taught me as a child to play golf and tennis. The Bingham family goes back to the Charge of the Light Brigade and all that. [Though] I don't think my father was a very good competitor and my mother wasn't bothered about it really."

In terms of why he moved from being an active sportsman to the organisational side of things, "I went into

---

100 Hon. Emily Ina Florence Bingham.

administration because I got a bit angry during the mess-ups at the 1968 Olympics; the jury couldn't make up their mind what to do. I was telling them what to do while still a competitor! I become a vice-president of the international association in 1968."

Robin continued to develop his sporting connections and was President of the Jury at the 1976 Winter Olympics, set up the Ulster Games Foundation in 1983, was appointed Chair of the Northern Ireland Tall Ships Council in 1987 and has been President of the British Bobsleigh Association since that same year. He has given support to the Irish Lighthouse Service and the British Field Sports Society and is a member of the Countryside Alliance.

Robin's family seat is in County Antrim, but he is descended from generations of Belfast businessmen. His family has been at the heart of Unionism since Irish partition in 1921. Upon the death of his father, the second Baron Glentoran, Dixon inherited his title and retired from business in 1998. The Right Honourable (Thomas) Robin Valerian Baron Glentoran (Lord Glentoran) is an extremely committed parliamentarian and was active in London's successful bid to host the Olympic Games.

As he says, "My life is full of accidents and it was another accident that got me into politics. When my father died and I inherited his title, I started to serve in the House of Lords. Margaret [whom he married in January 1990] was very keen that I had a responsibility and that I should do it. I enjoy it. I started when [the Conservatives] were in power during 1996 and then we went into opposition.

"By that time I was speaking in the Northern Ireland debates. One day I was sitting on the back benches and I was furious with our party – they'd got it all wrong and I divided the house. But our front bench decided that they were going to abstain. I lost the first division by nine and the second one by 12. I was absolutely furious. Particularly with my own front bench who, if they had voted with me, would have beat the government twice over.

"A month or so later I was having tea with Patricia Janet Scotland.[101] I told her, 'Patricia, I have to go and see my leader. I've been sent for to be carpeted.' She laughed and said, 'Robin, you're not going to be carpeted. They're just going to ask you to join the front bench and take the Northern Ireland portfolio.' And she was right! I've done it for over 11 years now. Once you've got into Northern Ireland politics, you get taken with it and build a team round you, people you can rely on."

Robin has three sons from his first marriage,[102] "Danny,[103] who was diagnosed as diabetic at the age of 16, was a beautiful athlete – he keeps fit. Works for the private and commercial bank Coutts, pretty near the top, number two. Andrew,[104] he's a headhunter – not sure what else he does – he's got a fulltime job at the moment running some company. Married to Karen Dixon MBE.[105] Patrick,[106] he does nothing, he's married to a stockbroker – they were all sportsmen in their own way but they were never competitive."

When Karen Straker first met Andrew Dixon she had no idea that his father was an Olympic champion. It was not until she visited the family estate in Ireland that she was

101 Baroness Scotland of Asthal, current Attorney General for England and Wales and Northern Ireland.

102 He and Rona Alice Gabrielle Colville were divorced in 1975.

103 Hon. Daniel George Dixon, born 26 July 1959.

104 Hon. Andrew Wynne Valerian Dixon, born 22 January 1961.

105 One of the world's leading three-day event riders. Having first represented her country at the age of 17, Karen has gone on to win medals at all levels. These include a team silver at the Seoul Olympics, team gold and individual bronze at the World Championships in Holland.

106 Hon. Patrick Dixon, born 3 April 1963.

nonchalantly shown the gold medal. She had won a silver medal in her first Olympic three-day event in 1988 at Seoul, alongside team-mates Ian Stark, Mark Phillips and Virginia Leng. Karen went on to represent Great Britain in Olympic three-day eventing in 1992 (Barcelona), 1996 (Atlanta) and 2000 (Sydney). Now the mother of Tara, seven, and ten-year-old Rory, Karen trains and sells horses in County Durham. She also still rides every morning.

Robin Dixon married for a second time in January 1979, but after almost exactly nine years he and Alwyn Mason were divorced. Altogether he has five grandchildren and a tremendous zest for life; he says his energy "comes from in here [he points to his head] but I can be lazy too."

His sporting activities are now confined mainly to golf. He once complained that a downside of the Troubles in his native Northern Ireland was that, "Golfers were driven out by the IRA."[107] But overall Robin seems fulfilled and appreciative of the richness of his life.

"I wouldn't change anything about my life. I've been unbelievably lucky. From where I came from, the things I've been able to do and the experiences I've had. Being a member of the Millennium Commission has allowed me to really get to know communities all over the country for 12 years. It is really phenomenal how many good and really committed people there are out there who have nothing – maybe with a child or two, maybe with a husband or not – doing things for their communities and trying to have an influence. Phenomenal! Wonderful people, all over the country, hundreds and thousands of them!

"I was particularly keen to sort the British Bobsleigh

107 Although the likes of Darren Clarke, David Feherty, Michael Hoey, Graeme McDowell, Rory McIlroy, Gareth Maybin, Graeme McDowell and Rohan Rafferty might question this opinion.

Association out. I took that on quite lightheartedly but I've spent an hour or two on it every single day since I started. The International Olympic Committee insisted that the bobsleigh and skeleton had to be represented as one organisation if they wanted to stay in the Olympic fold. UK Sport[108] had said they were not fit for purpose. The two separate associations could not agree on anything. I used my contacts within sport but had no idea what I was taking on. For 2010 I want to go as the President of the British Bobsleigh and Skeleton Association, with two competent teams for each of the disciplines and a good set of athletes."

After meeting Robin a couple of times, you get the sense that his work is a great energiser. His long CV stands as testament to his public service since entering the Lords:[109] Chair of Positively Belfast from 1992 to 1996, Chair of the Growing a Green Economy Committee from 1993 to 1995; Robin has been Shadow Minister for Northern Ireland, Shadow Minister for Sport, Shadow Minister for the Olympics and Shadow Minister for the Environment, Food and Rural Affairs. He is also a member of the British-Irish Parliamentary Body, was awarded a CBE in 1993 for his services to Northern Ireland and Industry and took over as the Tory spokesman for Wales in 2007. Looking back on his time as a parliamentarian, he says, "The good thing about the Lords is that you meet and work with such a wide range of people from so many different backgrounds and they get on and work together: union men and company directors, all great experts in their respective fields."

108 UK Sport is responsible for managing and distributing public investment. It is a statutory distributor of funds raised by the National Lottery and is accountable to Parliament through the Department for Culture, Media and Sport.

109 He is one of 75 hereditary peers that remained in the House of Lords after the passing of the House of Lords Act 1999.

Robin and Margaret[110] live in the family home, Drumadarragh House in Ballyclare, and also have a summer house in the luxury resort of Sotogrande, 20 miles from Gibraltar, a short distance from the Valderrama golf course (favoured by Prince Andrew) and Sotogrande's polo fields.

Robin remains modest about his sporting prowess and success, but admits that he "wouldn't have missed a single second of it all, being an Olympian means I belong to the very best club in the world. For us, it all amounted to more than just Innsbruck – it was a way of life for a while."

However, he may be more than just a sporting hero. In the summer of 2006, while sailing with a friend from Hampshire to Northern Ireland in his yacht, *The Lazy Life*, he helped to rescue a crew of five from a stricken yacht. Robin spotted *The Talisman* drifting off the Dorset coast; he raised the alarm when he saw red distress flares launched from the disabled yacht. On approaching the vessel, Robin discovered a man had fallen overboard and, in the cockpit, found an unconscious woman. He began to search for the man overboard as the coastguard rushed to the location east of Anvil Point.

With the assistance of his fellow sailor Ian Murdoch, an off-duty Belfast Coastguard watch manager, Robin came across an elderly man and hauled him aboard *The Lazy Life*. At the same time, the Portland Coastguard helicopter *Whisky Bravo* winched the comatose woman from *The Talisman*, taking her to Poole General Hospital. A lifeboat took the rescued man ashore, together with two women and a child who had also been aboard *The Talisman*, to be examined by paramedics as the rescued vessel was sailed into harbour by some of the lifeboat crew.

110 Formerly Margaret Ann Rainey, now aged 61.

After making port in Weymouth, Robin commented, "I did what any other yachtsman would have done and I'm just happy that we were there to help."

Ian Murdoch told how the injured man had been knocked into the sea by the boom as he had attempted to take the mainsail down. It was believed that the woman had been knocked unconscious at the same time. Murdoch said, "Lord Glentoran is a very experienced yachtsman and he was at the helm throughout the rescue. He did an exceptional job. We were very lucky to be in the area, there weren't any other yachts nearby."

The Portland Coastguard watch manager, Jim Anderson, praised Dixon and Murdoch. "I am pleased the man overboard was rescued and that we were able to quickly evacuate the lady who had sustained an injury.

"Ian and Lord Glentoran did an excellent job in finding and recovering this man and also keeping us up to date with information regarding the situation with the lady, who is now being treated in hospital."

Robin and Tony Nash were inducted into the British Bobsleigh Hall of Fame as a result of their success. But both these men are much more than sportsmen. While their achievements and experiences in the mid-1960's did much to inform and educate them, they are not – like so many who subsequently scaled the heights of sporting achievement – one-dimensional beings, starting and finishing their contributions within the confines of field or track.

While performances may have improved, with seconds being sheared from record times, sport's essential concern with the building of character seems to have largely vanished. This writer's conversations with Tony Nash and Robin Dixon coincided with a period in sport dominated by the return of Michael Phelps, after suspension for drug offences, and the purchase of Cristiano Ronaldo's loyalty by enough money to build and equip a large hospital in the decaying Fontainhas slum area of Lisbon. I'm sure I'm not alone in wondering if we have gained much less than we have lost.

Some years ago I went on a skiing trip in Andorra. I was amazed to find my group was guided by a former French Foreign Legionnaire who I had met when he was a recruiting sergeant in Marseille. One evening we were having a drink and got to talking about the Legion's concept of honour. He said something that has come to my mind many times in the course of writing this book: "Honour has to be based on truth; without truth there is no honour, and the truth is honourable in itself." The truth, be it about bolts or battles, winning or losing, is the source of all honour in this life.

Veracity is inextricably linked to integrity. Nearly half a century on from their heady sporting days, Nash and Dixon have an intimate understanding of this. It is the foundation of the ethos of the Corinthian spirit. It is embodied in the all-embracing commitment to fairness championed by Eugenio Monti and the instinct for adventure of Vic Emery and his Canadians. It may survive only in small corners in future Olympics, but perhaps the story of these men and their times will do something to fan the flames of authentic sporting passion; the soul of sport that cannot be bought or manipulated by the all-intrusive global electronic media.

That one bright moment so long ago, Britain's Olympic Gold Run, now has the mythical resonance and meaning of a Valhalla, an Asgard. As Eugenio Monti told us, "The brakes are for stopping at the end" – but reflecting on the lives, times and examples of Tony Nash and Robin Dixon may dissuade us from throwing out the anchors just yet.

EPILOGUE:
THE MONTI
BOLT GESTURE

In the light of very recent events, my thanks to Vic Emery for the following:

Just after Brian Belton put this book to bed, in November 2009, I was invited to attend a January 2010 inauguration of a new intermediate start on the St Moritz bob track. The start will be between Sunny Corner and the Nash-Dixon corners, and is being named the Monti's Bolt Start to honour Eugenio Monti for his generosity toward the British team in the heat of the 1964 Olympic boblet competition. Without Monti's famed gesture with a replacement bolt, the British chances of beating him for the Olympic Gold could have been seriously jeopardised.

However, the story that never got out was that the bolt the British used was *not* Monti's! In the typical manner of the true sportsmen of our era, Nash and Dixon kept quiet when the Monti's bolt story was distorted by the press. For them the gesture was the important thing, so they kept quiet about what really happened until Brian dug deep in his research.

The Monti's Bolt Start will undoubtedly be seen for generations to come as the ultimate commemoration of sportsmanship, for which Nash and Dixon stand equal alongside Monti, who is honoured by its naming. I have no doubt that, if Eugenio was alive today and learned what had really happened in 1964, he would smile and welcome Tony and Robin with open arms as true fellow sportsmen. That the story has lasted until now actually seems to enhance the new start's naming, whether based on myth or reality.

When I received the invitation to the inaugural ceremony, I immediately telephoned Fritz Burkard, the man behind the Monti's Bolt Start, in Switzerland about the true story. After explaining what had really happened and how this book would reveal all, Fritz easily grasped the *double entente* and decided to carry on with the programme unchanged. I was so pleased to find that, some 45 years later, there continue to exist, in this mad world of professional sport, sportsmen like Fritz who understand the true meaning of what transpired in 1964.

Victor Emery, November 2009

THEY ALSO SERVED

It is important to both Robin Dixon and Tony Nash that the Britons who accompanied them on their Olympic odyssey are recognised and remembered. More is known about some than others; many distinguished themselves in other fields, from motor racing to commerce, but it would be remiss to provide biographies when all could not be similarly represented.

This being the case, I hope that the following will at least delineate the doubtlessly huge contribution each of them made to British Olympic bobsleighing. As in all teams it is probable that some were perhaps able to give more than others, but all of these individuals were as committed to their sport and their country as the two gold medallists were.

FOUR-MAN[112]
John Blockey
Martin Boyle
David Evans
Roy Freeman
Walter Lewis
Guy Renwick
Robin Seel
Robin Widdows

TWO/FOUR-MAN
Andrew Hedges
William McCowan

FOUR-MAN
Harold Brown
John Evelyn
Guy Renwick
Timothy Thorne
Robin Widdows

TWO/FOUR-MAN
John Blockey
Roy Freeman

112 I have designated squad members by their roles in the two and four-man teams, but in practice every athlete contributed to both team efforts.

BIBLIOGRAPHY

Bossley, M. M. *Cracked* Orca Book Publishers, 2007

Brimmer, L. D. *Bobsledding and the Luge* Grolier, 1997

De Agostini, C. (ed.) *Monti. Il Rosso volante* GiorgioNADAEditore, 2006

Ice Skating Institute of America *Olympic Bobsledding* Regensteiner Publishing, 1979

Lechenperg, H. *Olympic Games of 1964, Innsbruck Tokyo* A. S. Barnes & Co/Thomas Yoseloff, 1964

Mrakawa, R. J. *The Greatest Challenge* Rupert J. Mrakawa, 1964

Phillips, B and Goldsmid, C. (eds.) *The British Olympic Association Official Report of the Olympic Games 1964* BOA, 1964

Robson, G. *Ford Escort Mk1* Veloce, 2006

US Olympic Committee *Bobsledding* Griffin Publishing, 2002

JOURNALS/NEWSPAPERS

Daily Express
Daily Herald
Daily Mail
Daily Mirror
Daily Sketch
Daily Telegraph
Evening News
Life Magazine
London Evening Standard
News of the World
The People
Sports Illustrated
Sunday Express
Sunday Mirror
Tatler
The Times

ARCHIVES

British Library
British Library Newspapers
Canadian Broadcasting Company Digital Archives
Guildhall Library

FILMOGRAPHY

The Essential Winter Olympics BBC1 2006
Mercury of the Mountains – Torino Olympics NBC 2006
Sporting Heroes BSB 1998